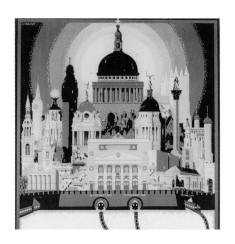

The Moving Metropolis
A History of London's
Transport since 1800

Edited by Sheila Taylor
Introductions by Oliver Green

The Moving Metropolis

A History of London's Transport since 1800

Edited by Sheila Taylor
Introductions by Oliver Green

In association with
London's Transport Museum

Laurence King Publishing

First published in Great Britain in 2001

Paperback edition first published in 2002
by Laurence King Publishing
71 Great Russell Street
London WCIB 3BP
Tel: + 44 20 7430 8850
Fax: + 44 20 7831 8880
e-mail: enquiries@laurenceking.co.uk
www.laurenceking.co.uk

This book was designed and produced by Laurence King
Publishing Ltd, London, in association with London's Transport
Museum

A catalogue record for this book is available
from the British Library.

Hardback ISBN 1 85669 241 8
Paperback ISBN 1 85669 326 0

Design: Karen Stafford

Printed in Singapore

Acknowledgements

The following people have contributed their knowledge and time in helping to publish this book: Nick Agnew, Mike Ashworth, Roger Brasier, Jean Coleman, Ken Glazier, Mike Horne, Ruth Kelly, Simon Murphy and David Ruddom. Special credit must go to Patricia Austin, Ian Bell, David Ellis, Oliver Green, Hugh Robertson and Sheila Taylor, whose time and dedication to this project brought it from an idea to reality.

London's Transport Museum would also like to thank Denis Tunnicliffe, former Chief Executive of London Regional Transport, for supporting this project.

All images included in the book are from the photographic archive of London's Transport Museum unless otherwise stated.

Page 1
Detail from the poster *From Euston to Clapham Common: The Transformation is Complete* by Richard T. Cooper
1924

Pages 2-3
Detail from the poster *London's Freedom* by Charles Paine
1926

Contents

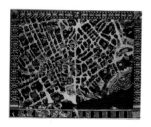

The Londoner's Transport ... some of the means

Shanks' Pony • Roman Litter • Roman Carruca • Hammock Waggon 1100 • Chare 1220 • Horse Litter 1330 • Travellers 15th Century • Whirlicote 13th century • Common

Thames Waterman 1680 • London Hackney Coach 1715 • Wayfarers 1720 • The Machine 1740 • Stage Waggon 1740 • Sedan Chair 1745 • Stage Coach 1750 • Posting Carriage 175

Tilbury 1825 • The First Omnibus 1829 • Chaise 1829 • Cabriolet 1829 • Mail Coach 1830 • Gurney's Steam Carriage 1828-30 • Hancock's Steam 'Bus 1833 • Boulnois' Cab 1835

London's First Horse Tramway. Train's Patent 1861-2 • "Growler" 1865 • "London General" Omnibus 1869 • Thames Penny Steamer 1890 • Omnibus 1898 • Steam Omnibus 1902 •

The Metropolitan The First Underground Railway 1863 • • • The City and South London 1890

Overground and UNDERGROUND

The First Tube

172/2500/1 6.26.

London:
The First
World City

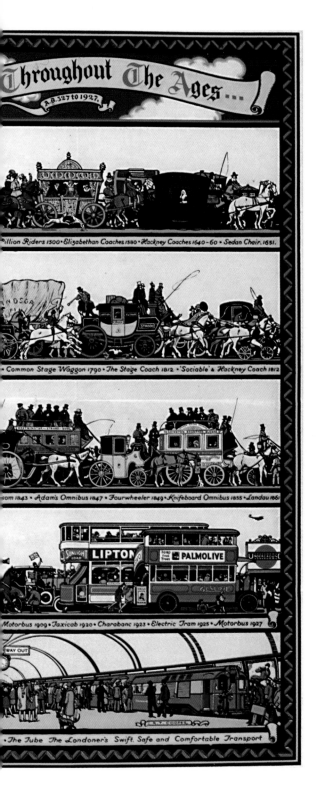

*The Londoner's Transport throughout the
Ages* **by R. T. Cooper**
1929

Poster commissioned to mark the centenary
of Shillibeer's omnibus service.

London: The First World City

The growth of London over the last two hundred years has been closely linked with the expansion of public transport services. Although London was founded soon after the Roman invasion of Britain in AD 43, it remained a relatively small settlement throughout the Middle Ages and during the sixteenth and seventeenth centuries. It was not until the end of the eighteenth century that the rapid growth began which created the urban giant of Victorian London, the largest and most important city in the world.

In 1801, when the first census was taken, the population of London was just under one million. By 1901, the year of Queen Victoria's death, it had risen to 6.6 million. London's built-up area continued to expand outwards until the mid-twentieth century when it was curbed by Green Belt planning legislation. At the start of the twenty-first century, London is no longer the largest city in the world, but it remains one of Europe's leading financial, commercial and cultural centres. The economic geography of the city continues to influence, and be influenced by, its intricate and extensive public transport networks. Without these systems the life of the city would soon come to a standstill.

Blackfriars Bridge from the south side, 1798. Blackfriars was a toll-free bridge built in 1760.

Transport in 1800

Until the nineteenth century the River Thames was London's main traffic artery. The first public transport was provided by watermen using small rowing boats called wherries. As the main built-up area of London extended no more than a mile from the river, these water taxis offered the fastest means of urban transport.

On land it was usually easier to walk than ride in the narrow, uneven streets. The only road vehicles for public hire were four-wheeled coaches called hackneys. The name was derived from the French word *hacquenée,* meaning a strong horse hired out for journeys.

Strict licensing regulations limited the number of hackneys and also gave licensed operators a virtual monopoly of public transport in central London. Anyone wishing to travel further to an outlying village such as Highgate or Hammersmith had to take a short stage coach. These services usually ran from inn yards in Westminster and the City. They were not allowed to compete with hackneys by picking up or setting down passengers along the route until they were outside 'the stones', as the paved central area of London was known.

The horse bus

The early years of the nineteenth century saw the arrival in London of two new forms of transport – the cab and the omnibus – both of which originated in France. They were the horse-drawn forerunners of the modern taxi and bus. Between the late 1820s and the 1840s they replaced all the existing hackney and short stage coaches in London.

The omnibus, which became the more important of the two, was not a new type of vehicle but offered a novel service. It was a long, box-shaped coach similar to the existing short stage coaches, but passengers could get on or off anywhere along a short, fixed route. The name omnibus, meaning 'for all' in Latin, was first used to describe such a service by Stanislaus Baudry, a French coach operator who founded *L'Entreprise des Omnibus* in Paris in 1828.

George Shillibeer, an English coachbuilder who had worked in Paris, introduced the omnibus to London a year later. He was refused permission to run a service in the central area because of the hackney coach monopoly, so he chose the busy New Road route round the edge of London, from Paddington to the City via

Oil painting of George Shillibeer's omnibus of 1829, outside his Bloomsbury workshop.

Horse bus services were in high demand during the Great Exhibition of 1851. Illustration by George Cruickshank.

Islington. Shillibeer's fares of sixpence (2½p) and one shilling (5p) were far beyond the means of most working people, but were much cheaper than short stage coaches. Unlike the stage service, omnibus departure times were guaranteed whether a vehicle was full or not, and it was no longer necessary to book in advance as a uniformed conductor rode on the omnibus to collect the fares.

After a Government enquiry, the hackney coach monopoly was ended in 1832. Other operators were then quick to follow Shillibeer's example by introducing omnibus services all over London. Competition was fierce, with the drivers racing each other and conductors using any means they could to poach a rival's passengers. After 1838 individual licences were required for both drivers and conductors after complaints about their uncouth behaviour from the travelling public.

Early omnibuses did not carry outside passengers, but by the late 1840s vehicle capacity was increased by adding a back-to-back 'knifeboard' bench seat along the roof. This double-deck arrangement was encouraged by the sudden traffic boom created by the Great Exhibition of 1851. In the business slump that followed, many omnibus owners accepted takeover bids from the newly created London General Omnibus Company (LGOC). By the end of 1856, the LGOC's first year of operation, it had acquired 600 of the 810 omnibuses then running in London and had become the largest single omnibus operator in the world.

The horse tram

A tramcar running on smooth iron rails can be pulled much more easily by horses than an omnibus running over an uneven road surface. Two horses can comfortably haul a tramcar weighing a couple of tonnes and seating up to 50 passengers – about twice the weight and capacity of a standard horse-drawn omnibus.

Passenger-carrying street tramways originated in the USA, where they operated in New York and New Orleans from the 1830s. It was an American, George Francis Train, who

Lithograph showing one of the first successful horse tram services, 1870.

introduced the tramcar to London in 1861. He laid three short demonstration lines but made the mistake of using rails that protruded above the road surface and endangered other vehicles. This led to the compulsory removal of all three lines by the authorities after only a few months in operation.

Three further tramways in London were authorised by Parliament in 1869 and built with track laid flush with the road surface. The Metropolitan Street Tramways Company began operations between Brixton and Kennington on 2 May 1870. A week later the North Metropolitan's line opened from Whitechapel to Bow, and on 13 December the Pimlico, Peckham and Greenwich Tramway introduced its first services. Here, for the first time, was a method of public transport that the majority of Londoners could afford to use and that served less affluent districts. While tracks were soon laid along most of the main roads into the suburbs, trams were not allowed in either the City or the West End, which were still dominated by the omnibus.

Steam underground

The passenger railway first came to London in 1836 with the opening of the London & Greenwich Railway, which had its city terminus at London Bridge. Within a few years a series of termini had opened for main lines from all parts of the country, including Euston (1837), Paddington (1838) and King's Cross (1852). Most of these stations were built some distance away from the central business area because Parliament wished to avoid the extensive demolition and disruption that would have taken place if each railway had been allowed to penetrate the heart of the capital. Anyone travelling by rail to central London was therefore forced to complete the journey from the station by cab or omnibus.

As more goods and passengers arrived by rail, they generated increased road traffic, and street congestion became a growing problem. By the 1850s it often took longer to cross central London than to travel up to the capital by train from Brighton, 50 miles away. One proposed solution, which was later adopted by cities all over the world, was to build an underground railway as a rapid transit link between the mainline stations and the city centre.

In 1854 Parliament agreed to allow the Metropolitan Railway Company to build an underground line from Paddington to Farringdon Street via King's Cross. Work began six years later when enough capital had been raised to finance the project. The route lay mainly below the Marylebone and Euston Roads (the former New Road used by Shillibeer's first omnibus service) which allowed the use of 'cut and cover' construction. This involved digging a wide trench, supporting the excavation with side walls, roofing over the track bed, and restoring the road surface above. Only a short section under Clerkenwell required the excavation of a true tunnel.

The first urban underground railway in the world was opened to passengers in London on 10 January 1863. Despite gloomy predictions in *The Times* that Londoners would never take to travelling underground, the Metropolitan was an immediate success and within five years extensions had been added to both ends of the original line.

A second underground company, the Metropolitan District Railway, opened its first section of line in 1868 from South Kensington

An early view of the world's first underground railway at Praed Street Junction, Paddington, 1863.

LONDON: THE FIRST WORLD CITY

to Westminster. Services were then extended along the newly constructed Victoria Embankment on the north bank of the Thames towards Tower Hill, linking the mainline railway termini of Victoria, Charing Cross, Blackfriars and Cannon Street. Eventually in 1884 the District and Metropolitan were joined up at both ends to form an Inner Circle underground railway, but in the interim both underground companies had found it more profitable to tap suburban traffic with overground extensions into London's countryside. The District spread west and south-west towards Ealing, Hounslow, Richmond and Wimbledon, while the Metropolitan extended a branch line north-westwards from Baker Street through St John's Wood to Willesden, Wembley, Harrow and beyond.

Before the revolution: London's transport dominated by horse and steam power, 1897.

A technical revolution

Transport in London was revolutionised at the end of the nineteenth century by the use of new methods of underground railway construction and new sources of motive power for both road and rail services, challenging the dominance of the horse and the steam engine.

Compressed air, gas, oil, steam, battery electric and cable tramways were all tried out in the 1870s and '80s with varying degrees of success. However, it was the use of electricity generated at a central power station and picked up by individual trams connected to a system of supply that was to transform the capital's tramways in the 1900s.

Electric traction was successfully demonstrated by Werner von Siemens at a Berlin exhibition in 1879, and the first electric railway in England was opened along the Brighton seafront by Magnus Volk only four years later. Electric tramways developed rapidly, especially in the USA, but London's first electric tram services were not introduced until 1901, when the London United Tramways opened two routes running into the western suburbs from Shepherd's Bush.

Fourteen separate electric tramway systems were opened in greater London over the next five years, the most extensive being operated by the London County Council (LCC). Outside the LCC boundary, operation was divided between three private companies in the northern, western and southern suburbs, together with ten local authorities in east and south-east London. Between them these tramways were carrying over 800 million passengers a year by 1914.

Unlike trams, buses need an independent and portable source of power for each vehicle. None of the experiments at the turn of the century with steam, battery electric and petrol-driven motor buses initially showed any great promise. The first regular service in London using petrol-engined vehicles, introduced in 1899, lasted for only just over a year.

Excavating a station tunnel with Greathead's shield, on the Great Northern & City Railway, c. 1903.

More reliable engines were developed, however, and in 1905 the first boom in motor bus operation took place with a series of small independent companies entering the field. Three years later the LGOC, which still operated the largest horse bus fleet, made a successful takeover bid for two of its largest rivals. The technical expertise of all three companies was then pooled to develop a new standard motor bus for London. This eventually emerged in October 1910 as the famous B-type bus. It was so successful that within a year the LGOC was able to replace all its remaining horse buses. Routes were no longer limited in length by the need to change horses at intervals, and the network grew dramatically.

Underground railway development in central London was held back by the limitations of 'cut and cover' construction. It caused considerable disruption to any street under which a line was built, and wherever the path of the railway diverged from the street, property demolition was necessary. Digging tunnels at a much deeper level avoided these difficulties but became a practical alternative only towards the end of the nineteenth century. Three key developments made it possible. First, a reliable technique for deep-

level tunnelling; second, a safe means of vertical transport for passengers; and third, a non-polluting power source for the railway which could be used in deep, poorly ventilated tunnels.

Tunnelling through soft ground like London clay requires some means of protecting the excavation against collapse while the miners are at work. Marc Isambard Brunel designed a rectangular cast-iron shield for this purpose and used it to build the first tunnel under the Thames between Wapping and Rotherhithe. Opened in 1843 as a pedestrian subway, his Thames Tunnel carried the East London Railway from 1869 and is now part of the London Underground system.

Peter William Barlow developed Brunel's technique with a circular tunnelling shield that could be used to build a cylindrical tube tunnel. His Tower Subway, a short tunnel under the Thames, opened in 1870 and was the world's first tube railway. A small cable-hauled railcar carried passengers through the tunnel, and there was a steam-driven lift in the shaft at either end. The lifts incorporated safety features first demonstrated in the 1850s by Elisha Otis in the USA and later adopted world-wide. Unfortunately, neither

Poster advertising the Central London Railway, already called the 'Twopenny Tube' because of its single fare, 1905.

The City & South London showed the way forward for new underground railway construction in London. Six more deep-level tube lines were opened in quick succession at the turn of the century, each built by a separate company. These were the Waterloo & City (1898), Central London (1900), Great Northern & City (1904), Bakerloo (1906), Piccadilly (1906) and Hampstead Tube (1907). During the same period, the existing underground lines of the Metropolitan (Met) and District Railways were electrified to compete with the new tubes, although steam services continued on the outer main line of the Met. In less than 20 years electric travel underground, which had seemed a daring experiment in 1890, had become part of the daily routine for thousands of Londoners.

Suburban spread

The growth of public transport services in the nineteenth century allowed an increasing number of people to live some distance away from their place of work. Suburban development in Victorian London often depended on, and followed, the provision of local railway services. An early example was the impact of the District Railway's western extension, which provided a direct service to Westminster and the City from 1877. This prompted the development of Bedford Park, a new middle-class suburban housing estate adjacent to Turnham Green station, and helped turn the village of Hammersmith into a suburb for City clerks.

In the Edwardian period the first of the tube railways to reach the fringes of London had a similar effect. The Hampstead Tube opened in 1907 between Charing Cross and Golders Green, then in open country. Within five years a completely new suburb had grown up around the station, while just to the north the first section of Hampstead Garden Suburb had been laid out. In 1921 Edgware was still a tiny village in rural Middlesex, but as soon as the Hampstead Tube was

method of locomotion proved reliable, and both the lifts and railway were removed after only a few months' operation.

The first successful tube railway was built in the 1880s by James Henry Greathead, the contractor for the Tower Subway, using an improved version of Barlow's shield. This was the City & South London Railway, opened in 1890 between Stockwell and King William Street, near the Bank of England. Originally intended for cable operation, it was adapted for electric traction during construction. Hydraulically operated lifts were used to convey passengers to and from the deep-level station platforms.

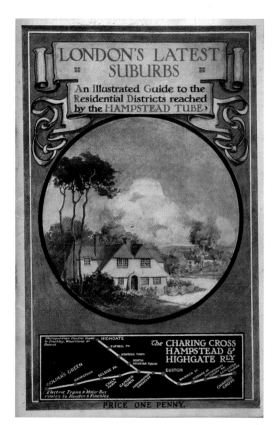

A 1910 brochure promoting new suburban housing on the Hampstead Tube.

extended northwards from Golders Green in 1923–4, speculators began buying up land for houses and shops. By the late 1930s the population was more than ten times greater. Similar new streets of semi-detached houses followed the extension of the same line south to Morden in 1926 and the projection of the Piccadilly line north of Finsbury Park to Cockfosters in 1932–3.

The Metropolitan was the only railway to become directly involved in the commercial exploitation of land adjacent to its line. By the turn of the century a number of new housing estates had appeared on railway property close to stations such as Wembley Park and Pinner. The name 'Metro-Land' was coined in 1915 to publicise the districts served by the railway, and in 1919 Metropolitan Railway

Country Estates Ltd was established to develop the area more extensively, in accurate anticipation of a post-war housing boom.

During the 1920s estates were built all down the line, allowing the Metropolitan to build up a captive market of season-ticket holding passengers who lived in Metro-Land but commuted daily to the City by train. There was a certain contradiction between the Metro-Land dream of a new home on the edge of unspoilt countryside and the reality of the suburban sprawl that soon engulfed many of these areas. Nevertheless, for many middle-class families who moved out of inner London, Metro-Land represented a way of life in which they hoped to enjoy new, and formerly inaccessible, pleasures and comforts.

Amalgamation

The cost of building the new tubes and modernising London's other road and rail services with new forms of power was enormous. A number of the private companies involved either went bankrupt or were forced to sell out to larger concerns with more secure financial backing. It was in this way that the Underground Electric Railways of London Co. Ltd (UERL), founded in 1902 by American financier Charles Tyson Yerkes, came to dominate London's public transport operations. Over a period of eleven years, the UERL grew rapidly by taking control of the District Railway, five tube companies, all three private electric tram companies and the main bus operator, the LGOC.

Some of the old company names survived, but they all became subsidiaries of the Underground Group, and by 1914 a large part of London's public transport was in the hands of one giant private holding company. However, it was not yet a monopoly. Still outside the Underground Group and jealously guarding their independence were the Metropolitan Railway, the various council tramways and the suburban services of the mainline railway companies.

Competition between the remaining transport operators effectively ceased during the First World War (1914–18), but new rivalries arose in the early 1920s. The LGOC found its dominance of bus operation challenged by a number of small independent companies, many of them using vehicles supplied by manufacturers on hire purchase schemes. These 'pirates', as they were commonly known, often worked only over busy existing routes, creaming off the profits that the LGOC used to subsidise its under-used local and off-peak services. Rival bus crews raced and blocked each other on the roads, and several accidents were caused by dangerous driving in the frantic battle for passengers.

Unrestricted competition of this kind was clearly not in the public interest, and a series of reports to the government suggested that the best way forward was to create a single authority responsible for all London's public transport. The result was the formation of the London Passenger Transport Board (LPTB), which from 1 July 1933 took over the Underground Group's road and rail operations, the council tramways, the Metropolitan Railway, and all the independent bus companies. Only the local suburban services of the four mainline railway companies were excluded.

London Transport, as the new authority soon became known, was a public corporation with total control of bus, tram, trolleybus and underground railway services over some 2000 square miles of London and its surrounding countryside within a 20–30 mile radius of Charing Cross. Management of London Transport was dominated by the leading figures of the Underground Group, with Lord Ashfield as chairman and Frank Pick, the UERL Managing Director, as Vice Chairman and Chief Executive.

For the first time it became possible to plan and co-ordinate London's public transport development effectively. In association with the mainline railways, London Transport drew up proposals for new Underground extensions, primarily in north and east London. The schemes involved construction of new lines and electrification of some existing steam-worked suburban branches of the London & North Eastern Railway, which were to become part of the Underground system. Collectively these projects were known as the 1935–40 New Works Programme. A substantial part of the construction work was completed by 1939–40, when a new branch of the Bakerloo line and some of the planned extensions to the Northern line were opened. By this time, however, the country was at war again, and all further improvements to the system were necessarily postponed.

During the 1920s buses lost nearly all traces of their horse-drawn beginnings and

Morden, southern terminus of the Northern line, with feeder bus services 1936

All the housing beyond the station had been built in the ten years since the completion of the Tube extension.

Poster advertising LGOC Sunday excursions
to London's countryside by motor bus, 1913.

began to resemble modern vehicles. However, each advance in design had to be won as a concession from the licensing authorities. They included a gradual increase in seating capacity, enclosed top decks (1925), pneumatic tyres (1925), and enclosed drivers' cabs (1930). From 1923 onwards, LGOC buses were regularly carrying more passengers than either the trams or the Underground.

The LGOC moved progressively towards standardisation of both its vehicles and overhaul procedures, using an extensive purpose-built works, which was opened at Chiswick in 1922. When London Transport took over in 1933, it continued the LGOC's policy of placing large orders with manufacturers for vehicles based on just a few standard types. Double-deck buses remained the standard London vehicle, with some single deckers for hilly or lightly used suburban and country routes. Single-deck coaches were also required for excursion services and for use on the new Green Line routes, introduced from 1930 onwards, running out to the towns in the surrounding rural area. One of the new Board's first decisions in 1933 was to use oil (diesel)

The rapid development of bus design in the 1920s demonstrated at Marble Arch in 1930. In the centre is a K-type of 1919, on the right the latest ST-type.

LONDON: THE FIRST WORLD CITY

Trolleybus to Kingston by F. Gregory Brown, 1933. This shows one of the original LUT trolleybuses.

tram and a bus. It is electrically powered, using an overhead supply, but instead of running on rails, it has rubber-tyred wheels like a bus. This gives the trolleybus much greater flexibility than the tram, allowing it to be driven to the kerbside at stops, and to avoid obstructions in the road.

The LUT decided to invest in new, faster and more comfortable tramcars on its busiest routes, but to convert others to trolleybus operation. New twin overhead wiring was required, but the trolleybuses could use the same power supply as the trams, and the track, which was expensive to maintain, could be taken up. In 1931, 20 years after the first British trolleybus systems opened in Leeds and Bradford, the LUT introduced trolleybuses over 17 miles of former tram routes in the Kingston area of south-west London. The conversion was carried out at less than half the estimated cost of tramway modernisation.

When London Transport took over all London's tramways in 1933, the LUT's successful experience in trolleybus operation led the new Board to plan further conversions. Between 1935 and 1940, when the programme was interrupted by the war, more than half London's tramways were converted to trolleybus operation. After the war there was less financial benefit in re-using the ageing tramway electrical distribution system, and

engines in its buses because they had been shown to save some £120 a year in the running costs of each vehicle. All London Transport's subsequent new orders were for diesel buses, but, because of the war, conversion of the existing petrol-engined fleet was not completed until 1950.

London's tramways began to lose money in the 1920s. Passengers deserted them for the new buses, and the tramway operators could not afford the essential modernisation necessary to win back their customers. One company, the London United Tramways (LUT), saw that adopting the trolleybus offered a way out of its difficulties. A trolleybus is essentially a cross between a

The Underground Group's roundel and type-face as used by London Transport in the 1930s.

diesel buses were used to replace the remaining trams in 1950–52.

Post-war developments

Six years of war took a considerable toll on London Transport. When it ended in 1945, a vast amount of repair work to bombed or neglected property and vehicles was necessary. Reconstruction began almost immediately, but a period of post-war austerity lay ahead. London Transport was nationalised in 1948, along with the four mainline railway companies and found itself low on the government's list of priorities for new investment.

Rehabilitation – It Takes Time, one of a series of four posters by Fred Taylor, 1945.

REHABILITATION

23 railway stations, 15 bus garages and 12 trolleybus and tram depots had direct hits or suffered severe damage from enemy action. Replacements and repairs are in hand — but

IT TAKES TIME

Coincidentally, London Transport carried more passengers in its first year of nationalisation than ever before, but the numbers then started to fall steadily. The decline was mainly in the use of the central area road services and was matched by a dramatic increase in car ownership. Between 1950 and 1965 the number of private cars licensed in the London Transport area quadrupled. Increased traffic on the roads led to congestion, making daytime bus services less reliable and encouraging even more travellers to turn to private transport. The rapid growth of television viewing meant that people also made fewer evening bus journeys to entertainment facilities outside their homes such as cinemas and sporting events.

The application of Green Belt planning legislation, preserving an undeveloped band of countryside around London, ensured that the city did not continue to expand unremittingly after the war. In fact, the population of Greater London began to decline, while beyond the Green Belt, in the London Transport country area, it grew steadily, as people moved out to the New Towns like Stevenage and Crawley. This brought an increase in the use and provision of Country Bus and Green Line coach services in the 1950s and early 1960s. Electrification of the two outermost country sections of the Underground network, the Central line beyond Epping and the Metropolitan beyond Rickmansworth, was completed in this period, finally ending London Transport's use of steam-hauled passenger trains in 1961.

As full electric traction took over on the Underground, it was abandoned for road services. In the 1950s operating electric trolleybuses was no cheaper than using diesel buses, and their environmental benefits were not fully appreciated. London Transport decided in 1954 to replace its trolleybuses once it had perfected its new diesel bus, the Routemaster. The entire trolleybus network, once the largest in the world, was scrapped between 1959 and 1962 as the new

A new Routemaster bus in Parliament Square, 1961.

New tubes

Routemaster fleet came into service.

A shortage of operating staff, especially on the buses, was a serious problem in the 1950s. It was partly solved by making permanent, from 1951, the wartime policy of recruiting women as conductors, and by direct recruitment of new staff from the West Indies after 1956. Driver-only bus operation, previously confined to a few country services, was adopted on a growing number of suburban routes in the 1960s to ease the continuing staff shortages. By the 1970s when one-person operated double deckers were introduced, the main reason for doing it was to cut costs. There was a progressive changeover to driver-only operation throughout the 1970s and '80s as new front-entrance buses were introduced all over London. However, conductors have been retained on some heavily used routes in central London where the open platform Routemasters still provide the quickest service.

The Victoria line, first proposed in the late 1940s, was finally built in the 1960s. This was the first new tube railway to be constructed under central London for 60 years. The route chosen provided a direct West End link for north-east and south London, as well as a rapid cross-town connection between four of the main line

Cut Travelling Time – Victoria Line **by Tom Eckersley, 1969.**

railway termini. New tunnelling techniques were used, and a novel method of automatic train operation was introduced for the line. When it opened in 1968–9, the Victoria line was the most advanced underground railway in the world, and was soon being used by 1.25 million passengers a week.

Two significant developments took place on the Underground in the 1970s. The Piccadilly line was extended to Heathrow in 1977, making London the first capital city in the world to be linked directly with its busy international airport by underground railway. The second project was the Jubilee line, another new tube railway planned to run under central London from the north to the south-east. The first stage was completed and opened in 1979. Instead of completing the Jubilee line eastwards through Docklands in the 1980s, a cheaper alternative was found in light rail technology. This meant the return of the electric tram to London in modern form. The Docklands Light Railway (DLR), the first section of which opened in 1987, uses lightweight rail vehicles that can handle steeper gradients and tighter curves than conventional trains. Operation is fully automatic, with sophisticated computer control of the driverless trains.

However, it soon became clear that the DLR was insufficient to meet the growing public transport needs of Docklands, which was being rapidly redeveloped as a business and residential area in the late 1980s. A ten-mile extension of the Jubilee line was eventually authorised once a funding contribution had been agreed with the private sector developers of Canary Wharf in Docklands. Construction began in 1992, and the new line, running south of the river, through Docklands to Stratford, opened in 1999. It has interchanges throughout with mainline, DLR and other Underground lines and dramatic new station designs. The extended Jubilee line has been a massive and complex engineering project, completed 20 months late and well over budget, but it is as impressive and important an addition to London's transport infrastructure as the Victoria line was 30 years earlier.

London Bridge Jubilee line station concourse 1999

The new Jubilee line station at London Bridge was built beneath the bus station, and the existing Northern line station was upgraded. Both link to this spacious vaulted concourse beneath the mainline railway viaduct.

Managing change

In 1970, control of London Transport passed from central government to the Greater London Council (GLC), which had been created as a new governing body for London in 1965 to succeed the London County Council. Operation of the Green Line and Country Bus services, which ran largely outside the GLC area, was transferred to the National Bus Company.

London Transport became the GLC's responsibility at a time when it was already requiring public subsidy as operating costs increased and passenger numbers fell. Losses on the buses were partly offset in the early 1970s by operating surpluses on the Underground, buoyed up by the new Victoria line, but by the late 1970s road and rail services were losing both money and traffic. The GLC began raising fares each year above inflation levels to increase income, but only succeeded in driving away more passengers.

The question of just how heavily London's public transport should be subsidised and private transport controlled soon became a major political issue. A radical Labour GLC administration elected in 1981 cut bus and Tube fares dramatically under its 'Fares Fair' scheme. This attracted passengers back to public transport but not enough to cover the loss of income, which required a supplementary rate demand by the GLC from the London boroughs. The south London Borough of Bromley, which was not served by the Underground, challenged the legality of the GLC's policy in the courts. The case was lost, then won on appeal to the House of Lords. The GLC was forced to increase fares again early in 1982 by nearly 100%, and again passengers were lost. The real loser in this, as London Transport became a political football with no consistent policy, was the travelling public.

Further changes in control did little to resolve the key issue of how best to plan and fund London's future transport. The Conservative Government removed London

Cover of Greater London Council opinion poll 1982

The GLC commissioned an independent opinion poll to discover what Londoners felt about London's transport system. The opinion poll offered five approaches, including 'Fares Fair'.

Transport from GLC control in 1984 as a preliminary step to the full abolition of the council two years later. The new London Transport authority, briefly known as London Regional Transport, but soon reverting to its old name, was a public holding company with two main subsidiaries, London Buses and London Underground. In tune with the prevailing government policy of privatising public services, London Transport was now required to invite competitive tenders for service provision, and from 1985 onwards the private sector became increasingly involved in operating bus services in London. In 1994 London Buses' operating subsidiaries were sold to the private sector, but co-ordination and regulation of services was still carried out centrally. Although London Underground remained in the public sector, private finance initiatives were developed in the 1990s to help fund major investment projects such as new trains, smartcard ticketing technology and new power supply arrangements.

Into the 21st century

The Labour Government elected in 1997 did not reverse the privatisation of public transport but adopted a public/private partnership approach. It was also committed to reintroducing a strategic governing authority for London. In July 2000, fourteen years after the GLC's demise, the Greater London Authority came into being, led by an elected Mayor with full executive powers who is answerable to an elected Assembly. One of

the Mayor's major tasks is to draw up and implement an integrated transport strategy for London through a new executive body, Transport *for* London (T*f*L). T*f*L has taken over London Transport's role, together with the management of the road network, regulation of taxis and London River Services.

Planning and providing safe, reliable and economic transport facilities is both a responsibility and a challenge for the Mayor, the GLA and Transport *for* London. As the history of London's transport in the last century shows, it is a difficult and complex business. The quality of life in twenty-first century London and the daily travel experience of millions of people will depend upon its success.

A 21st-century view of Westminster Bridge, featuring the London Eye.
Photograph: Hugh Robertson

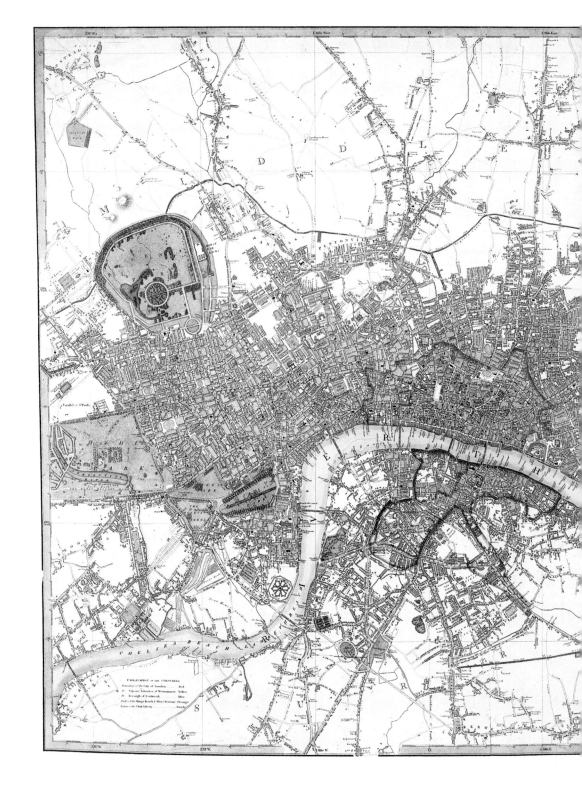

Horse Power and Steam Power

Transport for a Growing Metropolis 1800–1850

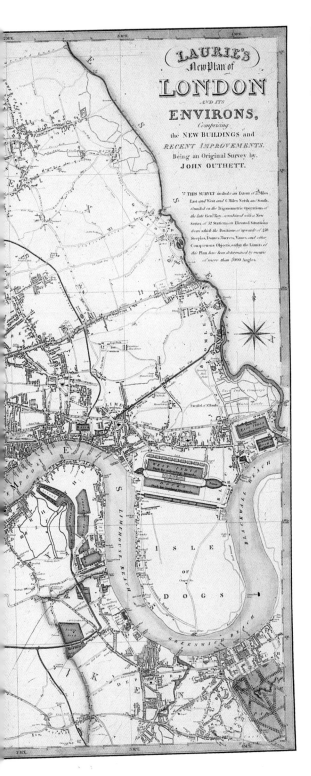

Map of London
1821

In 1800 London was the largest city in the world with nearly a million inhabitants, yet the main built-up area rarely extended more than a mile from the River Thames.

Horse Power and Steam Power
Transport for a Growing Metropolis, 1800–1850

Bashful men, who have been looking down the hatchway at the engine, find… a subject on which they can converse with one another… steam.
'Wonderful thing steam sir.' 'Ah! (a deep-drawn sigh) it is indeed sir.' 'Great power, sir.' 'Immense – immense!' 'Great deal done by steam, sir'. 'Ah! (another sigh at the immensity of the subject and a knowing shake of the head) you may say that, sir'. 'Still in its infancy, they say, sir.'

'The River' in *Sketches by Boz* by Charles Dickens, 1836

London in 1800 was the industrial and commercial centre of the nation. Its importance was symbolised by two building projects that were under way at the turn of the century: the construction of the great London Docks on the Thames and the major rebuilding of the Bank of England in the heart of the old City of London. Trade and finance were already fuelling the rapid expansion of the metropolis, which would see London's population more than double by 1850.

Very few Londoners or visitors to the capital could afford to ride around town,

London's Transport throughout the Ages
(detail) by R. T. Cooper
Poster
1929

although street congestion was already quite a problem for those who did. One of caricaturist Thomas Rowlandson's humorous *Miseries of London* cartoons depicts a traffic jam of private carriages as early as 1807. The caption reads: 'In going out to dinner (already too late) your carriage delayed by a jam of coaches which choke up the whole street and allow you at least an hour or more than you require to sharpen your wits for table talk ….' In 1807 private carriages would have been jostling in the narrow streets of London with about a thousand licensed hackney carriages available for hire and a similar number of short and long-haul stage coaches running out to the villages of Kensington, Richmond and beyond.

All these vehicles were, of course, horse-drawn, and because horses were expensive

MISERIES OF LONDON.

In going out to dinner (already too late) your carriage delayed by a jam of coaches — which choak up the whole street, and allow you least an hour or more than you require, to sharpen your wits for table talk —

***Miseries of London* by Thomas Rowlandson**
1807
Guildhall Library

Thomas Rowlandson satirised the problems of London life in the early nineteenth century in this series of prints. Here a rich couple on the way out to dinner encounter a jam of short stage coaches. By the 1820s about 600 short stage coaches operated from the City and the West End to the new suburbs such as Paddington and Camberwell.

to feed and maintain, fares on the early public services were high. When Shillibeer introduced the first omnibus service in 1829, he was able to undercut the fares of the short stage coaches but he was not going downmarket. His omnibus was advertised as 'a new carriage on the Parisian mode', and the proprietor stressed that 'a person of great respectability attends his vehicle as conductor and every possible attention will be paid to the accommodation of ladies and

London & Greenwich Railway viaduct
c. 1836

Most of the route for the London & Greenwich Railway was supported on a brick viaduct to avoid the expense of blocking existing roads or demolishing buildings. The Railway was also able to rent out the arches for warehouse space, and even for private homes and a pub.

children'. The omnibus was from the start a middle-class mode of transport, and was to remain so throughout the nineteenth century.

In 1839 there were 620 omnibuses in London, most of them licensed to carry 15 passengers in vehicles smaller than Shillibeer's original three-horse coach. By 1850 there were nearly 1300 omnibuses licensed, many of them seating up to 22 passengers. The vehicles were no larger, but up to nine of the seats were now 'outside' beside the driver and along the roof on the back-to-back 'knifeboard' bench. The standard London omnibus had become a rather primitive double decker.

The only mechanical competition for the horse-drawn omnibus in this period was on the river. Steamboats first appeared on the Thames in 1815 and were soon offering cheap and regular services all along the river from Greenwich to Chelsea. By the 1850s 15,000 people were travelling into London every day

The Thames below London Bridge
1839

Steam boats first appeared on the Thames in 1815, and paddlesteamers soon became very popular with pleasure-trippers as well as commuters, replacing most of the traditional wherries by the 1840s.

by paddlesteamer, and there was considerable excursion traffic up and down the river.

Steam had a less immediate impact on land travel in London. Although the first passenger-carrying railway in the capital, the London & Greenwich, was in effect a suburban service, most of the subsequent lines opened in the 1830s and 40s were primarily for long-distance traffic. Building these main lines required massive property demolition through great swathes of inner London with no benefit to those who were displaced. The poor could not afford to move further out, and the railway companies had not yet recognised the potential for middle-class commuter traffic from the suburbs. Even so, the effect of the railway on the character and shape of the Victorian city was already obvious to contemporary observers. Anthony Trollope wrote in his novel *The Three Clerks*, published in 1857, that:

'It is very difficult nowadays to say where the suburbs of London come to an end and where the country begins. The railways, instead of enabling Londoners to live in the country, have turned the countryside into a city. London will soon assume the shape of a great starfish. The old town, extending from Poplar to Hammersmith, will be the nucleus, and the various railway lines will be the projecting rays.' This was a perceptive prediction.

effect on the structure. In May 1924, because of increased river scouring, one of the main piers failed. Temporary repairs were carried out but it took another 10 years to begin demolition of the damaged bridge.

With delays caused by the outbreak of the Second World War, the formal opening of the present bridge did not take place until 10 December 1945.

◖ Waterloo Bridge under construction
opened 1817
London Metropolitan Archives

The River Thames was an important transport artery which divided the north from the south of London. As the city grew, so did the demand for a river crossing that was safer and more reliable than the weather-dependent ferry boats.

The first stone for the new Waterloo Bridge, designed by the engineer John Rennie, was laid in 1811, and the bridge finally opened on 18 June 1817.

The construction in the 1860s of the Embankment, upstream, and the growth in traffic on the bridge, were to have a severe

◖ Model of late Victorian Thames wherry
National Maritime Museum

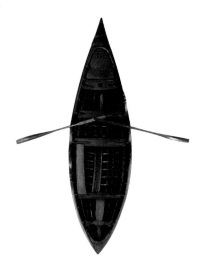

◖ Waterman's arm badge

The first public transport in London was provided by watermen using small rowing boats called wherries. The watermen wore distinctive uniforms and large metal arm badges.

◖ Waterloo Bridge
completed 1942
London Metropolitan Archives

This, the first all concrete bridge to span the Thames in London, was designed by Sir Giles Gilbert Scott and opened in December 1945, replacing Rennie's Georgian structure.

Within central London the strict licensing of hackney carriages gave them a virtual monopoly on the streets. Competition was introduced by the 1832 Stage Carriages Act, which allowed short stage coaches and omnibuses to compete in the central area for the first time.

🜂 **Cabs and carriages at Hyde Park Corner**
1820

Cheapside
1823
Museum of London

Hackney carriages dominated the City of London before omnibuses were allowed into the heart of the city.

Reynold's new patent safety cab
1846

The nineteenth century saw many competitions and private efforts to produce 'improved' vehicles. Reynold's design, however, is unlikely to have been judged sufficiently different from existing cabs, and may have progressed no further than this illustration.

Model of a 'coffin cab'
1824

Cabriolets were light, two-wheeled carriages, first used in France, and came to London in the 1820s. They were pressed into service as hackney carriages, competing with the more common four-wheeled vehicles then in use. When restrictions on numbers were lifted in 1831, the speedy cabriolet soon became popular. The abbreviation 'cab' was considered vulgar at first, but soon became commonplace. These early types were known as 'coffin cabs' because of the shape of the seat.

Cab with 'Patent Mile Index'
1847

Cab fares were set by various public authorities, including in turn the Hackney Carriage Office, the Stamp Office and finally the Public Carriage Office. They were based on a standard charge per mile. In the early days passengers depended to a large extent on the honesty of the driver. The 'Patent Mile Index' on this four-wheeled 'growler' was an early attempt to provide an independent check on distance travelled.

Harvey's 'Curricle Tribus'
1848

Seating only three people, this curious overgrown Hansom cab, complete with a conductor, like a bus, was introduced by Mr Harvey of Lambeth House. His publicity assured potential passengers that 'cab fares only' are charged. The idea seems to have sunk without trace.

Model of a Hansom cab
1873

This vehicle was named after Joseph Hansom, who patented an improved, safer cabriolet in 1834. Although his company was bought out by John Chapman, whose vehicles were substantially different from Hansom's original, Hansom's name stuck. This model shows the Hansom in its final form, which Disraeli dubbed the 'gondola of London', as developed by coach-builders Forder & Co.

SHILLIBEER'S SERVICE

George Shillibeer, 1797–1866

three steps, where the conductor stood. Inside were longitudinal seats, with room for around nine people each side. What distinguished the omnibus from existing short stage coach services, however, was the way it was operated. This involved running to a fixed timetable, whether or not the vehicle was full. The provision of a conductor – to collect fares – and easy access to the vehicle's single deck made 'short hop' journeys practical.

The first service was operated with two vehicles, which took between 40 minutes and an hour to traverse the route. This compares well with the three hours often taken by short stage coaches. The fare was one shilling. Despite opposition from local residents, the operation was a success, and within nine months Shillibeer's fleet had grown to twelve vehicles.

Reconstruction of Shillibeer's omnibus for the Lord Mayor's Show
1929

This reconstruction was built in 1929, to mark the omnibus centenary, and is still in the collection of London's Transport Museum.

George Shillibeer began his career as a coach-builder and stable-keeper. He started his omnibus service in London in 1829, but within two years, competitors forced him into bankruptcy. In 1831 the first horse bus association was formed to limit competition, with Shillibeer elected Chairman. However, after two spells in prison – for insolvency and for smuggling brandy – he withdrew from the bus scene, ending his days as a funeral director.

The design of Shillibeer's omnibus was not new, resembling the long stage coach that had been common from the end of the eighteenth century. A long, high-sprung box van with a flat roof, it was drawn by three horses. At the rear was a door approached by

'Shillibeer' horse bus at Horse Guards Parade
1830s
London Metropolitan Archives

After Shillibeer's withdrawal from bus operations, his name was appropriated by other operators anxious to establish their credibility, appearing on the side of buses on several routes in the 1830s.

Partnership agreement between George Shillibeer and William Morton
1832
Public Record Office

Shillibeer and Morton went into partnership when they introduced buses on to Oxford Street. The service was not competitive, and the partnership was dissolved in 1834, marking the demise of Shillibeer's bus interests.

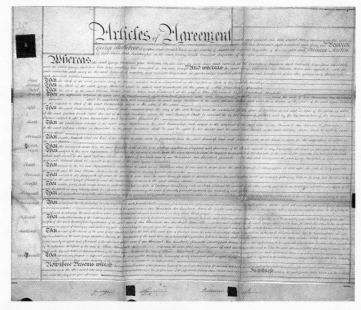

Detail from commemorative sundial designed by Edwin Russell at Tower Hill station, October 1996

The first omnibus service in London ran from the Yorkshire Stingo at Paddington, along the New Road to the Bank.

↻ Model of a short stage coach
1820s

Before the railways, stage coaches provided inter-city travel and covered shorter routes from cities such as London to nearby towns and villages. Closer stopping places on such routes led to the name 'short stage'. They were the main competition for Shillibeer's first bus service. Fares were high because of heavy taxes and road tolls.

◐ Parisian omnibus
1828

The world's first horse bus service was started in Paris, introduced by Jacques Lafitte in 1819. The name 'omnibus' was adopted by Stanislaus Baudry, who ran a service between Nantes and Richebourg. In 1828 the Paris Police authorised Baudry to operate a fleet of 100 buses across Paris. Shillibeer was inspired by Baudry's success, and may also have built buses for Lafitte.

◑ 'Favorite' horse bus
1845

In 1831 the first of many horse bus 'associations' was formed. These regulated the service, controlling the number of vehicles operating on a route and allocating times for different operators to run. The association name – 'Favorite' in this case – was usually painted on the side of the bus, which, together with its colour, gave a useful quick indication of the places served by a particular vehicle.

◑ Paddington 'Conveyance Association' horse bus
1830s

Shillibeer's buses were found to be rather cumbersome in crowded central London streets. As bus transport developed during the 1830s a smaller two-horse vehicle seating twelve people became the norm.

🎧 *The Rival Omnibuses*
1837

Efforts to establish new bus routes and build up the number of passengers using them led to keen competition between rival operators. Objections abounded as to sharp practices, crawling and obstruction. Once full, buses would then frequently race one another in an effort to claim any prospective passengers along the route.

🎧 *The Conductor*
c. 1840

The conductor, or 'cad' as he became known, secured the success of the omnibus. It was his job to help people on and off and collect the fares. In practice, competition focused his efforts on keeping the bus as full as possible. A cad portrayed by Dickens boasts 'that he can chuck an old gen'lm'n into the buss [sic], shut him in, and rattle off, afore he knows where it's a-going to'.

🎧 Hunnybun & Venden's 'New Patent Safety Omnibus'
1846

Ease of access was a key factor in the success of bus services, and the publicity accompanying this illustration claimed that its 'remarkable low construction' enabled passengers to board without the aid of a step. Nevertheless, one can be seen beneath the conductor's perch.

💧 Model of a 'knifeboard' horse bus
1850s

💧 Stockbrokers travelling to the City
1845

By the mid-1840s the newer buses had curved roofs, and at busy times the more athletic male passengers would clamber on the roof and sit back-to-back.

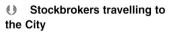

In 1847 a new type of omnibus with a clerestory roof was introduced. It provided a convenient place for 'outside' passengers to sit. By the 1850s the clerestory had acquired a long, padded, back-to-back seat. These vehicles were dubbed 'knifeboard' buses because of the seat's resemblance to a knife-cleaning board. Access to the new 'top deck' was by iron rungs alongside the door at the back.

Hancock's 'Autopsy', 'Era' and 'Infant' steam buses

Practical steam traction had evolved during the first three decades of the nineteenth century, leading in due course to the great railway revolution. Steam road vehicles also seemed full of promise. Relatively cheap to run and capable of speeds between 10 and 20 mph, they could easily compete with horse buses. Walter Hancock built nine in all, many of which saw service in London, until the idea was killed off in the 1840s.

James Clephan's London Railway
c. 1845

The 1840s was a period of 'railway mania', with many practical and impractical schemes proposed. The problems of constructing lines within London, where the need for transport was at its greatest, produced some remarkable schemes. One was James Clephan's London Railway of 1845–6. Designed to be worked by atmospheric power, it was to encircle London on a broad, elevated shopping arcade but was never built.

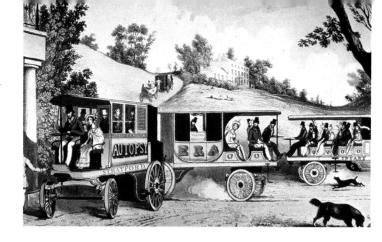

Dr Church's steam coach
1833

Steam coaches operated briefly on long-distance routes as well as in London. In addition to incessant breakdowns, they damaged road surfaces, despite the use of wide wheels. This resulted in punitive tolls on road steamers by the road authorities.

ten miles out, was the closest station to its terminus at Euston, the many intermediate stations coming later. Constructing the line involved much heavy engineering, including a major tunnel at Primrose Hill, as it ran through the Hampstead ridge, just north of the terminus.

London Bridge Station
1845

London Bridge Station was opened in 1836 by the London & Greenwich Railway. The company offered the use of its facilities to two other companies, the London & Croydon, opened in 1839, and the London & Brighton, which began carrying passengers in 1841. To cope with the traffic, a new joint station, designed by Henry Roberts, was opened in 1845. This Italianate building survived for only five years, since the joint users squabbled and began building separate sections at the station.

Surrey Iron Railway
1803–48

Early horse-drawn waggonways are associated with the industrial areas of England, where many early lines were constructed.

The Surrey Iron Railway, opened in 1803, was constructed in south London to link the important industries of Croydon and the Wandle Valley with the River Thames at Wandsworth. The Surrey Iron Railway was pioneering in being the first line in Britain that accepted goods for transportation from the public. Extended beyond Croydon in 1805, the line fell into disuse following the construction of steam-operated lines during the 1840s.

Primrose Hill Tunnel on the London & Birmingham Railway
1838

The London & Birmingham Railway (L&BR) built one of London's first inter-city rail links, marking a decisive break from the short, local lines that joined London to its immediate outskirts. In fact, Harrow, over

Invitation to opening ceremony of the London & Greenwich Railway
14 December 1836

London's first railway, the London & Greenwich, was four miles long, and conceived primarily as a commuter line in competition with a popular short stage coach route. The line terminated on the south side of London Bridge, close enough for city workers to walk to work.

⟳ Chalk Farm Bridge, with the city in the background
c. 1840

The bridge was built during construction of the London & Birmingham Railway.

⟳ Locomotive engine house, Camden
c. 1840
Public Record Office

This illustration shows the locomotive engine house at Camden on the London & Birmingham Railway, with a train changing from cable to locomotive haulage.

⟳ The locomotive roundhouse at Camden
1847

Built in 1847 on the London & Birmingham Railway, the roundhouse fell into disuse during the 1850s and has since seen many different uses, including a gin store, before becoming the performing arts space used today.

◐ Blackwall Station
c. 1840

Blackwall Station, designed by William Tite, was the terminus of the London & Blackwall Railway, which connected the Victorian city with the rapidly growing docklands of east London. Opened on 6 July 1840, the line ran from Fenchurch Street to Blackwall. The first section passed through a densely developed area. To minimise the demolition of property, it was built on a lengthy brick viaduct, which fell into disuse in the 1960s. Parts of it were reused by the Docklands Light Railway in 1987.

◑ The Euston Arch
1838
Public Record Office

Much of the architecture of the London & Birmingham Railway was on a grand scale. The famous Doric Euston Arch was designed by Philip Hardwick in 1838 and constructed as a triumphal entrance to both station and railway. This photograph was taken around 1910. Unfortunately, the arch was demolished during reconstruction of Euston in the 1960s. The stones, numbered for possible re-erection, are believed to lie at the bottom of the River Lee in east London. An image of the arch can be seen on the tile motifs on the platform at Euston Underground station.

◑ Tile motif of the Euston Arch
1968

THE THAMES TUNNEL

The Thames Tunnel was designed by Marc Isambard Brunel, a prolific inventor and royalist exile from Revolutionary France, who came to England via America in 1799. He quickly made his fortune in London making boots for the army and pulleys for the navy, but was bankrupted by the end of the Napoleonic Wars. Languishing in prison, he observed the tunnelling prowess of the common shipworm *teredo navalis*, which inspired the tunnelling shield used in the Thames Tunnel, his most ambitious project. The shield was composed of twelve separate frames with three cells, each measuring six by four feet. They covered the tunnel face, allowing up to 36 miners to dig simultaneously. The shield was advanced by a screw, 4½ inches at a time – the width of a single brick. The Thames Tunnel was

Marc Isambard Brunel, 1769–1849

This portrait of 1813 by James Northcote is in the National Portrait Gallery, London.

eventually opened in March 1843. Ten men had died during its construction, which took over 17 years and cost £614,000.

Although Brunel's company could not afford to build the great spiral 'descents' that would have allowed carriages under the Thames, more than a million people passed through the tunnel in the first four months. It was converted to railway use in 1869 and is now part of the East London line of the Underground, connecting Wapping and Rotherhithe. In 1995 London Underground Ltd proposed closing the dilapidated tunnel for seven months to re-line it using the spray concrete method used on the new Jubilee Line Extension tunnels. At the last minute English Heritage stepped in to ensure a more sympathetic restoration. The whole project took three years.

Wapping side of the Thames Tunnel *c.* 1843

Brunel's tunnelling shield

The design of the shield was inspired by the common shipworm.

The Tunnel or Another Bubble Burst
Guildhall Library
1830s

Although this satirical print makes fun of the work, it was no joke. At some places tunnelling took place only four metres below the river bed; there were constant leaks, often including raw sewage, and several major floods, and 10 men perished during construction.

Brunel's tunnel during refurbishment
1996

Plaque from the Institute of Civil Engineers honouring Brunel

INTERNATIONAL HISTORIC
CIVIL ENGINEERING LANDMARK

THAMES TUNNEL

CONSTRUCTED 1825-1843

FIRST SHIELD-DRIVEN SUBAQUEOUS TUNNEL

SIR MARC ISAMBARD BRUNEL
CIVIL ENGINEER

PRESENTED 25 SEPTEMBER, 1993

INSTITUTION OF CIVIL ENGINEERS
AND
AMERICAN SOCIETY OF CIVIL ENGINEERS

ERECTED BY KIND PERMISSION OF
LONDON UNDERGROUND LIMITED

The tunnel after refurbishment and resumption of East London Line services
1998

◉ Early disc signals on the Great Western Railway
c. 1844

◉ ◯ Early railway signalling
c. 1841

Since the beginning of the railways there has been a need to communicate to the train crew the conditions ahead to ensure the safe and efficient operation of the line. Although hand signalling was used on the early lines, it became necessary at such places as junctions to have fixed signal posts. Various designs were in use, but these disc signals are typical of those used at junctions on the Great Western Railway, in west London. The discs, hand operated on site, could be rotated to show simple 'stop' or 'proceed' indications. The discs were often repeated on high posts so as to aid train drivers in advance.

The junction in south-east London at New Cross Gate, on the London & Brighton Railway, saw the first installation of semaphore signals in 1841. These were to become the standard type of railway signals on all British railways. The arms are pivoted on the post and can show three indications: horizontal for 'stop'; lowered by 45 degrees for 'caution'; and vertically down for 'proceed'. By the use of associated lanterns and coloured lenses, these indications could be repeated, making the signals more visible at night.

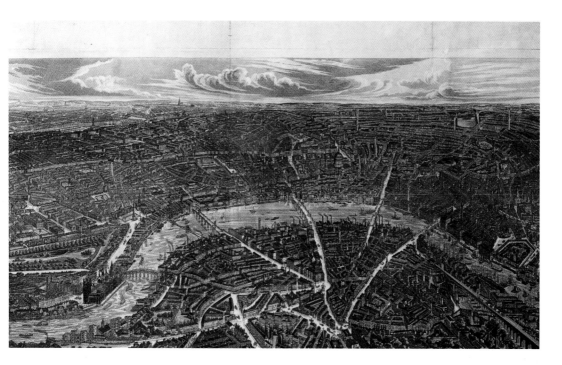

⌒ Panoramic view from Southwark to Hampstead
c. 1851

Around 1851, crossing the river would have meant using one of the bridges shown here, users being charged a toll for the privilege in most cases. Visible between Westminster and Waterloo Bridges is Hungerford Suspension Bridge, designed by Isambard Kingdom Brunel and opened in 1845. The brick piers still remain as part of Hungerford Railway Bridge, while the chains now support the Clifton Suspension Bridge over the Avon at Bristol.

↻ *London, 1800–1850* by Zero (Hans Schleger)
1936

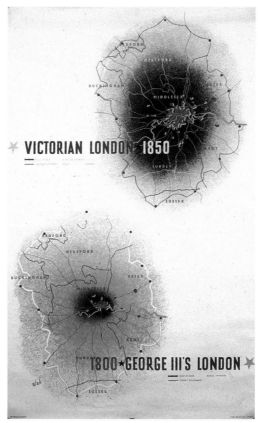

This poster clearly illustrates that after 1800 London expanded rapidly in all directions. By 1850 the population had reached nearly two and a half million.

Swing Sash

4 INCH DRAIN PIPE

LEVEL OF RAILS

SECTION ON LINE

Overground and Underground

The Circle Squared 1850–1900

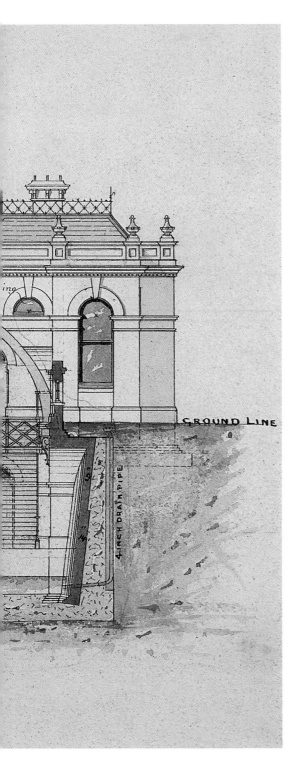

GROUND LINE

4 INCH DRAIN PIPE

St James's Park station

Architectural drawing of the station, which opened in 1868.

Overground and Underground
The Circle Squared, 1850–1900

Once upon a time the Strand was 'up', and the London 'bus was drawn by horses. The bus driver, threading his way painfully through the dishevelled traffic, looked over his shoulder, and called to his front seat passenger: 'A damned fine city London will be, sir – when it's finished!'

Reminiscences of J.B. Booth, Victorian journalist, *Sporting Times*, 1938

City & South London Railway carriage and locomotive.
Photograph: Printz P. Holman

Hyde Park Corner
1888

The Great Exhibition of 1851 was the biggest show the world had ever seen, and was London's first large-scale visitor attraction. In the six months that it was open in Hyde Park, six million visitors flocked to see it. For transport operators this was their first experience of dealing with huge crowds of trippers and tourists, and the temporary traffic boom brought chaos and only short-term profits. Omnibus proprietors were inevitably soon faced with a subsequent slump in traffic, which made them vulnerable to takeover bids from an ambitious new organisation, the London General Omnibus Company (LGOC), set up in 1856.

The LGOC never achieved a monopoly of horse-bus operations in London, but it quickly came to dominate the market. With the removal of most remaining tolls and taxes, the LGOC was able to make fairly good profits throughout the second half of the century. Although there was competition on some routes from the new tramways and underground railways, the number of

omnibus passengers continued to rise steadily. In 1885 the LGOC carried nearly 77 million passengers; by 1890 this figure had risen to over 112 million.

When permanent street tramways were opened in London from 1870 onwards, they catered for a different market. By using larger vehicles with twice the capacity of an omnibus, tramway companies could afford to offer lower fares. Like the railways from the 1860s, they were also obliged by law to provide special workmen's tickets, usually at half price, in the early morning and after 6pm. The first tram on the North Metropolitan system was at 4.45am. Omnibuses, by contrast, did not start running before 8am, too late for working-class travellers but well timed for City clerks. The last 30 years of the century saw an almost continuous increase in traffic on both omnibuses and trams. In the

**Stained-glass window from the offices of the
Metropolitan District Railway**
c. 1880

mid-1870s the LGOC, its 200 associates and a handful of independent omnibus operators were carrying about 70 million passengers a year, while the three tramway companies carried about 50 million. Twenty years later both had more than quadrupled their traffic to about 300 million and 280 million passengers respectively.

The social contrast between the two forms of transport was pointed out in an article in the *Cornhill Magazine* in 1890. London omnibuses, the writer observed, were becoming more comfortable and convenient to use, and, as a result, 'ladies and gentlemen, officers, members of first class clubs even, all patronise the once despised 'bus'. At the same time 'the working man is rarely seen on the upholstered cushions; he feels himself uncomfortable and *de trop*. The tramcar is *his* familiar vehicle and he can ensconce himself there in his mortar splashed clothes without restraint.'

Suburban railway traffic in London was also booming from the 1860s onwards, both to and from the mainline termini and on the two new underground railways that linked them, the Metropolitan and the Metropolitan District. The former, opened triumphantly as the world's first undergound railway in 1863, was carrying about 40 million passengers a year on its extended line by the 1870s. The District, opened in 1868 and then also progressively extended, carried about half as many passengers. Both underground companies followed the example of the main lines by developing overground suburban extensions to generate more traffic before completing what is now the Circle line by linking their original lines at both ends.

The Inner Circle underground railway was finally created in 1884, by which time there was rather less enthusiasm for the experience of underground railway travel. It provided a rapid and easy way of getting round Central London. However, with steam locomotives a trip was invariably smokey and unpleasant. The day after the Circle opened *The Times* commented that 'a journey from King's Cross

to Baker Street is a form of mild torture which no person would undergo if he could conveniently help it'. The condensing apparatus on the locomotives reduced, but did not eliminate steam emission, and the open sections and 'blow holes' in the 'cut and cover' tunnels did not provide adequate ventilation. Little could be done to improve matters until electrification transformed the experience of underground travel at the turn of the century. By then the combination of a safe, deep level tunnelling method and a non-polluting power

Horse tram at Stamford Hill
1888

source had been demonstrated on the world's first deep level electric tube, the City & South London Railway, opened in 1890. It was, however, by no means obvious at the time that this pioneering little line represented a revolutionary way forward for urban transport. Its successors were to do so in a remarkably short period of time.

CUT AND COVER

Until the advent of the Metropolitan in the early 1860s, nobody had built an underground railway, so the appropriate technology had to be developed. Construction proceeded on what came to be known as the 'cut and cover' principle. To simplify matters the railway followed the street wherever possible, as burrowing beneath buildings could lead to complications and extra expense. Broadly speaking, the road surface was lifted, excavation took place below, retaining walls, tunnels and track were installed beneath the street, and the roadway was finally replaced, or 'covered over'. This method of construction was extremely disruptive for road-users.

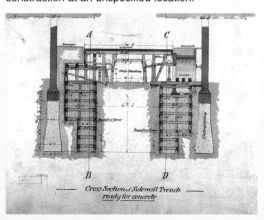

⬏ **Cut and cover**
October 1861

Engraving showing, with a touch of artistic licence, a view of 'cut and cover' construction at an unspecified location.

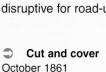

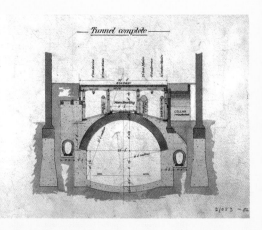

⬏ **'Cut and cover' construction below Cannon Street, showing work in progress (above left) and the finished tunnel (above right)**
c. 1884

THE METROPOLITAN (UNDERGROUND) RAILWAY.—WORKS IN PROGRESS AT KING'S CROSS.

🎧 Cut and cover
1862

Contemporary engraving showing 'cut and cover' construction of the Metropolitan line at King's Cross, with the 10-year old mainline station recognisable from its clock tower in the background.

🎧 Cut and cover construction at South Kensington
1868

The scale of the excavation work required for the cut and cover method of tunnel building is evident in this view, showing the twin tunnels of The District Railway under construction near South Kensington.

Metropolitan heraldry

The earlier version of the Metropolitan Railway coat of arms. Railway coats of arms were often arbitrary affairs, cobbled together from various sources. The Metropolitan was no exception, appropriating the St George Cross with the sword of St Paul from the City of London, albeit hopefully inscribed 'We work for all'.

Director's pass
pre-1900

Staff travel pass belonging to a director of the Metropolitan Railway.

Metropolitan Railway Illustrated Guide
1888

This guide features an elaborate Victorian gothic cover. Most of the locations mentioned would still be featured on today's tourist trail, with the possible exception of Lambeth Palace.

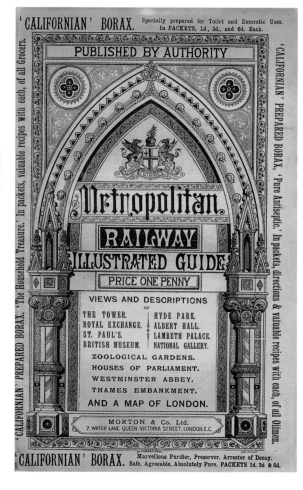

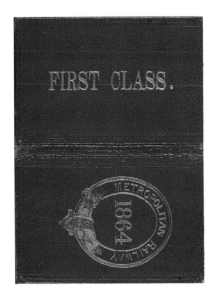

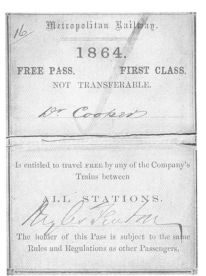

⊕ First class staff travel pass
1864

Metropolitan Railway First Class Free Pass for 1864, the year following the opening of London's first underground railway. The pass has been signed by Myles Fenton (1830–1918), General Manager of the Railway from 1863 to 1880. He was knighted in 1889.

⊃ Sir John Fowler, 1817–98
National Portrait Gallery

One of the greatest Victorian civil engineers, Sir John Fowler was the chief engineer to both the Metropolitan and District Railways. The technology that made possible the construction of the Underground was largely his.

Opening of the Metropolitan Railway
1862

Seated amidst a forest of top hats in the broad-gauge trucks of the contractors, Messrs Smith & Knight, an assemblage of Victorian worthies enjoy the novelty of underground travel on the celebrated Metropolitan Railway trial trip of 24 May 1862. Engineer John Fowler in light coloured "topper" leaning his elbow on the side of the truck sits next to William Gladstone, then Chancellor of the Exchequer.

'Fowler's Ghost'

This locomotive was so-called because for many years there was some doubt as to whether it actually existed. Designed by Sir John Fowler and built by Stephenson's, it attempted to solve the problem (never successfully dealt with) of using steam propulsion underground without creating an intolerable atmosphere. Designed to be 'smokeless', a small firebox pre-heated a combustion chamber in the boiler containing fire-bricks, which were supposed to maintain a head of steam while the engine was working in the tunnel. The experiment was not a success.

Bayswater station
1868

Newly completed as part of the Metropolitan Railway extension from west of Edgware Road to Gloucester Road, this photograph shows Bayswater station shortly after it opened in 1868.

King's Cross Station

One of the original stations on the first stretch of the Underground to open in 1863 was King's Cross, here shown with mixed gauge tracks to accommodate the broad gauge trains of the Great Western Railway. Strictly speaking the station is not underground at all, and boasts a traditional nineteenth-century elevated glass and iron train shed to help dispel smoke and fumes.

A steam classic

Quickly falling out with the Great Western Railway, which had agreed to provide it with locomotives and rolling stock, the Metropolitan was forced to come up with something suitable of its own. The result was the classic type of 4-4-0 condensing tank locomotive built by Beyer Peacock between 1864 and 1886, which almost monopolised services on both the Metropolitan and Metropolitan District Railways for as long as steam lasted. Dating from 1866, locomotive No. 23, now in London's Transport Museum, is seen here restored to its 1903 condition.

⟲ **Metropolitan Railway timetable**
1883–4

The Metropolitan offered express horse bus services between its Portland Road (now Great Portland Street) station and the mainline station at Charing Cross, to attract passengers to its services.

◑ **The finger of competition**
1886

There was never any love lost between the Metropolitan and District Railways. This was largely due to the clash between Sir Edward Watkin, Chairman of the Metropolitan, and James Staats Forbes, Managing Director of the District, whose personal antagonism bedevilled entire areas of railway politics. Although both railways had grudgingly co-operated to complete the Circle line in 1884, this poster shows that battle still raged, with the Metropolitan attempting 'one-upmanship' at

the expense of the District by claiming that their services were quicker and cheaper.

◑ **Baker Street station**
1863

The Metropolitan opened the world's first underground railway between Paddington and Farringdon in 1863. Baker Street was one of the original stations. However, unlike King's Cross, the platforms were truly underground. The suspended globes contained gas lighting, although daylight penetrated through the brick recesses, which were initially glazed. The glass was taken out in the late 1860s in an attempt to cope with the ever present problem of ventilation.

◌ Tile from Baker Street station
1863

Believed to be a rare survivor from the earliest Metropolitan Railway station, this decorative ceramic tile was salvaged from the platforms at Baker Street during building work in the late 1980s.

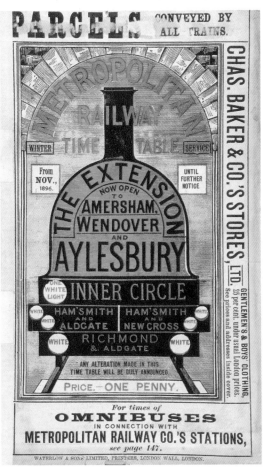

◌ Aylesbury extension timetable
1896

The Metropolitan gradually edged northwards from Harrow, opening its service to Aylesbury via Amersham and Wendover in 1895, an event commemorated on the cover of this timetable. By 1897 the Railway had pushed on to Verney Junction, more than 50 miles from Baker Street.

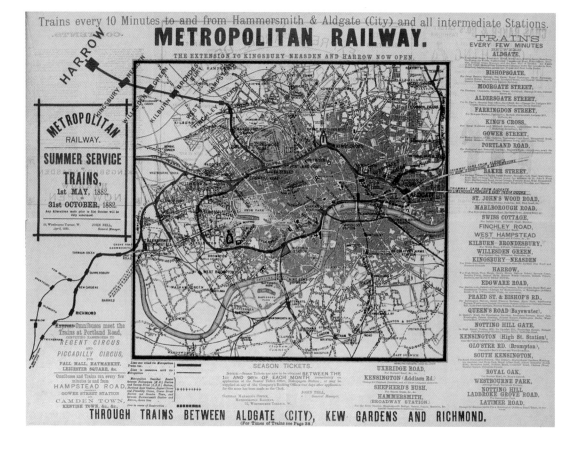

Metropolitan Railway map
1882

In 1868 the Metropolitan became responsible for running an apparently insignificant branch line, the Metropolitan & St John's Wood Railway. Unremarkable as it seemed at the time, this was the Metropolitan's first move towards what was to become its outer suburban empire known as 'Metro-Land'. By 1880 the Railway had reached Harrow. This map from the 1882 timetable proudly announces that this recent extension is open.

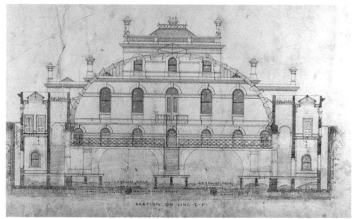

Sectional drawing for the Metropolitan Railway station at Gloucester Road
c. 1867

The Metropolitan Railway opened an extension from Praed Street junction to Gloucester Road in 1868, built under the supervision of the Railway's chief engineer Sir John Fowler. The design for the surface building at Gloucester Road conforms to the neo-classical style adopted for all the stations on the extension, although it is unusual in having a second storey.

Rounding the Circle
c. 1866

The Metropolitan's Notting Hill & Brompton extension authorised the Railway to extend from Paddington to South Kensington, forming what is now the western curve of the Circle line. This photograph shows the construction of the twin tunnels of the Gloucester Road section, with five rings of brickwork superimposed upon iron. The number of attendant navvies hints at the enormous size of the workforce. The Inner Circle was not completed until 1884.

Metropolitan Railway tickets
1879–96
Public Record Office

These tickets are for 1st, 2nd and 3rd class travel from various stations on what became known as the Inner Circle line. The bold 'I' on later tickets shows validity via the direct 'Inner Rail', as distinct from the other direction, the 'Outer Rail'. Second-class travel on the Metropolitan Railway ceased in 1906.

Gloucester Road station

Gloucester Road station is one of the best surviving examples of a mid-Victorian station, with its fine yellow brick Italianate exterior. The roof parapet has been restored, and the lower level canopy is a modern version of an original feature. In 1985 the station became a Grade II listed building.

Gloucester Road station refurbishment

c. 1990

The station was carefully integrated into a new development during the 1990s. Although the original arched open District line platforms were rafted over as part of the development, the preservation of the retaining walls, along with careful lighting, have provided a period feel for the station.

Ticket hall at Gloucester Road station

The original barrel-vaulted ticket hall leading down to the platforms has been restored as part of the refurbishment.

Notting Hill Gate station
1868

Metropolitan Railway's Notting Hill Gate station ready for opening in 1868. The iron and glass windshield of the high roof dominates the photograph.

Ticket hall at Rickmansworth station
1934

A typical rural station on the Metropolitan Railway, little changed from Victorian times.

Concrete Side Walls rendered in Cement

In 1884, when the 'Albert Hall Subway' was proposed, it was intended to run under Exhibition Road from South Kensington station to the Royal Albert Hall. Ticket offices and turnstiles leading from the subway to the South Kensington museums were also planned but never built.

🎧 Map of District Railway & Connections
1892

By the end of the nineteenth century, London was ringed and crossed by a bewildering variety of connecting railway services. Using the connections, it was possible to travel the length and breadth of London but most people used the railways for short hops to avoid being held up on a horse bus in a traffic jam. In 1902 this map was updated to include the Whitechapel & Bow Railway and showed connections with the London, Tilbury & Southend Railway to Southend.

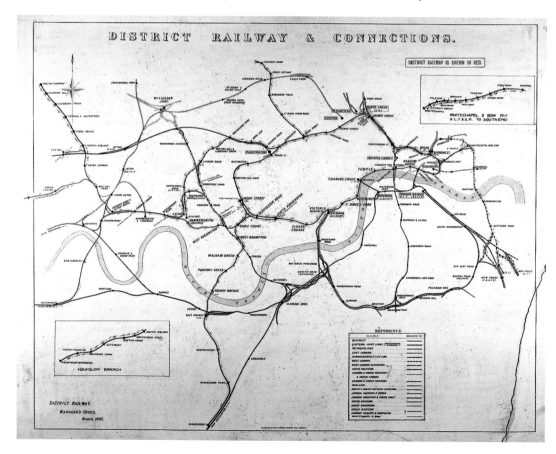

Sir Joseph Bazalgette, 1819–91

Thames Water

Chief Engineer to the Metropolitan Board of Works, Sir Joseph Bazalgette probably did more for London than any other individual since Sir Christopher Wren, and yet his name is now relatively unknown. His great achievement was to transform London into a far healthier city by engineering the great system of sewers on which its well-being still depends. Part of that system is enclosed beneath the Thames Embankment, and so it is fitting that his memorial should have been placed on the Victoria Embankment close to Hungerford Bridge.

Beneath the Embankment

1867

A cross section of Joseph Bazalgette's Victoria Embankment, dating from 1867 when it was under construction. The upper subway contains public utilities, gas and probably water, whilst the lower carries the sewer. The District Underground Railway was accommodated beneath the Embankment between Westminster and the City. The railway running left to right in the foreground is the Whitehall & Waterloo pneumatic tube, proposed in 1865, partly constructed but never completed. In the background are Hungerford Bridge and the South Eastern Railway's Charing Cross terminus.

🎧 **Initials of the Metropolitan Board of Works on a lamp standard on the Embankment**

🎧 **West Brompton station**
1876

Established in 1855, the Metropolitan Board of Works (MBW) was London's first centralised administration. Not only was it responsible for appointing Bazalgette to mastermind the sewer system, but also for vital street improvements, including the Thames Embankments, which reduced traffic congestion. The MBW was replaced by the London County Council in 1889.

A District Railway train at West Brompton in 1876 when the station was still a terminus, before the opening of the Putney Bridge and Fulham extension in 1880. Locomotive No. 10 was one of the first batch of Beyer Peacock 4-4-0 tanks to enter service with the District and is seen here in original condition

displaying much brass and copper. Prominent are the connecting pipes across the firebox top to allow water vapour created by condensing to escape. The four-wheel carriages were oil-lit.

🌀 **Charing Cross**
1894

A steam-hauled Inner Circle line train entering Charing Cross (now Embankment). This part of the station is in its original state, with the elliptical glazed roof (removed about 1914) still in place. Advertisements for property, theatrical performances and Turkish baths jostle for attention behind the passengers.

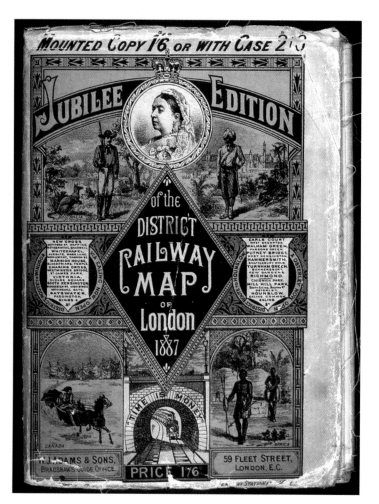

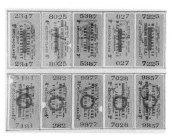

Metropolitan District Railway tickets
Pre-1900
Public Record Office

These second-class travel tickets define the correct route to be taken on the Inner Circle line by 'I' for Inner Rail (i.e. anticlockwise) and 'O' for Outer Rail (clockwise). Also shown are overprinted identifying initials of the destination stations to speed up ticket collection and reduce fraud. Second-class travel on the District Railway ceased in 1905.

Jubilee edition of the District Railway Map of London
1887

The District Railway was a prolific publisher of maps of London designed to encourage use of its services. The covers usually showed London scenes, but for Queen Victoria's Golden Jubilee celebrations the District had branched out to illustrate areas of the Empire not even it could claim to serve by direct services!

The Victorian Era Exhibition, *District Railway's Illustrated Guide*
1897

An exhibition was held at Earl's Court in 1897 to celebrate Queen Victoria's Jubilee. This cover uses transport as a theme to illustrate almost a century of progress, from stage coach to steam. The price of a District Railway ticket included entrance to the exhibition. A great attraction at Earl's Court exhibitions between 1894 and 1907 was the enormous Ferris Wheel, as popular in its day as the London Eye is now.

THE TOWER SUBWAY — THE FIRST TUBE TUNNEL IN THE WORLD

The Tower Subway was formally opened on 2 August 1870. A tunnel, only seven feet in diameter and 1430 feet long, was built under the Thames by the engineer Peter Barlow using an excavating shield that he patented in 1864. Each end of the tunnel was reached by a shaft, one at Tower Hill, the other in Vine Street. A railway track was laid along the tunnel, and a single carriage was hauled backwards and forwards by a wire rope attached at each end to a four horse-power, single-cylinder steam engine. However, this cable system was a failure, and the company was bankrupt in less than a year.

After the machinery was removed, the tunnel was used by pedestrians, who reached it by wooden staircases. More than a million people a year walked through the tunnel until the opening of Tower Bridge in 1894 made it obsolete.

◗ **Peter William Barlow, 1809–85**

Barlow was a noted bridge, canal and railway engineer, who built the Tower Subway.

◖◗ **'Advancing the shield'**
September 1869
Illustrated Times

The shield included a water-tight door through which the clay face was dug out by hand. The shield was then forced forward by manual screw jacks. The tunnel was lined with cast-iron rings bolted together.

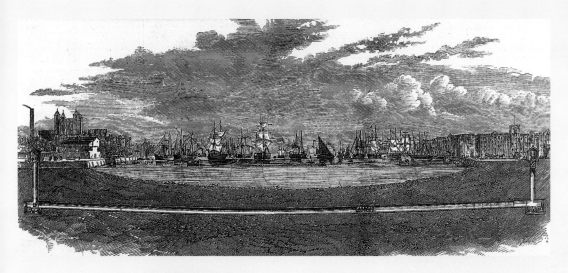

Tower Subway cross-section
1870

The tunnel dipped slightly towards the middle. Barlow hoped in vain that the slope would allow the carriage to build up momentum.

Tower Subway, Tooley Street 'station'
1870

Passengers descended 60 feet in a steam-powered lift to a small waiting room, somewhat pretentiously referred to as a 'station'.

Tower Subway carriage interior
1870

The iron carriage held up to 12 passengers. Journey time was optimistically estimated at 70 seconds.

⌒ Mansion House
1850s
Public Record Office

Pedestrians outnumber road vehicles in this view at Mansion House. The perspective has been widened to exaggerate the space, and perhaps to de-emphasise the traffic and crowding associated with this busy junction. The single horse bus is of the early type, without the addition of roof seating.

◔ Horse trams at Marble Arch
1861
London Metropolitan Archives

George Francis Train opened three short tram lines in London in 1861. Within 18 months all three had

been closed and the rails torn up. Although one line did run close to Marble Arch, this scene is largely fictitious, and the double-deck vehicle on the right is pure fantasy.

⌒ *St Pancras Hotel and station from Pentonville Road* by John O'Connor
1884
Museum of London

This painting of a sunset over King's Cross, with St Pancras in the background, shows horse trams struggling up Pentonville Road, for which a third horse was needed.

The 'Growler' survives
mid-1920s

Motor cabs began to take over from the 1900s but there were still horse-drawn cabs in the 1920s. This photograph shows a four-wheeler weighed down with Kelly's Directories outside Kelly's London office.

'Growler' cab in the Strand opposite the Law Courts
c. 1880
London Metropolitan Archives

Following the abolition of their City monopoly in 1832, London's cabs began a slow decline, although a minority of better off travellers continued to prefer them to horse buses. Four-wheeler cabs known as Clarences or 'Growlers' were cheaper than Hansoms.

'Knifeboard' horse bus on the Strand
1850s
London Metropolitan Archives

The first horse buses to add proper roof seating appeared in the late 1840s, and most others added them to cope with the extra demand during the Great Exhibition of 1851. The earliest examples had a single seat running down the length of the roof, with room for up to ten extra passengers sitting back-to-back.

T. H. Shepherd   Engraved by Read & Co   Published 1851.

REGENT'S CIRCUS, OXFORD S͏͏T

◑ Artist's impression of Regent's Circus
1851

Ranged either side of the military is a representative selection of mid-Victorian horse traffic, including Hackney cabs (four-wheelers), a private coach surmounted by bewigged coachman and emblazoned with coat of arms, a two-horse dray, and a pair of omnibuses, one a 'knifeboard' with passengers 'on the roof'. As a vehicle the bus was still evolving, and was to develop rapidly in this year of the Great Exhibition.

⤵ 'The Great Globe', Leicester Square
1851

The horse bus advertises what the impressive building contains – 'The Great Globe', a panoramic view of the Earth, 60 feet in diameter, built by geographer James Wylde. On the removal of Mr Wylde's attraction in 1862, Leicester Square rapidly deteriorated into a sort of embarrassing rubbish dump until rescued on behalf of the public by the financier Baron Grant in the 1870s.

🎧 London Bridge blockade
1857

This print showing congestion on London Bridge emphasises how, by the middle of the nineteenth century (and not for the last time) London was choking with traffic. Apart from the provision of alternative forms of transport, there was a clear need for new and better streets. Consequently a number of important thoroughfares, such as the Victoria Embankment, Queen Victoria Street and Holborn Viaduct were all completed between 1869 and the end of the century.

🔊 In the heart of the City
1851
London Metropolitan Archives

In this scene of 1851 at the Royal Exchange, the 'knifeboard' bus of the London Conveyance Company is featured in the middle foreground. The company succumbed to intense competition a year later as the horse bus came into its own. By October 1852 the company's 65 buses and 508 horses were up for sale.

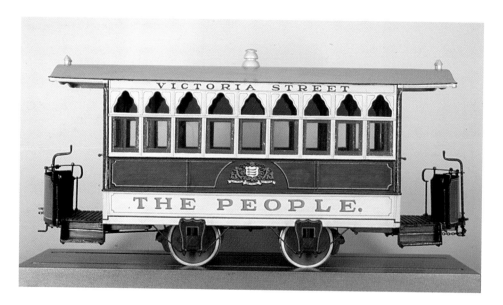

Model of one of London's first horse trams
1861

American George Francis Train built three tram lines in central London in spring and summer 1861. However, the L-shaped step rails of their track were unpopular, and had to be removed in a matter of months following legal action.

John Stephenson & Co horse tram
c. 1882

Stephenson trams were known the world over, and London's early tramway operators imported them direct from New York. This one is a 'garden seat' car of the London Tramways Company, which served a wide area of south London from Waterloo and Southwark to Tooting, Streatham and Greenwich.

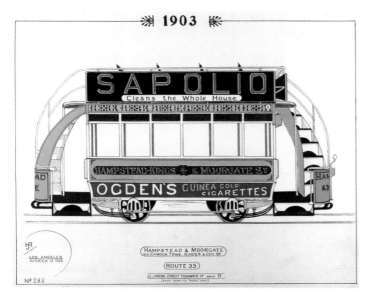

North Metropolitan horse tram
1903

A horse tram, owned by London's largest operator, the North Metropolitan Tramways Company. The reversible 'garden seat' design replaced the original 'knifeboard' seating in the early 1880s.

Horse tram interior
1870

Attempts to establish trams in London in 1869 with a new type of track were more successful than Train's efforts. The Metropolitan Street Tramways Company started its first service between Brixton and Kennington, in May 1870, carrying almost twice as many people as the average horse bus and for a lower fare.

LONDON STREET TRAMWAYS COMPANY TICKETS

By 1875 the London Street Tramways Company was issuing these colourful tickets. Minimum information about stages and fares was given under the advertisement on the reverse, and no doubt the advertising revenue was of more value to the usually impecunious companies. Most of the engravings are based on nursery tales, into which are introduced such useful products as 'Bonsor's Celebrated Tea' or 'Epps's Cocoa'. It is thought that another purpose of these attractive tickets was to encourage passengers to retain them so that conductors, who as yet did not have cancelling punches, would not be tempted to re-issue discarded ones.

London Street Tramways Company tickets

Horse tram ticket

This rare ticket was issued on the first day that horse trams ran between Euston Road and the 'Bull and Gate' at Kentish Town. It is on flimsy paper and is the size of a postage stamp.

Entertaining the men
1904

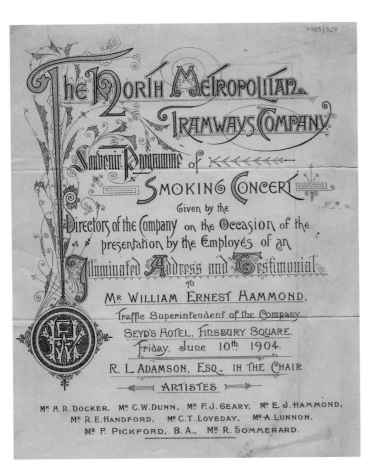

Souvenir programme of a 'smoking concert' given by the North Metropolitan Tramways Co. on behalf of senior employee William Ernest Hammond in 1904. Smoking concerts were strictly for 'men only'. Some of the 'artistes' may have been professional, or semi-professional, but were more likely to have been members of tramway staff performing their 'party pieces'. The absence of female company would allow some of the material to be a shade risqué, while without the ladies, the men could smoke to their heart's content. In 1904 a woman who smoked in public was 'not what she ought to be'.

Hampstead depot staff
1903

London Street Tramways staff pose for a group photograph outside Hampstead depot. The smart suits and white horses suggest a special occasion, possibly a Sunday outing.

◑ North London Tramways
Company tickets
c. 1886

The North London Tramways
Company was unique among
the Victorian tramway
companies of London in
operating steam trams. These
were supplemented at times by
horse-drawn cars, but the steam
operation continued from 1885
to 1892. These tickets, which
were issued on the steam trams,
were designed to be cancelled
by punching or tearing off the
appropriate diagonal corner for
the authorised journey

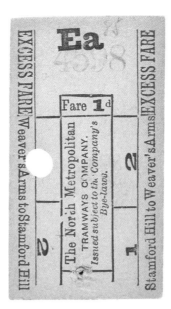

◔ North Metropolitan Tramways Company ticket
1884

◔ North Metropolitan Tramways Company ticket
1885

The North Metropolitan
Tramways Company ran an
extensive network of horse tram
services in north and east
London. The services they ran
used different coloured tramcars
according to the route on which
they operated. This 2d ticket
from 1884 is for the line from the
Archway Tavern to the City
Boundary (at Moorgate), which
was operated by red cars. The
ticket allows for two options for
the 2d fare and has been
cancelled with a ticket punch.

This blue 1d ticket from 1885 is
for issue between the 'Weaver's
Arms' at Stoke Newington and
Stamford Hill. It also has
provision to enable it to be used
as an excess fare, presumably
for over-riding or passengers
wishing to continue beyond the
point allowed by the ticket they
initially bought.

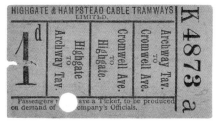

↺ ↻ **Cable tram tickets**
1891

↺ **Workmen's tram tickets**
c. 1900

These tickets were issued for the Highgate Hill cable tram, which was the first cable tramway in Europe. Note that while the 2d is solely for the ascent from the Archway Tavern to Highgate Village, the 1d allows for an ascent to be made over the top or bottom half of the route or a complete descent all the way.

It was mandatory for tramway companies to provide special cars at appropriate times of day for 'artisans and daily labourers', at cheaper fares. 'Two-journey tickets' were issued for a return journey. When presented with this ticket, the conductor would issue an 'exchange ticket' and retain the original for accounting purposes. These examples were issued for the Stamford Hill and Moorgate line by the North Metropolitan Tramways Company.

↺ **Horse tram traffic**
c. 1900

Trams of the north Metropolitan Tramways Company in service at Stoke Newington.

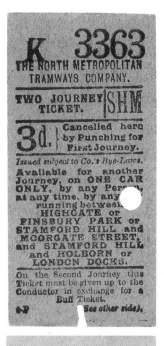

HIGH STREET, STOKE NEWINGTON.

◑ Steam trams

Several companies in London considered or tried steam trams, but the only enduring operation was by the North London Tramways Company. It ran 25 such trams exclusively on its Finsbury Park to Wood Green and Edmonton services between 1885 and 1891, when the company went into liquidation. The locomotives were a mixture of Merryweather and Dick Kerr machines, with deep skirt panels covering the wheels, as required for tramway operation. They hauled long wheelbase Falcon trailers, which had their bogies under the platforms so the passenger entrance steps were at an angle on the end corners of the cars.

◔ Cable-hauled trams

The first cable-hauled tramway in Europe opened in 1884 and ran between Archway Tavern and Highgate Village up the 1 in 11 gradient of Highgate Hill. It was operated by the Steep Grade Tramways and Works Company Ltd. The cars were hauled by a continuous moving cable in a conduit between the running rails, to which the car could be attached by a gripper. It had a chequered career, with two complete closures before it was finally taken over by the LCC in 1909 and closed for electrification.

◑ First cable tramway

This cable tramway was built in 1884 to service Highgate Hill.

Morning rush-hour at the Bank
1858

City workers alight from a jumble of 'knifeboard' horse buses at the Bank. At peak times as many as 600 buses per hour would cross this junction. The 'knifeboard' bus had improved ventilation and a clerestory roof to increase the headroom. This enabled a longitudinal seat to be fixed to the roof, reached by a series of metal foot rungs, outside passengers being carried at half fare. These buses were not immediately popular, as they were heavy and expensive, but they went into general use in the late 1850s.

'Improved' knifeboard bus

In 1881 the newly formed London Road Car Company introduced a new type of 'knifeboard', with improved access to the upper deck by means of a staircase at the front, and very small front wheels. These proved unsatisfactory and the front entrance unsafe, as passengers could go under the rear wheels if they fell. The front wheels soon reverted to the conventional size.

The 'garden seat' bus in the colours of the Atlas and Waterloo Omnibus Association
1881

After problems with the 'knifeboard' bus, the London Road Car Company designed a revolutionary new double-decker with its upper deck seats arranged in forward-facing pairs each side of a centre gangway. It became known as the 'garden seat' omnibus. The early examples had the same improved access to the upper deck, by a staircase at the front, as had been tried on the company's 'knifeboards'. This arrangement proved unsatisfactory and was soon abandoned, the stairs being moved to the conventional position at the back as seen here.

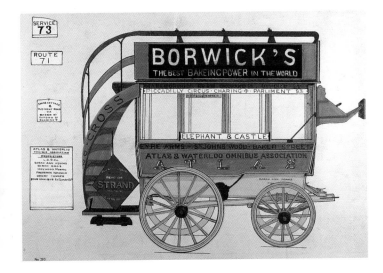

LONDON GENERAL OMNIBUS COMPANY (LGOC)

The LGOC was set up by a French political refugee, Joseph Orsi, in collaboration with a Paris businessman, Leopold Foucauld, with the intention of developing a monopoly on the Paris model, which Orsi had helped create. It was therefore registered in Paris under the name 'Compagnie Générale des Omnibus de Londres'. The business was reconstituted as the London General Omnibus Company in 1856 but did not live down its foreign origins easily. The London Road Car Company snubbed the 'foreigners' as late as 1881 by flying the Union Jack on its buses. The LGOC set up its own coach factory in Islington in 1871 and continued to build bus bodies into the motor bus era. The company became the largest bus operator, working in association with the Tilling, Nationals and East Surrey companies, and become a major part of London Transport in 1933.

● **Company seal of the Compagnie Générale des Omnibus de Londres**

● **LGOC coach factory**
c. 1900

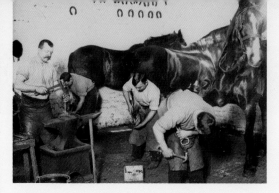

🎧 **Horses in an LGOC blacksmith's forge**
c. 1900

By 1900 there were over 40,000 horses working in London, but horse power was expensive. The standard two-horse bus needed a dozen animals for a working day of fourteen hours, each pair working a maximum of three hours. The supply of fodder was a major cost that could vary widely depending on the state of the harvest. Increases in a bad year could severely reduce the company's profit.

🎧 **'Knifeboard' bus**
1850s

This LGOC bus served the Caledonian Market to Pimlico route.

💠 **LGOC contract ticket**
1850s

No tickets were issued for normal fares on the first horse buses, but pre-paid contract tickets were available in books of 100. The price of a journey was high, reflecting the 'middle-class' nature of omnibus travel in the early days.

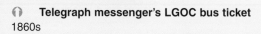

🎧 **LGOC horse bus conductor**
1890s

🎧 **Telegraph messenger's LGOC bus ticket**
1860s

A pre-paid ticket for a telegraph messenger in uniform to ride outside (on the upper deck) on an LGOC omnibus. The ticket bears the unusual watermark of an omnibus.

A typical LGOC bus conductor of the 1890s, in suit, waistcoat and bowler hat, stands on the narrow platform, bell rope in hand. The Bell Punch machine over his shoulder was first introduced by the LGOC in 1891.

Enamel licence badge issued by the Metropolitan Police.

◑ **Horse bus driver's enamel licence badge**
1890s

↻ **'The Pirate Bus' songsheet**
1890s

The term 'pirate bus' came into common usage in the 1890s, referring to unregulated itinerant independent operators, who hired buses on a day-to-day basis to 'muscle in' on the most popular LGOC and Road Car routes. Herbert Campbell was a popular music hall performer of the period, who died in 1901.

↻ **The Tilling horse bus**

A 'garden seat' bus on the Putney to Clapham service of Thomas Tilling Ltd. The advertisement on the side shows that, like many early bus proprietors, Tilling was a jobmaster, providing horses and carriages for weddings and other occasions, with buses as only part of the business. He started to run buses in the 1840s and had a fleet of 220 by 1901. The last recorded horse bus in London was a Tilling, which ran on 4 August 1914 between Peckham and Honor Oak Tavern.

Original Bell Punch
1880s

This original recording punch was manufactured by the Bell Punch Company. Known as the 'pistol' punch, this device was used by the London Road Car Company in the 1880s and by the LGOC from 1893. Separately coloured tickets for each fare value were held by the conductor who punched in the destination stage for each passenger. Only one ticket could be punched at a time, and the coloured clippings were retained in a sealed container within the punch. Any discrepancy in the number of tickets sold against the entries on the waybill and the cash handed in could be checked by laboriously counting the coloured clippings.

The Interior of a Bus by George Joy
1895
Museum of London

This painting, exhibited at the Royal Academy in 1895, shows how the seats were arranged to face inwards, with space for six people on each side. It looks calm, civilised, clean and comfortable, unlike earlier buses, which were described by one commentator as '… a strong stuffy box strewn with straw which disgusted the nose and had a filthy habit of clinging to the feet'.

Horse bus in Trafalgar Square

W.S. Birch & Son, a much-respected name in the bus industry for over 100 years, owned this bus, a typical 'garden seat' of the last quarter of the nineteenth century. It is working on the Swiss Cottage to Old Kent Road route of the Atlas Association, whose livery was light green. By this time most proprietors were members of associations, which controlled the allocation of 'times' to individual companies and ensured that timetables were co-ordinated. Each association worked within its own sphere of operation, which did not clash with the others, effectively creating voluntary monopolies.

⟳ Cannon Street station
London Metropolitan Archives

This was the South Eastern Railway's City terminus, opened in 1866. Victoria, Charing Cross and Liverpool Street were also authorised in the 1860s and '70s in the hope that they would reduce cross-city congestion.

⟳ Paddle steamers at London Bridge pier
1858

Paddle steamers were faster and cheaper than wherries and eventually wiped them out completely. At their peak in the 1850s steamboats carried several million passengers a year, mostly pleasure trippers, but also some commuters.

⟳ The workers move out
London Metropolitan Archives
1890s

A workmen's train disgorges its passengers at the Great Eastern terminus of Liverpool Street. The Great Eastern had cleared many tenement houses to make room for the construction of Liverpool Street, and rather than bear the expense of re-housing those displaced, it accepted a government requirement to provide cheap fares for workers who needed to move out to Edmonton and Walthamstow. The fare was a modest 2d for the return journey. Although the 1883 Cheap Trains Act made such services more widespread, Londoners were the greatest beneficiaries.

The arms of the London, Chatham & Dover Railway at Blackfriars Bridge

Gustav Doré's impression of traffic at Ludgate Circus
1872

A tangle of cabs, omnibuses and carts collide with cattle on their way to nearby Smithfield meat market, whilst a traffic policeman attempts to keep order.

Crystal Palace High Level

The London, Chatham & Dover Railway's High Level Station at Crystal Palace opened in 1865, more convenient than the Brighton Line's station down the hill, which involved passengers in a tedious walk up half a mile of corridors and staircases. After the closure of the Great Exhibition at Hyde Park, an enlarged Crystal Palace was relocated at Sydenham, re-opening in 1854. Gradually declining in popularity, the Palace burnt down in 1936, after which the High Level station fell on hard times. It finally closed in 1954.

➲ Pneumatic transport

Although steam ruled as a source of power during the nineteenth century, the ingenious still tried alternatives. In 1864 T.W. Rammell began operating an experimental pneumatic railway for passengers in the grounds of the Crystal Palace. Passengers were charged 6d return to be alternately blown and sucked through the 600-yard tunnel in the single broad gauge coach. It was successful enough to lead to the proposed Waterloo & Whitehall pneumatically operated tube to run from near Waterloo Station, under the Thames to Great Scotland Yard. Though partly built, the financial crisis of 1866 put paid to its completion.

◑ The Crystal Way, a proposal to the Parliamentary Select Committee of 1855

Throughout the nineteenth century, committees and commissions met to find solutions to London's traffic problems. One of the more whimsical suggestions, considered in 1855, was the Crystal Way, a five-level arcade of iron and glass apparently inspired by the Crystal Palace.

◑ Broad Street terminus
1890s
London Metropolitan Archives

An impression of the North London Railway's busy City terminus at Broad Street in the 1890s. Conceived as a means of conveying freight into the London docks, the North London became an immensely successful passenger carrier. Initially sweeping in an arc through the northern suburbs, its services quickly expanded south to Richmond and north to Gospel Oak and Hampstead. Willesden Junction was its focal point to the west, while Bow in the east became its administrative and engineering headquarters.

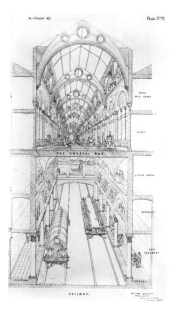

⟁ Booking office at Ongar station
1995

Ongar station was the eastern terminus of the Central line from 1948. It survived until closure in 1995 and is now part of a railway preservation scheme.

⟁ By North London to northern heights
Roger Brasier Collection

A North London Railway train destined for Muswell Hill passes Crouch End on the Great Northern's Alexandra Palace branch, hauled by one of William Adams's distinctive 4-4-0 tank engines at the head of a typical rake of North London four-wheelers. The raised 'birdcage' lookouts positioned fore and aft above the carriage roofs were for the guard.

⟁ Blake Hall station
1985

Blake Hall, on the furthest reaches of the Central line in Essex, was a quiet country station that was, almost by accident, welded on to the Underground system by the expansions of the mid-twentieth century. Constructed in 1865, it is architecturally typical of many rural stations built by the Great Eastern Railway.

○ **Platform canopies at Snaresbrook station**
c. 1900

Snaresbrook, on the Epping branch of the Central line, is one of the finest surviving stations of the Eastern Counties Railway, which opened the station in 1856. The station was, over time, extended to cope with growing commuter traffic that the line itself stimulated. These cast-iron brackets, supporting a timber canopy, are a typical feature of Victorian station architecture.

○ **Cast-iron decoration at Plaistow station**
c. 1900

Many Underground stations, such as Plaistow in east London (now served by the District line) still carry permanent reminders of their original operators. Here the platform benches and canopies still proudly proclaim ownership by the London, Tilbury & Southend Railway, which ceased to exist in 1912.

Southend & Westcliff-on-Sea for Sea Breezes
Anonymous poster
1908

Southend is the nearest seaside resort to London, and has always generated huge excursion and holiday traffic, particularly for East Londoners. The District Railway, and later the Underground, ran through-trains to meet the demand. Although these trains ceased to operate in 1939, it is still possible to buy a through ticket from any Underground station.

Interior and exterior views of a Waterloo & City Railway motor car
1899

The Waterloo and City was London's second deep level tube railway, and the first to abandon separate locomotives in favour of carriages with 'built-in' motors at each end. It opened in August 1898, with the specific purpose of moving commuters from the London & South Western Railway to the City. Then as now, the service was severely overcrowded.

CITY & SOUTH LONDON RAILWAY

The City & South London Railway (C&SLR) was opened on 4 November 1890 by the Prince of Wales (later Edward VII). Running from King William Street in the City to Stockwell, south of the river, it was the first part of London's deep-level tube system. It was also the first underground electric railway in the world. Today, save for the stub of tunnel from Borough to King William Street, it forms part of the Northern line.

The C&SLR was originally designed to use cable-haulage. However, the opening of electric tramways around the world prompted the radical decision to switch to the infant technology of electric traction. Mather & Platt supplied the electrical equipment, whilst the locomotives were designed by Edward Hopkinson, who had worked on early electric tramways in Ireland. Construction of the locomotives was subcontracted to steam engine builders Beyer Peacock. In practice, they turned out to be under-powered, but given the pioneering nature of the project, they were remarkably successful.

The C&SLR's carriages were designed without windows since it was reasoned that there was no view to see in the deep tunnels. This, together with the noisy and claustrophobic ride, dim lighting and high, button-backed seats, earned them the nickname 'padded cell'.

◊ **Edward Hopkinson, 1859–1922**

◊ **City & South London Railway locomotive**

Built by Beyer Peacock, these were the world's first electric railway locomotives.

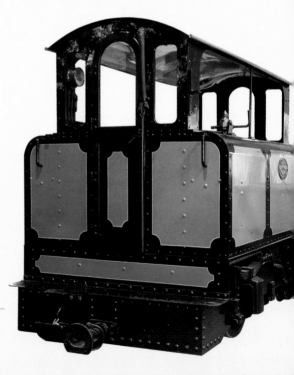

◊ **Decorative tiles from the City & South London Railway**

The station tunnels on the C&SLR were built of brick and decorated with glazed tiles. These tiles were recovered from Kennington station.

🎧 **Interior of a City & South London Railway carriage**

The absence of windows required the gatemen, who rode on the platforms at the end of the carriage, to call out station names on arrival.

🎧 **King William Street station**
1890

Among the radical features of the C&SLR were its classless carriages and 2d flat-fare system. No tickets were issued; passengers simply paid and entered through a turnstile.

🎧 **Station master's cap badge**

Some of the directors of the C&SLR had connections with the Great Western Railway (GWR), and the uniforms worn by station staff were quite similar to those on the GWR. This ornate 'laurel leaf' station master's cap badge is in typical railway style.

🎧 **Invitation to opening of the City & South London Railway**
1890

This ticket was issued to Mrs Grindle, wife of one of the line's electrical engineers, George Grindle.

🎧 **Stockwell station**
1890–1915

The C&SLR relied on its station buildings to attract passengers. Designed by T. Phillips Figgis, the distinctive domed buildings were built on prominent corner sites. Today, only Kennington station retains any of its original character.

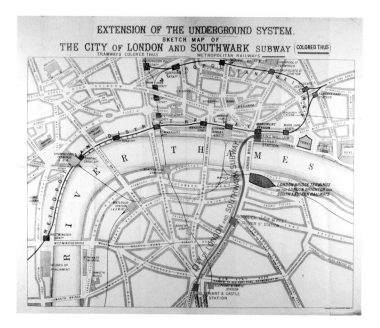

EXTENSION OF THE UNDERGROUND SYSTEM.
SKETCH MAP OF
THE CITY OF LONDON AND SOUTHWARK SUBWAY (COLORED THUS)

○ **Proposed route of City of London and Southwark Subway**
1884

The City of London and Southwark Subway Company was formed in 1884 to build a tube from the Elephant and Castle to King William Street in the City. In 1887 a bill was passed to extend the railway southwards to Stockwell three miles away. Initially intended to be operated by cable haulage, the line opened in 1890 as the City & South London Railway, using electric power.

◑ **Detail from commemorative sundial designed by Edwin Russell at Tower Hill station, unveiled 7 October 1996**

This section of sundial depicts the locomotive and carriages of the City & South London Railway.

○ **James Henry Greathead, 1844–96**

This statue was erected as part of the redevelopment of Bank station and unveiled on 17 January 1994. The engineer James Greathead was born in South Africa and possessed an inventive talent. His tunnelling shield, developed in conjunction with Peter Barlow and influenced by Marc Brunel's shield, provided the means to safely dig tunnels deep under London. This enabled the construction of today's deep-level tube system. The Greathead shield remains in use to this day.

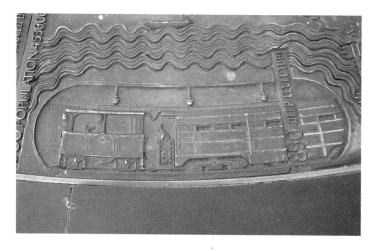

The Greathead shield being dismantled at the Moorgate cross-over
c. 1903

Bodnant (formerly Sir Charles MacLaren), who was Chairman of the Metropolitan Railway from 1904 to 1933. Prominent in the design are London Bridge and the twin tube tunnels of the City & South London Railway beneath it, flanked by the arms of the City of London and Southwark.

London's sub-soil is a mixture of clay and water-bearing sand and gravel. Conventional hard rock tunnelling – itself a hazardous activity – was quite impossible. Greathead's tunnelling shield solved the problem: an iron cylinder protected the miners while they worked at the tunnel face, and allowed the lining to be built within its circumference, making the tunnel safe, before it was jacked forward to continue excavation.

tunnels also provided a conduit for power and telegraph cables, and a hydraulic water main that was used to power the station lifts.

City & South London Railway enamelled silver medallion pass
c. 1911

This staff pass, allowing free travel on the railway, was issued to Baron Aberconway of

Cross-sectional drawing of City & South London Railway tunnel
1890

At a maximum of 10' 2" diameter, the tunnels of the City & South London Railway were narrow by today's standards. Squeezing a passenger carriage and pioneering electric locomotive into a tunnel was a major technical challenge. As well as the track and trains, the

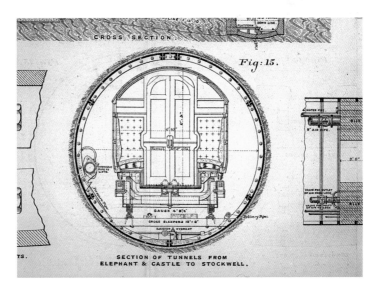

Electric Power and Petrol

From City Smoke
to Suburban Dream
1900–1914

Hampstead Railway non-stop services
Poster
1910

Electric Power and Petrol
From City Smoke to Suburban Dream, 1900–1914

The former steam railways – at least the Inner Circle portion – had one advantage, which disappeared with the steam locomotive. In the old days they provided a sort of health resort for people who suffered from asthma, for which the sulphurous and other fumes were supposed to be beneficial, and there were several regular asthmatical customers who daily took one or two turns round the circle to enjoy the – to them – invigorating atmosphere. But today the sulphur has all gone, except in the speech of a few irritable travellers, and has been replaced by an indescribable atmosphere of squashed microbes…

E.L Ahrons on the Metropolitan & Metropolitan District Railways in 'Locomotive & Train Working in the Latter Part of the Nineteenth Century', *Railway Magazine,* 1924

LONDON, BLACKFRIARS BRIDGE.

In 1900 the horse-drawn and steam-driven transport systems of Victorian London were creaking under the strain of ever increasing usage as the city's population continued to grow and become more mobile. The new technology of the electric motor and the petrol engine now brought sweeping and very rapid changes to London's transport in the early years of the new century.

LCC trams on Blackfriars Bridge
c. 1912

London did not pioneer electric tramways in Britain, but once the first route in the capital had been opened in 1901 by London United Tramways (LUT), others followed rapidly. The LUT network spread

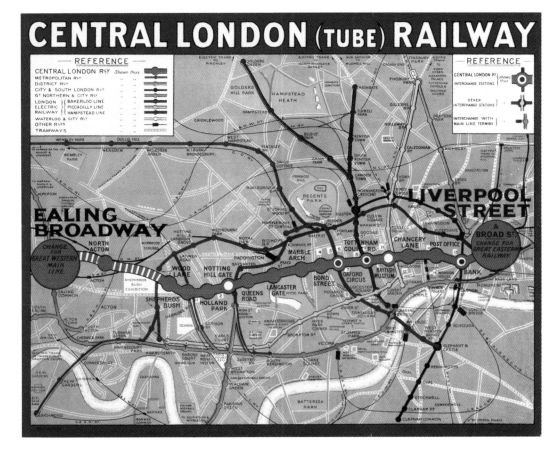

Map of the Central London Railway
1912

Running east–west, along the line of Oxford Street, the Central London Railway was the first of the Tube lines to penetrate the West End. This map shows its connections with other Tube railways.

over the western and south-western suburbs, and the Metropolitan Electric Tramways (MET) electrified much of north London and Middlesex. The LUT and MET were both private companies that soon became subsidiaries of the Underground Group. In south and east London ten local councils, including Croydon and West Ham, each developed their own electric tramway systems. The largest and most important network was built and operated by the

London County Council (LCC) covering most of inner north and south London. Trams were still excluded from the City and the West End, but the LCC's lines reached the edge of both, with the lines from south London crossing three of the Thames bridges and running along the Victoria Embankment. A link with the lines from north London was provided by building a tram subway from the Embankment under Aldwych to Holborn.

The LCC saw the provision of cheap public transport in London as part of its progressive drive to improve living and working conditions in the city. Trams were agents of social policy. The first LCC electric line, opened by the Prince of Wales on 15 May 1903, was from Westminster Bridge to Tooting, where it terminated at one of the council's large new housing estates. The number of workmen's tickets sold on this one

***Underground – the Moving Spirit of London* by
Thomas Robert Way**
1910

Lots Road power station looms out of the dawn
mist at Chelsea Creek in this poster.

line alone leapt from nearly 600,000 in the last year of horse trams to 3.34 million in 1906–7. Cheap, fast electric trams soon enabled many working-class families to move out of crowded tenements in central London to new cottage estates in the suburbs.

The new electric tube railways opened in this period brought rather different changes to London. The Central London Railway, opened in 1900, was the third London tube but the first to have a major impact. In particular, it was the first railway to run under the West End serving both the Oxford Street shops and the business heart of the City. This gave it the best route of the three pioneer tubes and helped ensure financial success from the start. Its nickname, the 'Twopenny Tube', came from its flat fare and was in popular use almost immediately.

The City & South London and Central London Tubes both began operations using electric locomotives to haul their trains. However, these are inconvenient for short, busy lines because of the time taken running the locomotive round the train at the terminus before making a return journey. The answer was multiple unit control, a system devised by Frank Sprague in Chicago in the 1890s. Motors and control equipment are fitted to some of the passenger cars in a train, linked by a low voltage control circuit. This allows operation from one controller in the cab of the leading car. With a cab at both ends of the train it can be driven in either direction like a tram. The solution made locomotives redundant.

In 1903 the Central London became the first railway in Britain to be worked entirely by multiple unit trains. The system was adopted for all other tube lines and for the larger trains introduced on the Metropolitan and District Railways, when these were electrified in 1905. Power supply and current collection arrangements, which varied between the early electric lines, were gradually standardised. A giant power station built in 1902–5 at Lots Road, Chelsea,

A packed B-type bus en route to Windsor Castle
c. 1912

eventually took over the supply to all lines except the Metropolitan, which had its own power station at Neasden.

Unlike the LCC's electric tramways, the electric underground railways were built for profit not social purpose. In practice this was always difficult and sometimes impossible to achieve. The core of the present London Underground system was created in this period, much of it funded from international sources and influenced in particular by American methods of urban transport operation, both in technology and management. The Underground Electric Railways of London (UERL) established by the Chicago financier Charles Tyson Yerkes became the dominating force in this. The last three tube railways to be completed in 1906–7, the Bakerloo, Piccadilly and Hampstead (now Northern) lines were all part of the Yerkes Underground Group, though Yerkes himself died in 1905 before his schemes were fulfilled. The Yerkes tubes all used American-influenced electrical engineering in everything from power supply and signalling systems to station lifts and rolling stock.

The most significant American influence of all on the Underground Group was Albert Stanley, the dynamic young General Manager appointed in 1907 to run the UERL. Stanley, later to become Lord Ashfield, was born in England but brought up in the USA where he started his meteoric career in the competitive world of American tramway management. He was to become one of the leading figures in the creation of a co-ordinated public transport system for London. Another was Frank Pick, who joined the UERL in 1906 from the North Eastern Railway and quickly made his mark as a skilful commercial manager for the Underground, particularly through the innovative use of pictorial posters to promote the company's image and services.

The successful mechanisation of London's buses was soon to supplement the new electric tram and underground railway services. Petrol engines looked more promising than battery electric or steam power for buses, but early attempts to develop regular services proved unsustainable. The technology had to become sufficiently robust for London's demanding conditions, with constant stopping and starting in heavy traffic. The conservatism of the LGOC, still the major horse-bus operator in the 1900s, worked to its advantage as smaller rivals over-invested in unproven motor vehicles. After buying out two of its struggling competitors in 1908, the LGOC was able to combine expertise and develop its own standard motor bus, the B-type. It looked primitive, with its wooden open top body almost unchanged from the horse bus, but it was rugged, reliable and cheap to run.

By October 1911, exactly a year after the first B-type went into service, the LGOC withdrew its last horse bus. Within another year the LGOC was itself absorbed by the Underground Group, and the profitable new motor bus network was developed to feed into and link up with the rail services rather than compete with them. The LGOC's bus building operation was immediately turned into a separate manufacturing concern, the Associated Equipment Company (AEC) which remained the main builder of London's buses until the 1960s.

⌐ **The Key to London is the Central London Railway**
1909

The Central London Railway was nicknamed the 'Twopenny Tube' because of its initial flat fare of 2d. The name stuck, as seen in this anonymous poster, despite the introduction of graduated fares in 1907, forced upon the line by bus competition.

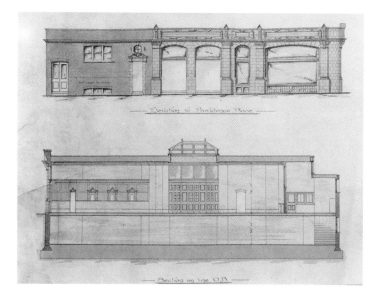

⌐ **Elevation of Shepherd's Bush station, Central London Railway**

Shepherd's Bush was the western terminus of the line when it opened on 30 July 1900. The building, designed by Harry Bell Measures still exists, though the interior has been extensively altered over the last century.

⟳ **Constructing the Central London Railway**
1897

Construction started on the Central London Railway in 1896. The men are working here within the protection of the Greathead shield at Tottenham Court Road in 1897.

◐ Central London Railway rolling stock
1900-1903

The line opened using large 'camelback' electric locomotives, which hauled the train carriages behind them. However, these locomotives, along with track problems, caused serious vibrations in the properties above the line and were soon replaced.

◐ Booking office, Shepherd's Bush station on the Central London Railway
1900

There was a flat fare of 2d when this photograph was taken in 1900.

◐ Central London Railway multiple-unit stock at Wood Lane depot
1903

The 'camelback' CLR locomotives were replaced in 1903 by multiple-unit stock with motors spread throughout the length of the train. This stock soon became widespread on other tube railways. The centrally situated single electric conductor rail is clearly visible.

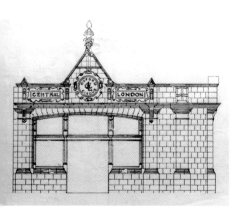

⋒ Front elevation, Oxford Circus station

The Central London Railway had the benefit of running parallel to Oxford Street, then well on the way to becoming London's premier shopping destination. The station at Oxford Circus, designed by architect Harry Bell Measures, was, in many respects, the heart of the line.

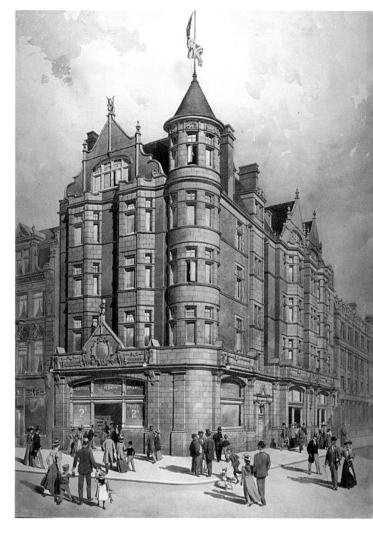

◑ Oxford Circus when it opened in 1900

⋒ Watercolour of Oxford Circus station
c. 1900

A four-storey office development by Delissa Joseph was built above the station soon after opening, *c.* 1900. The station façade still survives and is one of the best surviving examples of the salmon pink terracotta that Measures adopted for the stations on the Central London Railway.

➲ Advertising and publicity

Amongst the novelty giveaways issued to the public was this striking little folder showing a train at the station awaiting departure. The pillar box opens to reveal a string of photographs illustrating the CLR stations on the line.

◑ Postcards

Two images from a set of now highly collectable postcards drawn by the artist Phil May depicting scenes at each of the Central London Railway's stations in 1904. The people at

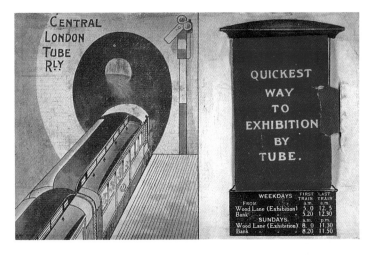

Bank station appear very staid in comparison to the couple at Marble Arch.

◑ Coronation souvenir

To coincide with the celebrations marking the coronation of George V in 1911, the CLR issued this lavish book. The book contains a description of the line, illustrated with specially commissioned watercolours of the stations.

JAPAN – BRITISH
EXHIBITION
SHEPHERD'S BUSH
LONDON
1910

OFFICIAL GUIDE 1/-

COPYRIGHT. PRINTED BY BEMROSE & SONS LTD. ENTERED STATIONERS HALL.

fares. However, on 1 January 1913 the dream of a unified system become reality as the Underground Group formally acquired the company.

Staff medallion
issued 1907

Senior railway staff enjoyed reciprocal free travel on other railways. This medallion was issued to Albert Stanley, the general manager of the UERL, by the Central London Railway. He was to enjoy this privilege until 1948.

Catalogue of the Japan – British Exhibition
1910

In 1908 the Franco-British Exhibition opened on a site at Wood Lane in west London. The white exhibition buildings led to the area becoming known as 'White City'. The Central London Railway opened a station at Wood Lane on the same day that the exhibition opened.

During the early years of the twentieth century, several major exhibitions such as the Japan–British Exhibition were held at White City.

Company stationery
1914

As an independent company, the CLR had co-operated with the other Tube railways over many issues such as publicity and

Invitation to the opening of City & South London Railway extension to Euston
1907

City & South London Railway, Euston Station
1907

The first northward extension of the City & South London Railway opened to Moorgate in 1900, involving a new alignment north of Borough station. A further extension to Angel was completed a year later, and the line was pushed through to Euston in 1907. It was formally opened by Sir Percy Harris, Chairman of the London County Council, on 11 May. Today it forms the city branch of the Northern line.

Bank station and church of St Mary Woolnoth
1900

A northward extension to Islington was planned for the City & South London Railway as early as 1891, only a year after it opened. Instead of extending from the City terminus at King William Street, however, it was decided to abandon the first tunnels under the Thames and build northward from Borough to London Bridge and on to Angel. After a court battle, the station at Bank was built, virtually in the crypt of the church of St Mary Woolnoth.

For the 1907 extension to Euston an ornate station building, designed by Sidney R. J. Smith, was constructed in white and green stone. It stood on Seymour Street (now Eversholt Street), until it was demolished to make room for the present Euston House. It had connections by subway to the mainline station and to the Charing Cross, Euston & Hampstead Railway.

generating station at Stockwell. Here, six boilers supplied steam to three vertical steam engines. Leather belts coupled the engines to 225kW Edison-Hopkinson generators. A fourth generating set was added in 1892. Despite the inevitable teething troubles, this pioneering venture worked well, and supplied electricity until replaced in 1901.

⊕ London Transport's power generation and distribution system, Greenwich
1948

With its massive network of railways, tramways and trolleybus routes, London Transport was a major generator and user of electricity. This 1948 diagram shows a sectional view of the old London County Council Tramways power

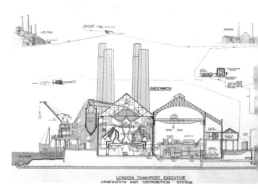

⊙ Power Underground by Edward McKnight Kauffer
1931

This striking poster in classic art-deco style used the theme of power generation in a great example of the 'soft sell' advertising favoured by the Underground.

⊙ City & South London Railway power house, Stockwell
c. 1892

Power for the City & South London Railway was supplied from a

station at Greenwich, and its 22,000 volt connections to the other major LT generators at Lots Road, Chelsea and Neasden.

⤴ **Turbine hall, Greenwich power station**
1905

The London County Council (LCC) electrified its first tramways in 1903. Conversion of the whole system swiftly followed, and the LCC opened a dedicated power station on the river at Greenwich in 1906. Its vertical steam engines (seen here) were rather old-fashioned, and were replaced with turbines in 1913. Further modernisation took place in the 1930s, when it was taken over by London Transport. Refitted with gas turbine generators in 1968, it remains in use today as a peak-load back-up to Lots Road power station.

◖ **Control room, Neasden power station**
1968

Neasden power station, originally built by the Metropolitan Railway, was taken over by London Transport in 1933. Extensions to the Underground in the 1930s, especially in north-west London, brought modernisation to Neasden, with an increase in capacity to meet the growing demand for power. It was finally abandoned in 1968, and power supply in that area was switched over to the national grid.

◖ **Turbine hall, Neasden power station**
c. 1905

Experiments in electrification were started on the Metropolitan Railway and the District line at the very end of the nineteenth century. Independent-minded as ever, the Metropolitan turned down offers for power supply from the Underground Group's power station at Lots Road, and built its own generating station at Neasden. It was fully commissioned by the end of 1904.

⟳ **Switchboard, Chiswick power station**
1901

London United Tramways (LUT), which operated in the Shepherd's Bush area, was the first of London's tram systems to abandon horses in favour of electricity. The London County Council and other municipal operators followed in a rush. In the Edwardian era, electric trams became the last word in modern transport and a powerful expression of civic pride, well illustrated by the ornate ironwork seen here in the LUT's power station.

🌑 **NorthMet Power Company sign outside the company show room at Wood Green, north London**

The North Metropolitan (NorthMet) Electric Power Supply Company was established in 1900 to supply electricity to a wide area of north London and Middlesex.

The company owned as many as seven generating stations at one point, the largest two being at Willesden and Brimsdown. Close ties were established with the Metropolitan Electric Tramways, and both became part of the Underground Group in 1913. The company went its own way when London Transport was formed in 1933.

🌑 **NorthMet Power Company certificate of service**

This certificate of service was signed by Lord Ashfield and presented to George Roden Willson after 20 years' service to the company in 1931.

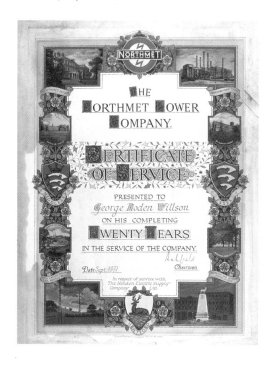

LOTS ROAD POWER STATION

In 1902 the Metropolitan District Electric Traction Company acquired a site for a power station at Chelsea Creek, christened Lots Road. When it was commissioned in 1905 it was said to be the largest generating station in the world. Lots Road power station's position on the Thames enabled coal to be brought in easily by barge, and provided a ready supply of cooling water. Conversion to oil-burning in the 1960s brought an end to the coal barges, and two of the original four chimneys were taken down.

After the Second World War, consideration was given to closing Lots Road and taking a supply from the new national grid. The new grid was, however, still under construction, and it was felt that London Transport had better retain its independent supply. Lots Road remains in use today and still supplies most of the power for the Underground.

🔊 **Detail from 'The TOT Alphabet' by Charles Pears**
1915

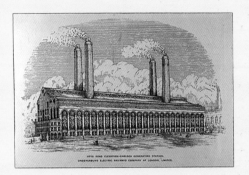

🔊 **Engraving of Lots Road Power Station**
1904

🔊 **Turbine Hall, Lots Road Power Station**
1990s

In 1969 Lots Road was refitted with new boilers, steam turbines and turbo-generators.

🔊 **Control Room, Lots Road Power Station**

Built in the 1930s, this remarkable, period control room is now disused.

🔊 **Lots Road Power Station at Chelsea Creek, 1990s**

The Metropolitan Railway Coronation celebrations
1902

The Metropolitan Railway was quick to extol the virtues of travel underground to those wishing to view the 1902 Coronation activities above ground. Perhaps wisely, they made no mention on this poster that the Inner Circle trains remained steam-hauled.

Leaflet announcing the opening of the Metropolitan Railway's Uxbridge branch
July 1904

First Metropolitan train to Uxbridge
30 June 1904

The first 'Met' train to Uxbridge is seen here at Ruislip. Although intended for electric train operation from the outset, trains on the branch remained steam-hauled for the first six months.

A new electric train
13 December 1904

The trial trip of the Metropolitan's new electric train on electrified track between Baker Street and Uxbridge. The event was reported in *The Times* the following morning: 'Everything which took place conveyed the impression that those present were celebrating the beginning of a new era in the history of the old underground railways from which smoke, dirt and discomfort will be nearly banished!'. Public service commenced on Sunday 1 January 1905.

Metropolitan Railway timetable cover
1916

Electric locomotive at Neasden 1906

For its mainline services the Metropolitan Railway acquired ten camel-back electric locomotives built by Metropolitan Amalgamated Carriage Co. with Westinghouse electrical equipment. Entering service in 1906, the locomotives were powerful enough to haul heavy passenger trains from Uxbridge via Harrow-on-the-Hill into Baker Street. Although reasonably successful, the camel-back design and centrally placed controls made driving awkward and visibility poor.

In 1907 the second batch of locos from British Thomson-Houston adopted a more familiar shape with cabs at either end.

Diagram of the Metropolitan Railway
1919

This diagram shows the remarkable extent of the company's lines. The lines to Brill and Verney Junction, a little over 50 miles to the north-west of London, into the counties of Oxfordshire and Buckinghamshire, were eventually closed or relinquished. However, the proposed extension to Watford did become part of the Underground's network.

Following the introduction of the roundel to London's Underground railways in 1908, the 'Met' rather grudgingly co-operated by introducing a red diamond variation on the roundel logo in 1914. This was used on stations, publicity and 'Met' buildings. Indeed, it can still be observed today on the façades of some stations such as Farringdon.

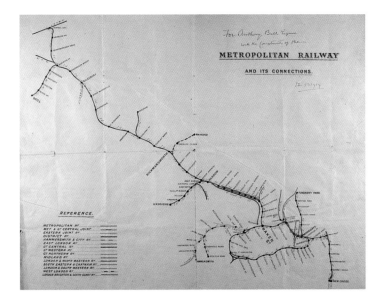

Metropolitan Railway timetable
1910

The cover illustrates well the majesty of the city linked via the 'Met' to the wooded delights of Harrow-on-the-Hill.

Metropolitan Railway 'Bogie' stock coach No 400
1899

Fifty-four coaches of this type were built between 1898 and 1900. The coaches became known as 'Bogie' stock, distinguishing them from the Metropolitan's earlier rigid wheel-base carriages. Between 1906 and 1924 all the stock was converted for electric working, running mainly on the Uxbridge and Stanmore lines. In 1939 No 400 was one of six coaches which reverted to steam working and is now preserved in London's Transport Museum.

Metropolitan trains
c. 1910

Like many railway companies, the Metropolitan lines were featured on commercially available postcards. Although this card shows a steam locomotive, the main subject is a train hauled by one of the British Westinghouse locomotives delivered in 1905. The loco, seen here approaching Willesden Green, was hauling a train that included a Pullman car. The latter was first introduced in 1910, and no doubt passengers approved of the new form of traction used on such a prestigious train.

Pullman car
1910

The Metropolitan Railway boasted two Pullman cars, named the Galatea and the Mayflower. Used on services between Baker Street, Aylesbury and (initially) Verney Junction, the cars ran until 7 October 1939 and had the distinction of being the first electrically hauled Pullmans in Europe.

⊙ Freight carrier
c. 1901
Roger Brasier Collection

A freight train saunters through Northwood about 1901, hauled by a new 'F' class 0-6-2 tank locomotive no. 93 still fitted with condensing apparatus. Far from being just a passenger line, the Metropolitan Railway also handled a healthy freight traffic. Coal to supply gasworks and for domestic use, building materials needed for suburban expansion, dairy produce from the Vale of Aylesbury, woodwork and footware from Chesham all created revenue.

device were added later to celebrate the power and efficiency of electric traction. This crest was photographed on the panel of restored coach 400 (see photo opposite).

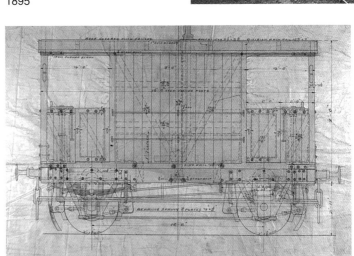

⊙ Elevation of a Metropolitan brake van
1895

◐ Metropolitan Railway crest
1899

The Metropolitan Railway crest incorporated the coats of arms of the City of London and the counties it served: Middlesex, Buckinghamshire and Hertfordshire. The clenched fist and sparks at the top of the

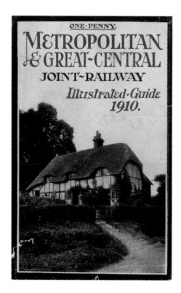

The Metropolitan & Great Central Railway Illustrated Guide
1910

Aspiring to join the ranks of mainline railways, the Metropolitan assisted the Manchester, Sheffield and Lincolnshire Railway to extend to London. Granted running powers over the Metropolitan south of Quainton Road, the MSLR opened its London service as the Great Central Railway (GCR) in 1899. In 1910 the Joint Committee formed to manage operation of the lines north of Harrow produced this guide to the rural delights of that northern section.

➡ London & North Western Railway residential guide
1913

The Metropolitan Railway was not alone in issuing guides as most of the mainline railway companies attempted to entice people to move out of London and become commuters. This illustrated guide includes descriptions of locations that were part of the countryside at the time but which are now embedded deep in 'suburbia', the very term used on this guide.

○ Country station
1906

The rural scene at Ickenham Halte looks very different today. The three-car train of 1905 Metropolitan electric multiple-unit stock provided the first electric service operated by the Met between Baker Street and Uxbridge. The wood-framed

platforms and waiting areas were all that was necessary before the development that the railway encouraged took place.

◐ London, Brighton & South Coast Railway electrification
c. 1910
Roger Brasier Collection

The introduction of electric trams and new tube services gave new competition to many of London's existing mainline commuter railways. In south London the 'Brighton' fought back by developing a suburban electrification system to replace slow, aged steam trains. Here, at Denmark Hill station, a rush-hour train draws up. The train pauses beneath the overhead electric wires that would be replaced by an electric third rail by the railway's new owners, the Southern, in the 1920s.

Great Eastern Railway suburban trains at Bethnal Green
1906
Roger Brasier Collection

A mixture of politics and finance meant that services from Liverpool Street remained steam-hauled until after the Second World War. In the 1920s this was the world's most intensive steam-hauled suburban service and was nicknamed 'The Jazz'.

UNDERGROUND

THE POPULAR SERVICE
SUITS ALL TASTES.

The Popular Service Suits All Tastes
1913

Designed as a 'willow pattern' plate, this poster makes a clever play on words. The Japanese pagoda in the background suggests that the station could be Kew Gardens.

(Getting and spending we lay waste our powers)

AT THE SHOPS

BY THE

UNDERGROUND

HUMOURS OF LONDON Nº 2

🎧 ***At the shops* by Tony Sarg**
1913

Before the widespread availability of private cars and vans, buses and taxis were the predominant motor vehicles on London's streets. This poster was one of a series promoting leisure travel issued by the Underground Group.

🎧 **The Bank–Royal Exchange intersection**
c. 1910

The City's busiest intersection, relatively uncongested in this scene at the beginning of the motor bus era, showing new motor vehicles sharing the streets with horse buses, carts and cabs and pedestrians.

🎧 **Piccadilly Circus**
1904
London Metropolitan Archives

Piccadilly Circus, still a relatively genteel haven of Edwardian exclusivity in 1904, before the motor bus and the Underground opened up the West End.

🎧 **Grooming LGOC horses**
1911

The London General Omnibus Company was London's biggest operator of horse buses. A single horse bus needed as many as 14 animals to keep it on the road for a working day. At its peak, the LGOC owned more than 17,000 horses. The cost of purchase, stabling, food, waste disposal, shoes and veterinary care constituted the single biggest expense for a bus operator, and employed vast numbers of people. Their jobs disappeared when motor buses took over.

🎧 **Breaking up LGOC horse buses**
1911

Building on earlier experiments, the move to motor buses gathered pace from 1908. The introduction of the B-type motor bus in 1910 sounded the final

death-knell for the horse bus, and within a year the last LGOC horse bus was withdrawn. Some were sold on to other operators, the bodies from others found a new lease of life as sheds and holiday homes. The majority met their sad end in the breaker's yard.

Motor bus driver's enamel licence badge

This type was first used on 9 October 1899, when motor buses began a service between Kensington and Victoria via Westminster Bridge.

Early motor cabs, Strand
1903

In 1897 a company called Bersey introduced a fleet of electric cabs – the first mechanically propelled taxis in London. The police approved, anticipating a marked reduction in congestion, as, without a horse, they needed less road

space. Bad reports in the press, however, lost them favour, and the horse-drawn cab enjoyed a brief respite. The Prunel cabs seen here outside the Savoy Theatre were the first petrol-engined taxis in London. Within ten years, horse-drawn cabs were completely eclipsed by the motorised newcomers.

Model of London's first motor bus

This model, which was commissioned for the centenary in 1999, is of the first motor bus to run in London. Operated by the Motor Traction Company with a Daimler engine, it ran from Kennington Gate to Victoria and

later Oxford Circus. It was withdrawn after just 14 months of service.

Model of Vanguard Fleet motor bus
1906

This model replicates a Milnes-Daimler motor bus of 1906 belonging to the London Motor Omnibus Company. The company used the fleet name 'Vanguard', by which they were better known, later becoming the Vanguard Motorbus Company. They were the first in London to use route numbers. This model is depicted on Service 4, which ran from Gospel Oak to Putney.

○ Bus driver's enamel licence badge

This type of badge was introduced in 1906.

⟳ Bus conductor's enamel licence badge

This type of badge was introduced in 1906.

○ 'Union Jack' bus

'Union Jack' was the fleet name used by the London Road Car Company, which had set up in competition with the LGOC in 1881, using the patriotic symbol to rebuff the General's French origins. The company pioneered the introduction of bus tickets, the 'garden seat' horse bus, and a true staircase and platform on its horse buses. It was one of the

two companies that amalgamated with the LGOC in 1908 to give the General an effective monopoly of motor bus operation in London, the other being Vanguard.

○ Clarkson steam bus
September 1905

The London Road Car Company bought at least 25 steam buses from Thomas Clarkson in 1905. At this time petrol engines were very noisy, smelly and unreliable, and many thought steam power preferable.

○ Coloured drawing of early motor bus

The LGOC tried out many types of motor bus before it started to build its own, among them being the Milnes Daimler. This thirty-

four seat body design was the standard in London for nearly twenty years.

○ *Trade Follows the All Red Route*
1913
This poster promotes advertising space on LGOC vehicles. The motorisation and numbering of all routes also meant a standard red livery for all General buses, replacing the various colour schemes of the horse-bus era.

○ LGOC 'winged wheel' cap badge
c. 1910

The 'winged wheel' logo of the LGOC was first used in 1905, when it was painted on to the buses. The same logo was adopted for cap badges from around 1910.

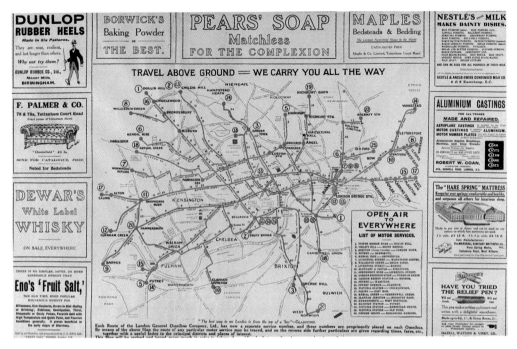

TRAVEL ABOVE GROUND == WE CARRY YOU ALL THE WAY

OPEN AIR
TO
EVERYWHERE
LIST OF MOTOR SERVICES.

○ First LGOC bus map
April 1911

London's first bus maps were produced in 1911 by the LGOC. At the time, horse buses were in decline throughout London, and the LGOC ran its last that year. Motor buses could cover longer routes than horse buses, and their adoption created a need for better route information. The slogan 'Travel above ground – we carry you all the way' reflects keen competition with the Underground, which had introduced its first maps in 1908.

⊃ Certificate of Incorporation of LGOC into the Underground Group
1912
Public Record Office

The idea of amalgamating the Underground Group and the General, London's biggest bus operator, was under active discussion from around 1909. The idea was to try to reduce competition, which was financially damaging for both operators, and, in the interest of efficiency, ensure that buses helped feed passengers on to the railways wherever possible. A formal merger was agreed in 1912. Subsequent legislation enabled fare receipts to be pooled, thus enabling the profitable buses to cross-subsidise the expensive Tube system.

TRADE
FOLLOWS
THE
ALL RED
ROUTE

Just as
the Flag

links the
Empire's Commerce,
so does the

GENERAL

link up the Trade Routes
of the world's greatest city

Certificate of Incorporation

I Hereby Certify,

London General Omnibus Company Limited

B-TYPE BUS

The X-type

Designed by Frank Searle at Walthamstow, the X-type was effectively the prototype for the famous B-type bus that followed.

B is for B-type Bus

This illustration by Charles Pears is for *The TOT Alphabet*.

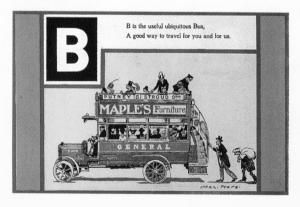

The B-type, London's first reliable motor bus, was not the result of any dramatic innovation, but was developed following experimentation, incorporating minor technical and design advances from many different buses. When the LGOC took over the London Motor Omnibus Co. ('Vanguard') in 1908, it also acquired that company's small overhaul works at Walthamstow and soon decided that the newly enlarged company should build its own buses on the site. The first model to be designed by the Chief Motor Engineer, Frank Searle, was the 'X', an unashamed amalgam of the best features of existing types which was rudely described by some writers as the 'Daimler-Wolseley-Straker'. An improved version, the B-type, was on the road by autumn 1910. It was so successful that the factory at Walthamstow was extended to produce 30 chassis per week, at one point reaching 60. By 1913 2,500 B-type buses had been produced.

One day's output of B-type chassis at Walthamstow
1913

Single deck B-type
March 1921

One of 60 double-deck B-type buses converted to single deck operation in 1920, with a new bigger body based on the K-type bus of 1919.

B-types at Cricklewood Garage
April 1911

Three new B-types entering service at Cricklewood Garage.

District Railway

Whitechapel & Bow Railway share certificate
1901

This certificate is a reminder that the Underground was initially funded by private capital with money raised on the promise of dividends. The Whitechapel & Bow, jointly promoted by the District and the London, Tilbury & Southend Railways, gave the District an outlet east into Essex. By 1902 trains were running beyond the historic terminus at Whitechapel and on to the widened Southend lines through Bromley-by-Bow.

District Railway map
1908

By 1905 the District Railway was electrified and formed part of the new Underground Electric Railways of London Group, which controlled the three deep-tube railways: the Bakerloo, Hampstead and Piccadilly, clearly shown as connections on this map.

District Railway promotion
1901

This letterpress poster is typical of the publicity of the Victorian era. Within a few years this style was to radically change under the influence of the new Undergound Group's commercial manager, Frank Pick.

🎧 **By train to the seaside**
c. 1902
Roger Brasier Collection

London, Tilbury & Southend Railway '37' class 4-4-2 tank locomotive no. 39, 'Forest Gate', passing through Hornsey Road on its way to Southend around 1902. When the District Railway later expanded out into east London and beyond, it shared the service with the Tilbury & Southend Railway.

〇 **Manufacturer's drawings of the District Railway's electrified B-stock**
1905

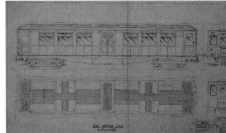

〇 **District Railway promotional poster**
1908

The electrification of the District, from 1903 to 1905, was indicative of the intervention of Charles Yerkes who helped to provide both the capital and technological knowledge that allowed the introduction of new electric rolling stock.

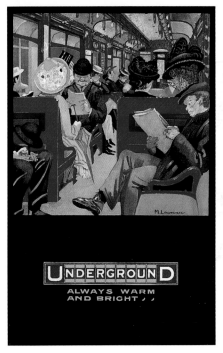

🎧 *Always Warm and Bright* **by Mark Lawrence**
1912

The interior of a District Railway car is well represented in this poster. It shows the clerestory ceiling, typical of the new stock and high enough to cope with the voluminous Edwardian hats worn by the passengers.

District Railway timetable
March 1903

By 1903 the District, as well as running intensive services in central and west London, was running services east along the Thames estuary to Southend and beyond, thanks to the Whitechapel & Bow extension.

Harry Wharton Ford FRIBA, architect to the District Railway, 1900–1911

Harry W. Ford was born in Hampstead in 1875. Appointed architect to the District Railway

in 1900, he was responsible for work on a number of stations connected with the electrification of the District that took place around 1905. Although he formally retired from the District in 1911, he continued to undertake commissions for them until 1916. He died in 1947.

Earl's Court station

Detail of the frieze at Earl's Court station, which was rebuilt by architect Harry W. Ford in 1906 to serve both the District, and the new Great Northern Piccadilly and Brompton Railways.

Architectural drawings for Charing Cross (now Embankment) station
1914

With the arrival of the Bakerloo and Hampstead lines at Charing Cross, the original District Railway station of 1870 required extensive redevelopment. These architectural sections and elevations prepared by Harry W. Ford show the station as constructed: a single-storey building clad in Portland stone.

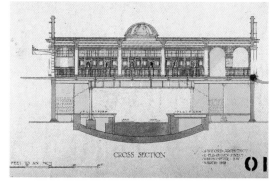

⌒ Architectural detail at Embankment (formerly Charing Cross)

Adorning either side of the Villiers Street entrance to Embankment station are these attractive bronze lamps. Flanked by Doric columns, they still illuminate the poster boards beneath.

⌒ Ticket office windows at Fulham Broadway (previously Walham Green)

The booking hall area of the glazed station arcade was rebuilt *c*. 1905 and was designed to incorporate shops, which directly faced the ticket windows in this photograph.

◔ *The New Charing Cross* by Charles Sharland 1914

A graphic poster of the work that went on below ground during reconstruction work, including the installation of the new escalators.

◔ Elevations for Walham Green (now Fulham Broadway) station 1910

Now listed, Ford's building at Walham Green station replaced the original 1880 station. In common with many other reconstructions of this date the opportunity was taken to include retail premises, the rents of which brought additional income to the railway. The station façade still exists today.

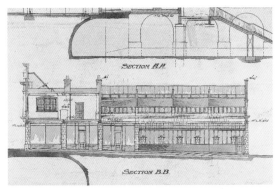

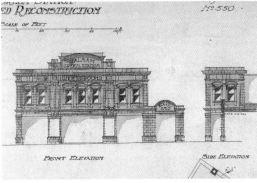

🎧 *Temple Station* by
Duncan Carse
1915

This luminous watercolour,
commissioned by Harry Ford,
shows a view of Temple station
following reconstruction by the
architect for the District Railway.
Local property owners insisted
that the building should not rise
above a single storey.

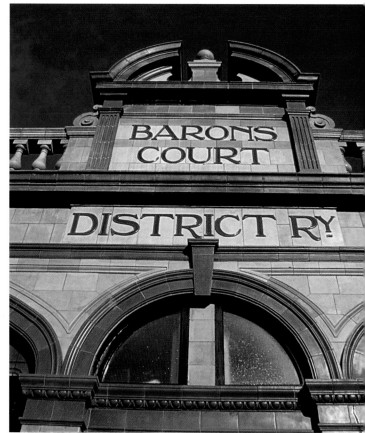

◖ **District Railway monogram at Barons Court station**

◖ **Ticket office at Barons Court station**

The interior of the office was clad with ceramic tiles in varying shades of green with matching ticket office window.

◖ **Barons Court station**
rebuilt 1905

The arrival of the Piccadilly Tube to west London in 1906 saw changes to certain District Railway facilities, including a new joint station at Barons Court where the new line surfaced. Here Ford designed a station that, in the use of terracotta-faced arches, loosely echoes Leslie Green's stations. However, the colours used, primarily a honey brown, and features such as the striking second-storey pediment, are unmistakably Ford's own.

KINGSWAY SUBWAY

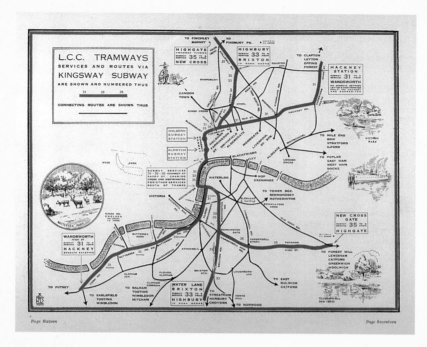

Kingsway Tram Subway medallion
1905

This medallion was struck to mark completion of the project.

The Kingsway Tram Subway was built as part of a great slum clearance scheme, and followed the line of two new streets, Aldwych and Kingsway. The subway was authorised in 1902, but obtaining authority for the connection along the Victoria Embankment proved difficult. When the subway first opened in 1906, trams had to terminate at Aldwych station, and the tunnels beyond were used as sidings. Powers to complete the extension were eventually obtained, and the connection to the Embankment was eventually opened on 10 April 1908. The Embankment was wide enough to accommodate a 'reserved track' for the trams, which helped to speed up the journey. By taking a tram via the subway, it was possible to travel from Bloomsbury to Westminster in as little as seven minutes – fast even by today's standards. The Kingsway Subway also connected the tram systems north and south of the river via the tram tracks laid across Westminster Bridge in 1906.

When it opened, the Kingsway Subway only had headroom for single-deck cars. The existing class 'F' trams had wooden bodies, which were not thought to be safe for operation in tunnels. Therefore trams, known as class 'G', were specially built, with bodywork made of steel throughout, for services running through the Subway. They were all withdrawn in 1930, when the Subway was rebuilt to take double-deck cars.

🎧 **Kingsway Tram Subway under Holborn**
1906

From 1906 until it was rebuilt in 1929–30 the Kingsway subway could only take single-deck trams. Here the tunnels can be seen passing under Holborn, just south of the entrance in Southampton Row.

🎧 **Model of class 'G' electric tram**
1906

The class 'G' electric tram was built specifically for services running through the Kingsway subway.

🎧 **Construction of Embankment entrance to Kingsway tram subway below Waterloo Bridge**
1908

🎧 **Tram at the northern entrance of the Kingsway Subway, Southampton Row**
c. 1908

The entrance was down a steep ramp, which still exists today. For many Londoners the sudden dive into the tunnels was as good as a funfair ride.

🎧 *Victoria Embankment* **by Monica Rawlins**
Poster
1926

⟳ Charles Tyson Yerkes, 1837–1905

Charles Tyson Yerkes, an American financier, founded the Underground Electric Railways Company of London (UERL) in 1902, taking control of London's floundering tube railway projects and raising £15,000,000 from mostly American sources. He acquired a controlling interest in the steam-operated District Railway, which was in poor shape when he arrived. Yerkes was responsible for electrification of the District and went on to secure finance for three new tube lines, known as Yerkes Tubes. These were the Baker Street & Waterloo Railway; the Great Northern, Piccadilly & Brompton Railway (GNP&BR); and the Charing Cross, Euston & Hampstead Railway. Yerkes died before any of the new lines opened.

◑ Publicity for the Baker Street & Waterloo Railway
1906

The first UERL Tube to open on 10 March 1906 was the Baker

Street and Waterloo Railway, quickly becoming the more familiar Bakerloo.

◑ *Visit the Zoo by Bakerloo*
c. 1910

This postcard suggests taking the Bakerloo Tube to Regent's Park station for a visit to the Zoo, although it was quite a walk from the station.

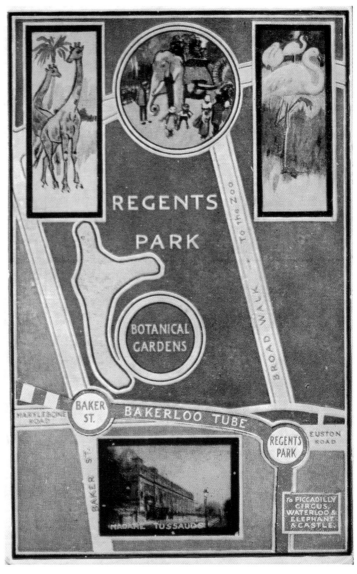

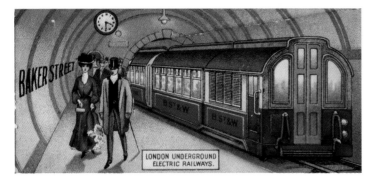

⬦ Early days on the Bakerloo
c. 1906

These Edwardian passengers have just got off a train known as gate-stock. The tiled platform walls are typical of all the Yerkes stations. Station names formed part of the platform tiling scheme.

⬦ Handbill for the extension of the Bakerloo railway from Queen's Park to Watford, 11 February 1915

One way of extending an Underground line out from

central London, thus tapping new suburban markets, was to co-operate with a mainline railway. By connecting with the London & North Western Railway's newly electrified Watford lines at Queen's Park, the Bakerloo reached the still relatively undeveloped, open country of Middlesex.

⬦ Commercial postcard depicting a platform at Piccadilly Circus station
c. 1906

The platform tiling, familiar on all the Yerkes stations, can be seen here in the station name and the geometric pattern running at waist and frieze height.

⬦ Publicity for the Great Northern, Piccadilly & Brompton Railway

The second UERL Tube to open was the Great Northern, Piccadilly & Brompton Railway (GNP&BR) on 15 December 1906, although not all the stations on this line were completed until the following year.

Interior of a Piccadilly Railway gate-stock car
1906

Mostly constructed abroad, the new trains for the UERL lines were very different from previous trains seen on British railways. Open plan, with no divisions into separate compartments or classes, they appeared open and airy. To reduce weight, and assist cleaning, the seats were made from woven-cane rattan.

Gate-stock train at Highgate station
c. 1907

One of the problems with early Tube trains was the limited number of doors, situated at the end of the cars, around which passengers had to crowd to enter or leave the train. Later designs, with more doors spread throughout the train, significantly helped improve loading.

The GNP&BR depot at Lillie Bridge
1907

The new lines required rolling stock and a depot. This postcard

shows the interior of the sheds at Lillie Bridge, close to Earl's Court in west London. Yerkes, as an American, had no compunction in buying abroad. The trains pictured here were built in France and Hungary.

Publicity booklet issued by the UERL
1907

Day trips out of the smoky city for organised parties, such as Sunday Schools, were a feature of Edwardian life. The Underground Group benefited from this trade, which had the advantage of being off-peak. Special arrangements and cheap fares were listed in booklets like this one.

GREAT NORTHERN, PICCADILLY & BROMPTON Ry. INTERIOR CAR SHED.

Approaching Hampstead station
1907

This impressive crossover tunnel, two hundred feet below the genteel streets of Hampstead, marks one of the deepest parts of the Underground network. Constructed of cast-iron lining segments, bolted together, it gives an impression of the scale of the engineering required to build London's deep tube railways.

Layout plan of Camden Town station
1907

This was the only subterranean junction station constructed on the original UERL system. The two branches of the Charing Cross, Euston & Hampstead Railway, the upper running to Golders Green and the lower to Highgate (now Archway station) can be seen with the lift shafts sitting between the two branches.

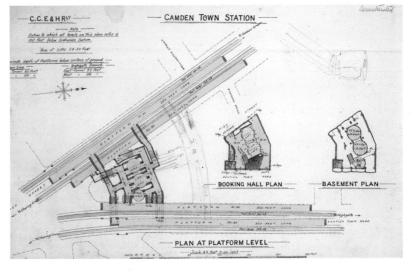

Map of the Charing Cross, Euston & Hampstead Railway – 'The Last Link'

The Charing Cross, Euston & Hampstead Railway opened on 22 June 1907. It was not until 1938 that the line's name became the more compact Northern line.

ARCHITECTURE OF LESLIE GREEN

Although the three new tube railways that formed part of Yerkes's empire were technically separate entities, he was determined that, unlike London's earlier Underground lines, they would form part of a cohesive network with a unified public face. To help achieve this, he employed a single architect, Leslie W. Green, to design the vast majority of the stations on the system. Green's designs for the three Yerkes Tubes, with their distinctive glazed terracotta finishes, the colour of oxblood, produced a remarkably cohesive set of stations, whilst at the same time being flexible enough to suit the demands of varying types

Leslie William Green FRIBA (1875–1908)
Mrs Vera Stubbs/D. Lawrence Collection

....

Born in Hampstead, Leslie Green was to leave the Underground with a legacy of Edwardian stations that are still treasured today. Unfortunately Green died of tuberculosis at the age of 33, just over a year after completion of his major work, the new stations for the UERL.

of sites. In the short space of three years, Green designed more than 40 stations with the assistance of Stanley Heaps and Israel Walker.

Architectural elevations for Hampstead (Heath Street) station
c. 1905

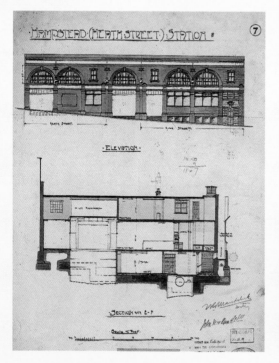

Architectural elevations for Strand (later Aldwych) station
c. 1905

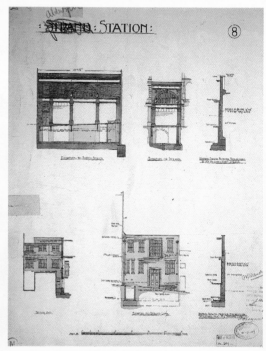

The interiors of Green's stations were also designed according to a unified style. Common elements used for the ticket halls were concrete floors containing crushed granite and walls decorated to shoulder height with bottle green tiling. The functional tiling could be easily cleaned, a necessary requirement in a heavily polluted city. The tiling was topped with a dado of relief tiles, moulded with an acanthus leaf or pomegranate design. The influence of Art Nouveau was evident in the faience ticket windows and the ornamental use of wrought iron on the lift shaft ventilation grilles.

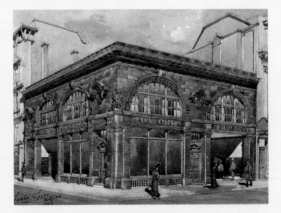

Watercolour of Oxford Circus station, as designed by Leslie Green
1905

This painting is signed by Green himself.

Brompton Road station on the GNP&BR
1907

The station façade hid a massive steel-girder frame that could support additional floors, whilst at first-floor level, behind the half-moon windows, sat the huge lift machines.

Elephant & Castle station
1914

This station was designed by Green as a multi-storey building for the Baker Street & Waterloo Railway.

Knightsbridge station
c. 1907

The most ornate example of the use of Art Nouveau style by Green, it was unfortunately demolished during reconstruction of the station in the early 1930s.

◌ Acanthus leaf motif

This was a common design used by Green for the panelled dado tiling.

◌ Pomegranate motif

This pomegranate design for the tiling frieze by Green is a rarer example.

◌ Restored platform tiling at Gillespie Road station (now Arsenal)
1999

◌ Faience ticket window by Green

The station name was spelt out in the tiled frieze. Unfortunately these rapidly became covered by commercial advertising or were simply redundant as station names changed, as in this example. Today they are, wherever possible, carefully restored. Directional information was also worked into the tiles adjoining entrances and exits.

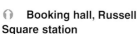

◌ Booking hall, Russell Square station

Leslie Green designed his booking halls to encourage passengers in the discipline of queuing at ticket windows. This station was typical with its faience ticket windows, elaborate light fixtures and barriers. Sadly, these features and the tiled walls topped by moulded dados no longer survive.

◌ Lift shaft ventilation grille by Green

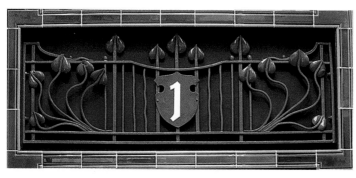

◊ *Zoo* by Sidney Thomas Charles Weeks
1913

The Undergound has long advertised the London Zoo as a major attraction, as in this poster, even though it is quite a walk from any of its stations. Both the Charing Cross, Euston & Hampstead and the Baker Street and Waterloo railways encouraged people to visit the Zoo using their services.

◑ Golders Green station
1911

Instead of terminating at Hampstead, as the name Charing Cross, Euston & Hampstead Railway implies, the line reached out to Golders Green, simply a crossroads amongst open fields at the time. Many thought Yerkes mad, but it was a deliberate and a very American-inspired move to stimulate suburban development and therefore traffic.

◊ *Golders Green for Bank Holidays*, publicity leaflet
1908

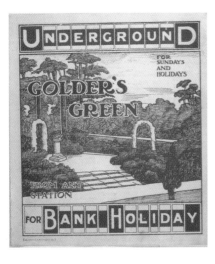

◑ Albert Stanley, later Lord Ashfield (1874–1948)

This photograph was taken in 1910 when Albert Stanley was the newly appointed managing director of the Underground Group. Born in Derbyshire, he emigrated to America in 1885 and changed his surname from Knattries to Stanley. Following a rapid rise in the tramway industry, he returned to England in 1907 as General Manager of the UERL railways. He brought with him a wealth of American expertise in the business of mass transit, knowledge that the fledgling group desperately needed. Knighted in 1914 and ennobled in 1920, he was appointed the first Chairman of London Transport in 1933, a post he held until nationalisation in 1947.

◑ Map of the London Underground railways
1908

Although by 1908 the Underground Electric Railways of London (UERL) dominated London's Underground, not all the lines shown on this map belonged to them. One of the real achievements of the UERL was to persuade other railways, such as the Central London, the City & South London and the Metropolitan Railways, to accept coordinated marketing, thus making the system appear seamless to the travelling public. This included use of the 'UNDERGROUND' logo that was to become a familiar sight to Londoners.

◑ Earliest logo for UERL
1907

The earliest logo for the combined lines was the result of a newspaper competition in 1907. The winner, a Mr Pawsey, combined the idea of tunnels under a London skyline with the motto 'swift and sure'. Some of the elements of this design continued in use after the widespread adoption of the roundel.

◑ UERL staff medallion
1907–8

The logo was used on publicity and, even more grandly, on the reverse of a hallmarked silver travel medallion issued to senior staff.

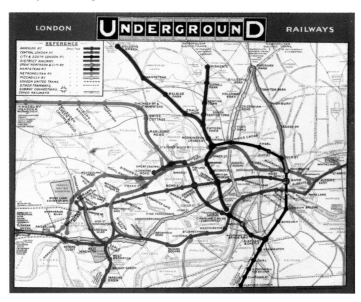

◔ The beginning of the roundel

The roundel, bullseye or bar and circle device evolved from several sources. Most notable were the red disc name boards that were introduced to Underground stations in 1908.

◔ Roundel as publicity

The roundel symbol soon came to be adopted on stations and on company publicity. Here it is used to reinforce the pleasantness of Underground travel. In comparison with the open upper deck of a bus, this was indeed weatherproof.

➔ *Points for Whitsuntide* by Charles Sharland
1912

A theory that the roundel device signifies London with the River Thames as the blue bar through the centre is given some credibility with this elaborate poster design showing the variety of places and activities reached by Underground.

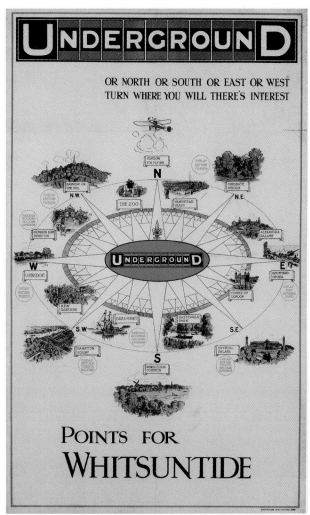

➲ *The Ghostly Driver*
1912

Ever quick to sell a good story the Underground was here featured in one of the popular magazines of the day. The London Electric Railway's rolling stock was fitted with a number of new safety features. Foremost amongst these was the 'deadman's handle', a device that ensures the train can move only when the driver's control handle remains depressed.

➲ *Moving stairway at Oxford Circus*
1914

Escalators were a novelty in 1914, and not everyone was confident about using them, hence this anonymous poster encouraging people to use them as a new and exciting innovation.

➲ **Technical drawing of a travelling footway**
1900

This proposal for a moving walkway stayed on the drawing board. The first use of this technical innovation was at Bank station, linking the ticket hall and the Waterloo & City line in 1960. Two travolators, as they are now known, were built at Waterloo as part of the extended Jubilee line.

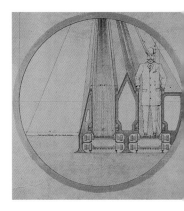

🎧 **Spiral escalator at Holloway Road station**
1906

🔌 ***L for the Lifts* by Charles Pears**
1915

Moving passengers from street to platform by lift quickly saturated capacity, and a novel solution was to experiment with a spiral escalator constructed in a lift shaft. The experiment was a failure and has never been repeated. Sections of this spiral escalator are now part of London's Transport Museum's Collection.

The use of illustrated alphabets was common in the early 1900s, not only to promote services, but also as an aid to poor standards of literacy.

L for the Lifts which go up and down,
To be found at our Stations in all parts of Town.

"BEG PAWDING"

"NO SMOKING IN THE LIFT"

THERE ARE MOVING STAIRWAYS NOW AT EARLS COURT, LIVERPOOL STREET, OXFORD CIRCUS, CHARING CROSS, BAKER STREET.

LONDON COUNTY COUNCIL TRAMWAYS

Far and away the largest operator of electric trams in London was the London County Council (LCC). Officially taking over responsibility for London's government from the old Metropolitan Board of Works in 1889, the LCC soon set about acquiring existing horse tramways with the intention of becoming the operator of a fully integrated electrified system. On 15 May 1903 the LCC's first electric service from Westminster Bridge to Tooting was officially opened by the Prince of Wales (later George V).

Covering much more of central London (apart from the City) than the privately owned tramways, the LCC's services predominantly benefited the labouring classes. At last ordinary working people felt that an up-to-date, affordable form of transport was theirs.

One significant decision, and debatably not a good one, was the LCC's decision to power its trams with current picked up from the slot conduit between the running rails, rather than overhead wires. These, it was felt, would deface the capital, something the conduit system avoided, but at greatly increased cost. Once a track was installed, re-routing it was also prohibitively expensive.

One of the advantages that the LCC's trams exerted over early motor buses was that top deck covers began to appear on them from 1904. The Metropolitan Police, uneasy about the stability of double-deck buses, condemned upper-deck bus passengers to the mercy of the elements until the mid-1920s, thus making the trams a more attractive proposition to the travelling public.

Construction of LCC Tramways electric conduit system on the Thames Embankment 1906

Trams to everywhere 1913

A 1913 map showing the extent of the LCC's tramways, with the system north and south of the Thames tenuously linked by the Kingsway Subway between Waterloo Bridge and Bloomsbury.

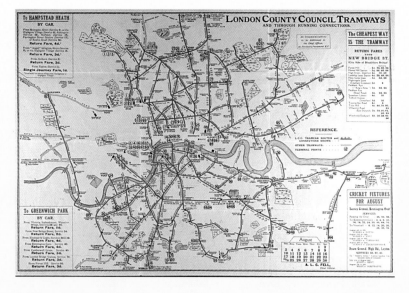

Trams for the millions
1903

The royal car, suitably decorated, making its way through the crowded south London streets at the official opening of LCC's first electric service from Westminster Bridge to Tooting by the Prince of Wales, 15 May 1903.

The dominant tram
c. 1910

In this photograph of about 1910, practically every type of LCC car in service is illustrated at Elephant and Castle, the heart of the Council's south London domain.

Current from below

This cross-section shows the traditional form of conduit construction used by the LCC, with the 'plough' for collecting the current suspended beneath the car.

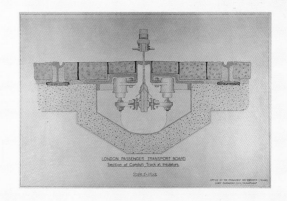

London County Council Tramways stop plates
1906

LCC Tramways helped to introduce the practice of fixed stopping places. These were identified by stop plates, manufactured from vitreous enamel, which were either suspended from a bar or in the case of 'clover leaf' shaped plates sat atop a post. These illustrations show both types.

◑ Bringing things together

By 1914 much of London's transport was supervised by one organisation, the Underground Group of companies. This included most of London's Tubes, the District Railway, the London General Omnibus Co. and the three privately owned tramways – London United, Metropolitan Electric, and the South Metropolitan. The latter, a small concern that operated services in the Croydon area, made up for lack of size with a resounding title: 'The South Metropolitan Electric Tramways & Lighting Co. Ltd'. This map shows how the services of all three companies were co-ordinated with those of the Underground.

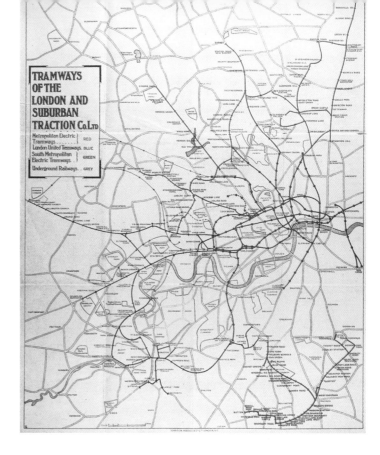

◔ From the suburbs into the country, designed by Fred Taylor
1915

The many scenic attractions reached by the Underground Group's three tramway systems are advertised in this handy little folding guide of 1915, which not only mentions obvious locations, such as Richmond Park and Hampstead, but also refers to Edgware ('Old-fashioned village on the Roman Watling Street'), Stanmore ('Pretty village on the Watford Road') and Sudbury ('Dairy-farming district in the Brent Valley…Special charm in haymaking time'). The burst of suburban development around the London area between 1900 and 1914 owed much to the electric trams.

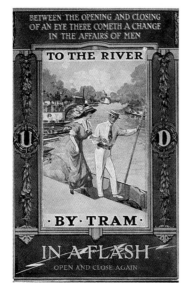

These two publicity leaflets aimed to show the integrated nature of the transport system at this time. Electric trains and trams could carry people seamlessly from their new homes in the leafy suburbs to the river for leisure. By this time most of London's Underground system and the privately owned electric tramways had come together within the Underground Group.

↻ **Electric revolution**

About 1900 London began to experience a profound transport revolution, much of which was due to the replacement of horse and steam power by electricity. Affecting both tramways and railways, it resulted in a fresh explosion of suburban development. This picture illustrates a crucial part of the pattern at Shepherd's Bush, where the interchange between the electric trams (introduced in 1901) and the Central London electric Tube connecting with the West End and the City (opened in 1900) enabled West London commuters to travel all the way, the modern way.

◑ Municipal enterprise
1912

The period from about the 1890s to 1914 was the great age of what came to be know as 'municipal socialism', and local urban authorities countrywide seized on the opportunity offered by the electric tram to bring city transport within the public domain. Their ideal was a publicly underwritten system, lavish but efficiently run with cheap fares, the local authority also providing the power supply. This was the aim of the LCC, demonstrated by this 1912 view of the busy junction at Commercial Road, Aldgate. Cars from the LCC and West Ham Corporation dwarf the 'General's' solitary bus.

◑ Metropolitan Electric Tramways 'G' class tram
c. 1909

Apart from London United, the other major private London electric tramway system was the Metropolitan Electric Tramways. Opening in 1904, it touched the LUT area at Acton, but predominantly served north London, including Finsbury Park

and Golders Green, extending out to Enfield, High Barnet and Waltham Cross. It was contracted to run services on behalf of Middlesex County Council, an arrangement made plain by this photograph of a 'G' class car, new in 1909.

6715 The Manor House.   Finsbury Park N.

◑ 'The gondola of the people'

This is how the electric tram has been described, and perhaps this picture of the lower deck interior of a MET 'C/1' class car shows the reason for such a colourful phrase. Although the photograph shows the lower deck after refurbishment in the 1920s, it still gives an excellent impression of the traditional tramcar interior, with inward facing perimeter seating and elaborately produced monitor roof. It somehow manages to combine a certain airiness with solidity.

◑ MET trams
c. 1904

Two electric trams of the Metropolitan Electric Tramways (MET) company are seen here at Manor House shortly after services began in July 1904. The first MET electric lines ran from the terminus at Finsbury Park to Wood Green and Seven Sisters Corner with a junction at Manor House.

◑ *Tram services to Finchley and Cricklewood*
1910

When the Metropolitan Electric Tramways line from North Finchley reached Golders Green in December 1909, the Underground arranged dual promotion with their Hampstead Tube service, doubling the number of peak time trains to provide a train every three minutes, as advertised in this anonymous poster.

HOUSING FOR STAFF AND TRAMS

During the first decade of the twentieth century, running public transport was a 24-hour business, requiring certain employees to live 'on the job'. London County Council Tramways built a three-storey foreman's house in 1905 as part of its new Poplar tram depot. The parlour and bathroom were on the first floor, while the area below the mansard roof contained that essential Edwardian domestic requirement, a good-sized box room.

Trams also had to be housed. The London County Council maintained several depots for its extensive fleet. Some, such as New Cross depot, which housed up to 300 cars, were very large, whilst Brixton Hill depot, details of which are shown here, was one of the later and smaller establishments. Opened in 1924, with its modest capacity of some 30 cars, it was run in conjunction with the more capacious nearby shed at Telford Avenue.

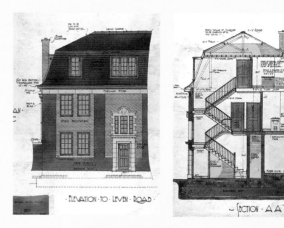

· ELEVATION · TO · LEVEN · ROAD ·

~ SECTION · A · A ~

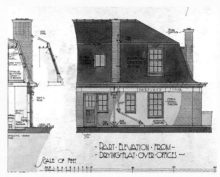

- PART · ELEVATION · FROM ~
- DRYING · FLAT · OVER · OFFICES ~

Architectural elevations for LCCT's foreman's house at Poplar tram depot

Architectural drawings for Brixton Hill tram depot

These drawings are signed by the LCC's architect at the time, G. Topham Forest.

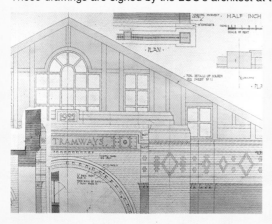

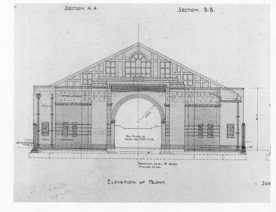

Local endeavour
1906

London County Council was not the only local authority in the London area to promote electric trams. Other boroughs were determined to prove how progressive they were by introducing them as well. In 1901 Croydon, then a distinctive Surrey town on London's outskirts, was one of the first, pre-empting the LCC. In this view a Corporation car wends its way towards West Croydon, while the tram tracks to Addiscombe can be seen turning into George Street. Recently reintroduced, trams once again proceed down George Street.

Serving the East End

West Ham Corporation Tramways car no. 102 of 1910, now preserved in London's Transport Museum, in the full Corporation livery that it would have carried until the formation of London Transport in 1933. West Ham was the biggest municipal operator after the London County Council. Beginning operations in 1904, it served the heart of the East End, and was also happy to take the cockneys to Epping Forest for a summer's day out.

LONDON UNITED TRAMWAYS

London was not among the pioneers of electric tramways, but once the electric tram arrived, it made up for lost time. By 1914 the London system was collectively the biggest in Europe. First in the field was London United Tramways (LUT). Under the directorship of James Clifton Robinson, the Imperial Tramways Co. acquired the run-down horse tramways of west London in 1894 and transformed them into London United Tramways. Opening its first routes in 1901, it stretched from Shepherd's Bush into west London suburbs such as Acton, Ealing and Chiswick, the pleasant surroundings of Hampton Court, and penetrating as far as Uxbridge.

The LUT built its own power station at Chiswick, designed by William Curtis Green. Work on the building started in 1899 and it opened at the same time as the tramway system. The amount of electrical equipment

◔ **James Clifton Robinson, 1848–1910**

James (later Sir James) Clifton Robinson is regarded by many as the man who brought electric trams to London.

installed rapidly increased to cope with expanding services to such suburbs as Tolworth, Kingston and Wimbledon.

LUT's new electric trams were overwhelmingly popular. During the Whitsun Holiday of 1903, 300 cars conveyed 800,000 passengers on all routes. By contemporary standards the electric tram was undoubtedly a modern vehicle, but those of the LUT were exceptionally decorative in a traditional style, a distinct colour identifying each route. With illiteracy still a problem, colour was an easy way to distinguish one route from another.

⋒ LUT coat of arms

The London United Tramways coat of arms graced the first electric tram from Hammersmith to Kew Bridge in 1901 and was subsequently displayed on all cars.

⋒ Model of car no. 7

One of the first 100 class 'X' cars owned by the LUT, it ran from Shepherd's Bush and Hammersmith to Kew Bridge and later to Hounslow.

⬆ **Bank holiday outing**
1903

A bank holiday crush at Shepherd's Bush caught by the camera in summer 1903.

⬆ **LUT car sheds at Chiswick**

The impressively austere new LUT car sheds at Chiswick, photographed at the beginning of the twentieth century.

⬇ **London United Electric Tramways ticket**
April 1901

Issued at the time of the opening of the first electric tramway lines in London.

⬆ **LUT power station, Chiswick**

The splendidly ornate cast-iron staircase in London United's Chiswick power station shows that the company intended to present itself with a certain amount of style. Though no longer a power station, the structure still survives.

⟳ *Hampton Court by Tram* **by Charles Sharland**
1913

This poster depicts the tranquil atmosphere of the river around Hampton Court in the hope of attracting travelling pleasure-seekers on to London United's trams.

◑ West Ham tram bell

In common with most London trams, and perhaps strangely for a vehicle powered by electricity, the bell was pneumatic. In practice the polite 'press once sharply' meant 'give it a good shove'. Conductors used to do this vigorously with the end of their wooden ticket racks.

◖ Leyton District Council tram

The driver of car no. 27 of Leyton Urban District proudly poses for the photographer in his brand new tram. Unlike the LCC cars, which were distinctively 'London', this one is virtually identical with the hundreds of similar vehicles serving counties all over the country. Leyton's tramways eventually suffered the fate of so many smaller municipal systems. The practical and financial burden of maintaining the infrastructure, especially during the First World War, proved heavy, and by 1917 the system was almost moribund. In 1921 the LCC began to run the system on Leyton's behalf, with finance being provided by Leyton Council.

◔ Rails in all directions
c. 1906

Thatched House tram junction, Leyton, is seen here under construction about 1906, showing the disruption caused by electric tramway construction. Leyton Urban District Council, typical of the smaller municipal operators on the fringes of the LCC area, opened in 1906 with a fleet of 40 vehicles. By 1910 services run jointly with the LCC brought Leyton cars to Aldgate and Moorgate.

⌂ Dartford Urban District Council team

Dartford Urban District Council was responsible for one of London's smallest tramways, with a mere 12 cars. Run on

behalf of the Council by J.G. White and Co. (later Balfour Beatty), the entire fleet was destroyed by a disastrous fire at this depot in 1917. Neighbouring Bexley Council immediately came to the rescue, operating

services with trams hastily purchased from the LCC until 1921, when the two authorities amalgamated their systems as 'Bexley Council Tramways and Dartford Light Railways'.

The Great War

From Home Front to Western Front 1914–1918

Theatreland **by MacDonald Gill**
1915

This pictorial map includes a Zeppelin flying above Lincoln's Inn in the top right-hand corner and beneath it the words *'NB a real bomb'*.

The Great War
From Home Front to Western Front, 1914–1918

But the general impression in London was of women at work everywhere. They were seen driving cars and drays, collecting tickets on the underground, working lifts at hotels and offices… On the trams and buses there were young 'conductorettes' in smart blue uniforms, hats with brims turned up at one side, skirts to their knees and leather leggings… War was proving a great equaliser, mixing the social classes… and breaking down old etiquettes – on trams and buses, for instance, in which junior officers who in 1914 would not have dreamed of using such plebeian transport were now everyday travellers, cheerfully handing their fares to the 'conductorettes'.

The Home Fronts 1914–1918 by John Williams, Constable, 1972

The First World War marked an interlude, not a break, in the development of public transport in London, although some new works, such as the extension of the Bakerloo line, still took place.

Less than 48 hours after the outbreak of war on 4 August 1914, a large number of London buses and their crews were 'commandeered' by the government for home troop movements. During the Boer War (1899–1902) London's bus companies had provided many of the army's transport horses. Now that the changeover from horse to motor bus operation was almost complete, it was natural for the companies to supply motor vehicles for military use. Within a few weeks over 300 London buses with volunteer drivers were being used in France and Belgium to carry troops to and from the battle areas. Altogether nearly 1000 buses, most of them B-types, were used for a variety of military purposes over the next four years and proved extremely reliable in the unusual conditions of the Western Front.

Back home London's transport systems had to cope with rapidly growing passenger traffic due to troop movements and the sudden development of war industries such as munitions. The LGOC's bus manufacturing

concern, the Associated Equipment Company (AEC), turned to the production of military vehicles and was able to provide only a few replacements for the commandeered buses. The result was service cuts and considerable overcrowding on those buses that did run.

There were soon serious staff shortages on the buses, trams and Underground as men were enlisted for military service. The obvious solution, the employment of women, was not immediately welcomed by either the trade unions or male management. In March 1915 a temporary policy of 'women substitutes' was reluctantly agreed by the Underground. When Maida Vale station on the new Bakerloo line extension was opened in June, it was staffed entirely by women, and by November London's first woman bus

In Watford by Edward McKnight Kauffer
1915

Even during the war, Frank Pick commissioned posters, such as this, depicting pastoral scenes. This was the first commission from McKnight Kauffer who was to dominate more than two decades of poster history.

conductor had started work on Tilling's route 37. Four months later the first female conductors to join the LGOC completed their training. By the end of 1916 there were over 1700, of whom nearly half gave their previous occupation as 'domestic servant'. Women undertook all sorts of transport work, usually at equal pay with their male colleagues, but had to give up their jobs when the men came home at the end of the war in 1918–19.

Few precautions were taken against an aerial attack on London in the First World War because it seemed an unlikely threat. When Zeppelin raids began in 1915 they caused more shock than damage at first, but over the next two years bombs dropped by German airships and later aeroplanes killed 670 people in London and wounded nearly 2000. The effect on the transport network was disruption rather than physical damage, with the introduction of blackout restrictions

and the first use of tube stations as air-raid shelters. However, the 31 air raids on the London area between 1915 and 1918 were an uncomfortable foretaste of the far more serious attacks of the Blitz in 1940–41. By the end of the First World War and the early months of peace in 1919 London's transport services were in poor shape with continued overcrowding, high fares and a serious shortage of buses.

Women on the Met

Metropolitan Railway guards at Neasden during the First World War.

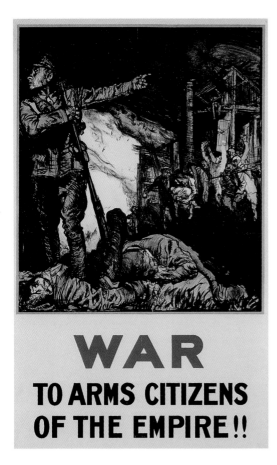

WAR
TO ARMS CITIZENS
OF THE EMPIRE!!

WHY BOTHER ABOUT THE
GERMANS INVADING
THE COUNTRY?

INVADE IT YOURSELF
BY **UNDERGROUND** AND MOTOR-'BUS

EASTER · 1915

Recruitment – War by Frank Brangwyn
1914

An Underground poster issued to assist army recruitment rather than publicise services.

Why Bother about the Germans Invading the Country? by the Brothers Warbis
1915

This Underground poster made a jaunty appeal to forget about the conflict and carry on as normal.

London Underground Railways Certificate of Service
1919

All women taken on as 'substitutes' during the war had to give up their jobs when the men returned. They were presented with Certificates of Service, such as this one, issued in 1919.

'Tis just a reminder, sincere lad and true.
To say that to-day we are thinking of you.

Christmas and
New Years' Greeting.

With heartfelt wishes for an early
safe and victorious return.
FROM THE
Office Staff, Traffic Staff, and Shed Staffs
OF THE
West Ham Tramways.

XMAS 1917

🎧 Front and inside of Christmas card
1917

Christmas card sent to colleagues in the forces by West Ham Tramways staff in 1917.

◑ Christmas present
1916

A tobacco tin sent as a Christmas present to Underground Group staff serving in the Forces by the T.O.T. (Train, Omnibus and Tram) benevolent fund in 1916. Inside the lid is inscribed 'T.O.T. Mutual Aid, Xmas 1916, with the compliments of the season, Electric Railway House, Broadway, Westminster'.

○ 1209 Men of these Companies Have Joined the Colours by Fred Taylor
1915

A poster issued to demonstrate the patriotism of Underground Group staff in volunteering for military service, but without revealing the companies' reluctant acceptance of 'women substitutes' to take their place.

⊃ Troop carriers
1917

Troops boarding London buses commandeered for war service at Arras on the Western Front, May 1917.

○ London buses at the Front

London buses in France during the First World War.

Model of LGOC B-type war bus

This model of a B-type war bus shows it boarded up and painted in War Department khaki for use as troop transport on the Western Front.

New use for a B-type bus

A B-type bus converted into a mobile loft for carrier pigeons, still widely used for army communications during the First World War.

Motormen and Conductors – Hostile Aircraft 1916

A poster giving special instructions for LCC Tramways staff posted at all depots in

November 1916, a few weeks after three staff and three passengers were killed when a tram was wrecked by a Zeppelin bomb at Streatham Hill.

London vehicle shortage

A 'lorry bus' used by the LGOC during the temporary vehicle shortage at the end of the war.

🎧 'Safety first' card

A 'safety first' card issued to bus passengers showing them 'The Right Way' and 'The Wrong Way' to get off a bus. These cards also promoted National War Bonds, a government scheme to raise funds for the war effort.

➲ *London Memories – Kew Gardens* by Fred Taylor
1918

Some of the posters published by the Underground during the war were intended for the troops overseas to decorate army billets and to 'awaken thoughts of pleasant homely things'.

🎧 *The Underworld* by Walter Bayes
1917
Imperial War Museum

This painting depicts Londoners taking shelter from Zeppelin raids at Elephant and Castle Tube station.

WOMEN AT WAR

*Female
Conductors
Wanted*
1916

LGOC
recruitment
poster.

FEMALE CONDUCTORS WANTED.

Height must not be less than 5 feet.
Ages between 21 and 35.

Applicants must apply between 10 a.m. and
1 p.m. on Week-days (Saturdays excepted) to

THE SUPERINTENDENT OF EMPLOYMENT,

L.G.O. Co.'s Training School,

Milman's Street,

Chelsea, S.W.

During the First World War women were recruited by the transport companies to replace men who had been called up. They worked in many capacities, for example as conductors on buses, ticket collectors, gatewomen or guards on the railways. The very first woman conductor in London worked on a Tilling's no. 37 bus on 1 November 1915. In March 1916 the LGOC first employed women conductors. By the end of 1917 522 women had been taken on for a wide variety of jobs.

Class of women conductors

This class is at the LGOC training school at Milmans Street, Chelsea. The instructor is explaining the fare stages on a Bell Punch ticket.

1914 to 1918   168   WOMEN AT WAR

Training women conductors

These women conductors at the LGOC training school are being instructed on how to use a ticket machine. They have not yet received their uniforms, unlike the women standing in the background.

Tea time

Tea at the end of the day's training at the LGOC training school. These recruits have just been issued with their new blue serge uniforms.

Trainee women conductors

This group of new recruits poses for the camera before going out on the road for instruction. Most of them have not yet been issued with uniforms.

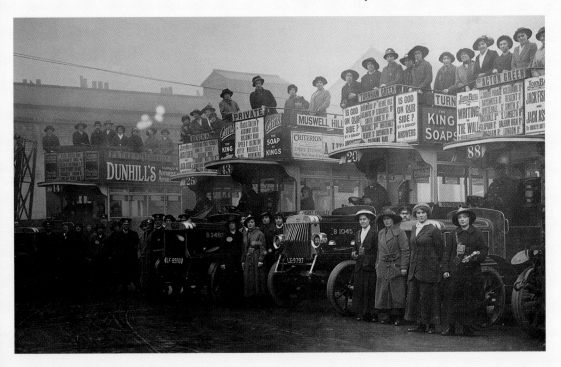

Woman conductor

LGOC woman conductor takes a fare.

Women bus cleaners

Women bus cleaners pause to have their photograph taken in the LGOC's Willesden Garage.

Pair of women conductors

These two Tilling's conductors were photographed at the Swan and Sugarloaf terminus in south Croydon some months after the first woman conductor had been employed in November 1915.

Women Underground staff

Two women painting Underground property during the First World War.

🎧 *War Work – Playing the Game: Women Painters* **by Archibald Standish Hartrick** 1918

🎧 *War Work – Playing the Game: Ticket Collector* **by Archibald Standish Hartrick** 1918

🎧 *War Work – Playing the Game: Lift Girl* **by Archibald Standish Hartrick** 1918

These lithographs are from a commemorative series by Hartrick, showing staff at work during the war. The borders of these images show war scenes, here depicting the troops on the Western Front, thus linking those at home with their colleagues fighting the war.

⮑ **Gatewoman**

A London Underground Railways publicity photograph of a gatewoman. Gatemen and women would normally open the gate on the platform side of the train but an exception has been made here for the convenience of the photographer. The gates were opened to allow passengers on and off individual carriages.

⮑ **A Metropolitan Railway guard**

⮑ **Railway cleaners**

Metropolitan Railway cleaners at the Hammersmith depot during the First World War.

🎧 **Victory celebrations**
1919

Front and back covers of the programme for a 'Victory and Welcome Home Celebration' held for Underground Group staff at the Albert Hall in 1919. T.O.T. (Train, Omnibus and Tram) was also used as the title of the first staff magazine.

➡ **Staff celebrate victory**
1919

Underground Group staff back from war service arriving at the Albert Hall for the Victory Celebrations in June 1919. Judging by the crutches on the bus, some of these men were wounded in action.

🎧 **Bank Holiday**
1919

In 1919 everyone in Britain would have remembered the August Bank Holiday 5 years earlier when war was only 24 hours away.

🎧 **Underground staff at Buckingham Palace**
1920

King George V (second from left) inspecting Underground staff ex-serviceman at Buckingham Palace in 1920. They arrived in one of the buses used in France during the war.

🎧 **Roll of Honour** by M. Greiffenhagen
1915

This poster produced by the Underground Group has spaces left blank for companies to name and honour staff who gave their lives during the war.

↻ **'Ole Bill'**

B-type bus no. 43, christened 'Ole Bill', was preserved by the LGOC and used for the Armistice Day parades. The names on the side of the bus record some of the battles in which London buses were used.

The Birth of London Transport

Designed for the Capital 1918–1939

Tooting Broadway station, designed by architect Charles Holden in 1925 as part of the Northern line extension to Morden.

The Birth of London Transport
Designed for the Capital, 1918–1939

Meanwhile, out in the Circus itself bedlam is let loose. All the chariots of London seem to be converging towards the fountain. The traffic is, as it were, in some great mortar, and a giant is pounding it with a half-seen shadowy pestle. Cabs, flivvers, Rolls-Royces, pleasure parties, country parties with dogs looking over hoods of their cars complacently without a bark – whistles, whistles, whistles, shrieks for taxis, tides of pedestrians, red buses like dragons swarming their way through scores of octopuses. Every bus-halt has its hundreds waiting to get home. For now is the great demobilization of pleasure – from the gay centre to all the humdrum suburbs and the stuffy box-spring beds.

Stephen Graham, 'Saturday Midnight at Piccadilly Circus',
from *London Nights*, John Lane, 1925

As early as 1863 a House of Lords Committee had suggested that a single transport authority was needed to co-ordinate and integrate transport services in London. Thereafter many government advisory bodies had reinforced that opinion. By the 1920s their argument was that the

conflict of interest between the Underground Group of companies, the mainline railway companies, the London County Council and other municipal tramway authorities and the independent bus operators, meant that the needs of the travelling public and London as a whole were not met. It was felt that co-ordination could be achieved only through a single authority responsible for all of London's public transport.

The Underground Group's method of amalgamation by takeover was impossible with the council-owned tramways and the mainline railways. The only way forward was by Act of Parliament. In 1923 all 120 railway companies in Britain except the London Underground and Metropolitan Railway were grouped together into just four private companies under compulsory amalgamation by the government. The 'Big Four' were the

Announcing the creation of London Transport
1933

The London Passenger Transport Board brought together the buses, Underground, trams and coaches in one company. It very swiftly became known simply as 'London Transport'.

Poster artwork by Tom Eckersley
1995

Based on a celebrated 1935 photograph of Boston Manor station, this 1995 poster was Tom Eckersley's last work for London Transport in a career that began in 1935.

Great Western, the Southern, the London Midland & Scottish (LMS) and London & North Eastern (LNER) Railways, all of which ran suburban services in the London area. In 1928–9 the Underground Group and the LCC each promoted a Co-ordination of Passenger

Transport Bill for London in Parliament. However, the new Labour government elected in 1929 disliked the idea of a private enterprise monopoly being created to run public services in London, and both bills were rejected. A way forward emerged largely through the collaboration of Lord Ashfield, the Underground Group chairman and Herbert Morrison, the Labour Minister of Transport. Despite their different political outlooks, these two formed a solution that remained generally acceptable even after the Labour government fell in 1931.

The four mainline railway companies would not agree to their London suburban services being included in a common management for all public transport in the capital, arguing that they could not be separated from their long-distance networks. They would, however, consider pooling fare receipts and establishing a joint committee to plan future developments. The main opposition to a new transport body for London came from the independent bus operators, who would be swallowed up, and the Metropolitan Railway, which considered itself both an urban underground railway and a full scale mainline concern serving the Home Counties. Despite active campaigning against it, the London Passenger Transport Bill was eventually passed, and London Transport came into being on 1 July 1933.

Under the new Board, ultimate authority was removed from the local authorities and shareholders of the various companies involved, the latter receiving either cash payments or shares in the new undertaking. There was some public control over new developments, but real power rested with the Board, which in practice was dominated by the leading individuals and established philosophy of the Underground. Lord Ashfield became Chairman, and Frank Pick the Vice Chairman and Chief Executive.

As the organisational strands of transport in the capital were brought together to create London Transport, there had already been considerable progress in the improvement of rail and road services since the First World War. London had continued to grow rapidly in the 1920s, and there were particularly strong pressures to provide or improve local railway services to newly developing suburban areas. The Southern Railway began a huge electrification programme covering nearly all the overground suburban lines south of the Thames by 1930. Only one tube line ran south of the river, the City & South London. This was extended in 1926 to Morden, where an LGOC bus interchange allowed the Underground to penetrate further into Southern Electric territory.

North of the river, the LMS electrified some of its overground suburban services, and the LNER met traffic demand by simply operating more suburban steam trains. The Metropolitan and the Underground led the way with new developments. The Met extended its electric services out to Rickmansworth and opened new branches to Watford (1926) and Stanmore (1932). As suburban Metro-Land grew there was an enormous rise in demand for season tickets. To take just one example, monthly season sales at Wembley Park rose from 3000 to just over 13,500 between 1923 and 1928.

The Hampstead Tube was extended overground from Golders Green to Edgware in 1923–4, stimulating more suburban growth around the new stations. At the same time the old City & South London Line was enlarged and linked to the Hampstead Line at Camden Town, creating what is now the Northern line. The Piccadilly line was also

Cover of Metropolitan Railway booklet promoting Metro-Land
1920

extended at both ends to reach Uxbridge and Hounslow in the west and Cockfosters in the north by 1933. In central London some of the busier interchange Tube stations were rebuilt, the most impressive being Piccadilly Circus, which re-opened in 1928 with banks of escalators instead of lifts and an elegant circular booking hall below the famous road junction. This modern underground transport hub at the very heart of the city was much admired by visitors to London from overseas and inspired metro development elsewhere, notably in Moscow.

During the 1920s the Underground Group developed a distinctive corporate design style that set it apart from other

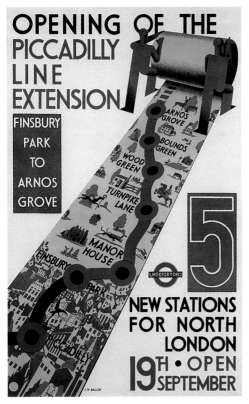

***Opening of the Piccadilly Line Extension* by
Cecil Walter Bacon**
Poster
1932

organisations. This came primarily from the influence of Frank Pick, who rose to become the group's Managing Director. Pick was an administrator but also had a firm belief that good design should be at the heart of all that an organisation did. The 'fitness for purpose' of a transport body meant that all it operated must both work properly and look right. This applied to everything, from the products of architecture and engineering through publicity and information systems to the details of seat upholstery, light fittings and litter bins. He believed the total effect of these should reflect London's bus and Underground services as modern, efficient, self-respecting and confident.

It was Pick who commissioned the leading calligrapher Edward Johnston to design a special display typeface for the Underground. This was used from 1919 onwards for signs, station nameboards, posters and eventually even bus destination blinds. Pick's thoughtful design management gave London Transport a powerful corporate identity that communicated and underlined the organisation's objectives very effectively. Johnston's lettering is still used by London Underground today. Pick also promoted the use of high quality poster artwork for publicity and worked with the architect Charles Holden to develop a modern design style for the Underground's environment, which is reflected in the new stations of the 1920s and '30s and the Underground headquarters at St James's Park built in 1927–9. Holden's work, particularly the new Piccadilly line stations of 1932–3, is now recognised as one of the most important contributions to modern British architecture in the interwar years.

The Underground's corporate philosophy of continuous improvement, high standards of design and efficient public service became those of London Transport after 1933. The New Works Programme of 1935–40 included more extensions and improvements to the Underground network, integration with mainline suburban services, converting the tram system to trolleybus operation, and introducing more efficient diesel buses. For Pick, as Managing Director, these were the practical outcomes of a broader vision: 'The Board's undertaking is a declaration of faith that its task is worthwhile and that its labours shall eventually contribute their appointed share to the transformation of our urban civilisation into some fine flower of accomplishment.'

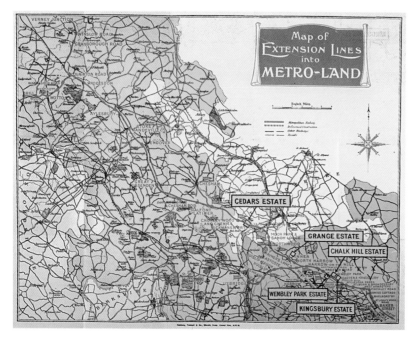

Map of EXTENSION LINES into METRO-LAND

CEDARS ESTATE

GRANGE ESTATE

CHALK HILL ESTATE

WEMBLEY PARK ESTATE

KINGSBURY ESTATE

◐ Map from *Metro-Land* booklet
1930

The Metropolitan Railway was involved through a subsidiary company in property deals on the surplus land adjoining its lines. The railway's publicity

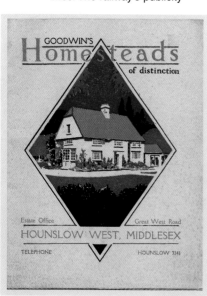

department coined the term 'Metro-Land' as a marketing ploy in 1915. This map shows the full extent of services to the north-west and highlights the five main estates established by their own Country Estates company, set up in 1919.

◑ Goodwin's Homesteads brochure

Estate Agents were quick to target areas around the new tube lines of the inter-war period, using the same kinds of imagery as Metro-Land's publicists, and often setting up offices near the new stations.

◑ *Cheap Fares to Metro-Land*
1922

Images of the modern, powerful new electric locomotives were a regular feature on Met publicity materials for the next 10 years. The locos came to be closely

identified with Metro-Land. In the later 1920s they were given names relating to historical figures and personalities associated with the areas through which they ran.

◑ *Metro Weekly Seasons*
1926

The Metropolitan Railway saw housing development as the route to a dependable long-term source of income through sales of season tickets. Their strategy worked.

METROPOLITAN RAILWAY

LONDON'S
PLEASURELAND

CHEAP FARE & PLEASURE PARTY
ARRANGEMENTS ON THE METRO.

↻ London's Pleasureland, brochure
1927

The Met publicised leisure travel, country walks and rambles in rural Metro-Land alongside its hard sell suburban re-settlement messages. However, the uncontrolled growth of London in the 1920s and 30s replaced many acres of open land with new housing developments.

↻ Metropolitan electrification
1925

Although the central area and the Uxbridge branch of the Metropolitan were already electrified by 1907, electrification

was not extended to Rickmansworth and the new Watford terminus until 1925. As part of this scheme, new electric locomotives came into use to haul the longer distance trains. The Metropolitan was very proud of these new trains and promoted the new and improved services heavily.

↻ A Tour through Metro-Land by E.V. Kealey
1921

In a bold marketing and publicity move, the Met produced these promotional booklets for an organised press tour of Metro-Land in July 1921.

METROPOLITAN
RAILWAY
ELECTRIFICATION

The Mark of Ⓜ *Efficiency*

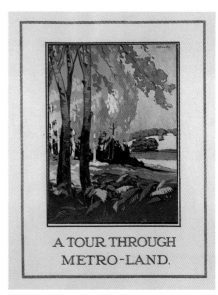

A TOUR THROUGH
METRO-LAND.

↻ Carriage door lock
1926

Never missing an opportunity to push their message, the Metropolitan Railway applied advertising to its carriage doors in 1926.

↻ New electric Metropolitan locomotive at Wembley Park
c. 1923

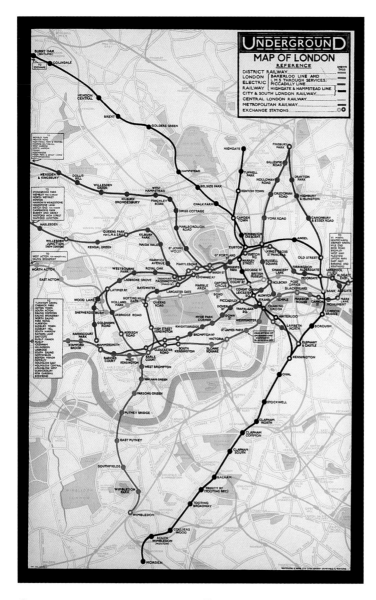

LEAVE THIS
AND

I never had any other desire so strong and so like to covetousness as that one which I have had always, that I might be Master of a small House and a Large Garden, with moderate conveniences joined to them.

MOVE TO EDGWARE

○ *Move to Edgware* by
William Kermode
1924

As the Underground grew, its prolific publicity machine issued innumerable posters exhorting Londoners to move out to the new suburbs that their lines were helping to create. London continued to grow without regulation until after the Second World War.

○ **Underground map**
1929

This unusual map by
F. H. Stingemore almost manages to show the full extent of the Northern line's extensions to Edgware and Morden in the 1920s.

○ *The New Quick Route to Stanmore*
1932

The Metropolitan Railway's last extension was from Wembley Park northwards to Stanmore. It was the first conceived with all electric working.

THE
NEW
QUICK
ROUTE
TO
STANMORE

🎧 *New Works* by Thomas Enoch Lightfoot
1932

The New Works Programme included a wide range of improvements to the London Transport network, including Tube extensions and station rebuilds over five years between 1935 and 1940. Budgeted at £40 million, much of the work was interrupted by the outbreak of war.

🎧 Bushey Heath station
1943

This sketch is by London Transport Architects Department. The New Works Programme included plans to extend the Northern line to Elstree and Bushey Heath. Postponed by the onset of war, plans remained on the table for another ten years, and appeared as a dotted line on maps of the Underground until 1949.

🎧 *More for You* by Beath (John M. Fleming)
1940

The use of a joint 'logo' on this poster shows the close association between the LNER and the London Passenger Transport Board.

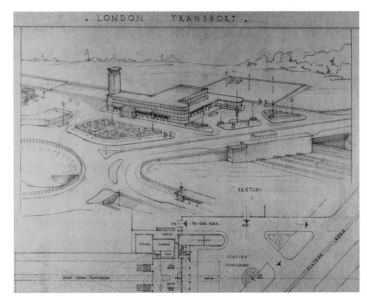

THE JOHNSTON TYPEFACE

One of Frank Pick's first responsibilities after joining the Underground Group was the poster campaign that he initiated in 1908. He became increasingly unhappy with the typefaces available for display work and asked the calligrapher Edward Johnston to design a company typeface. The Johnston typeface was first produced in 1916 in the form of wood letter blocks. The smallest sizes were produced in metal. By limiting their issue to a small number of approved printers, it remained in London Transport's almost exclusive use until 1979.

It proved admirable for its purpose and the typeface was to evolve and develop considerably during its long use by London Transport. Initially produced in a limited range of sizes – appropriate to poster printing – there were only capital letters and a range of punctuation marks. Lower case letters were designed in the 1920s, and the range of sizes and weights – bold, light and condensed – gradually increased. In order to squeeze all the information into limited space, London bus destination blinds used the special 'condensed' form of Johnston, where the space allocated for each letter is much narrower than with the standard Johnston typeface.

In 1979 the typeface was redesigned by Banks and Miles with the intention of retaining its distinctive character while improving its potential for application. 'New Johnston' is available in nine versions, including bold and light fonts, and italic and condensed faces. It has been adapted for computer typesetting and desktop publishing.

⬤ **Edward Johnston CBE, 1872-1944**
Holburne Museum and Crafts Study Centre, Bath

Born in Uruguay, Johnston studied medicine at Edinburgh University. A year later he abandoned his medical career, owing to ill health. He devoted the rest of his life to the study and teaching of calligraphy and lettering. The typeface he designed for the Underground Group was influential, and inspired subsequent sans-serif designs such as Gill Sans.

⬤ **'Johnston Sans' proof sheet**
1993

This sheet was hand printed from surviving original wood letter and metal type.

ABCDEFGHIJKLMN
OPQRSTUVWXYZ
abcdefghijklmn
opqrstuvwxyz
1234567890
&£,.;:'""?!--*//()

ABCDEFGHIJKLMN
OPQRSTUVWXYZ
1234567890
&£,.;:'""?!--*()

⬤ **Johnston wood letter printing blocks**

These were recovered from the Bournehall Press in 1985.

🎧 **Flowers – Spring by Freda Lingstrom**
1924

This poster is a fine example of the early Johnston typeface as it was designed to be used.

🎧 **Trackside destination sign in Johnston typeface, Holborn station**
1937

Johnston typeface was so widely used and became so familiar to Londoners that it earned the sobriquet 'London's handwriting'.

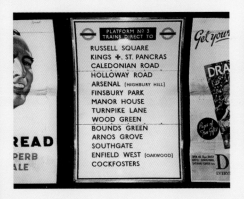

🎧 **Platform roundel, West Brompton station**
1920s

The 'crossed W' in this roundel sign is a relic of the earliest form of the Johnston typeface. The 'W' was soon redesigned to the simpler 'double V' form.

🎧 **Johnston's design guideline for the 'bullseye'**
1925

In 1916, Frank Pick asked Johnston to re-design the 'bullseye', or roundel. This 1925 drawing shows his fully lined-out 'standard' roundel, with the exact proportions and colours to be used, together with the 'pecked' UNDERGROUND lettering.

ABCDEFGHIJKLMN
OPQRSTUVWXYZ
abcdefghijklmnopqrstuvwxyz
1234567890&£,.;:'""?!--*()

🎧 **'New Johnston' designed by Banks and Miles**
1979

🎧 **Bus destination blinds, using the condensed form of Johnston**
1954

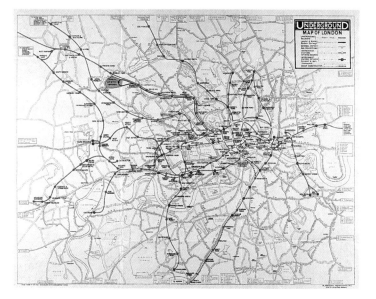

⌒ Combined bus and Tube map
1924

In the 1920s and '30s more emphasis was placed on road–rail connections than perhaps is the case today. This 1924 map shows the Underground network together with details of the numbers of connecting bus routes. Note the tube lines still under construction and the British Empire Exhibition site at Wembley.

⌒ Cover of *London Guide No. 3* by V. L. Danvers
1924

Several tourist guides were published in this series and usually included a bus map pointing out the sights to see by bus.

⌒ Bus queue in York Road, outside Waterloo station
10 August 1939

Just days before the outbreak of the Second World War, passengers patiently wait for a bus north, over the River Thames. Queuing for a bus was, in fact, a recent innovation at the time of this photograph.

⌒ Drying concrete bus stop posts at LT's Parsons Green workshop
28 September 1933

It was only in the late 1930s that fixed bus stops started to become the norm, and their introduction meant busy days for the workmen in London Transport's own concrete casting workshops. London Transport has a history of designing and manufacturing its own street furniture.

Bus and tram stop plates
c. 1928–34

During the late1920s the Underground Group started to experiment with the design of signs, in an effort to introduce a commonality of design. This series of plates shows the variation of the roundel from the 'Tramways' plate (left) of around 1928, through to the early 'London Transport' version (far right) of 1934. All are of vitreous enamel and bronze framed. The curved top, following the upper ring of the roundel, proved to be expensive to manufacture.

George James Shave, 1871–1933

George Shave was Chief Engineer of the London General Omnibus Company from 1918 and took on the additional role of Operating Manager between 1923 and 1931. He had great faith in the motor bus and was

entirely responsible for setting up the overhaul works at Chiswick, where production-line techniques represented a revolution in bus maintenance. He is pictured here in front of NS1. He was much liked by his staff.

Architectural elevation of bus passenger shelter produced by Adams, Holden & Pearson
c. 1935

During the 1930s London Transport, working with Charles Holden's architectural partnership, produced some remarkably futuristic street furniture, including bus shelters.

Strand
2 August 1923

Looking west down the Strand in 1923 one can observe three different types of bus: K-types, an S-type and, going away from the camera, a lone example of the then-new NS type heading for Barnes. However, no covered tops are yet allowed, and traffic is still two-way around Aldwych.

Regent Street
1930

Traffic is heavy in this 1930 view looking down Regent Street from Oxford Circus. Some buses of the NS-type now have the luxury of covered tops. Taxicabs are much in evidence, and one motor coach heads south towards Piccadilly Circus.

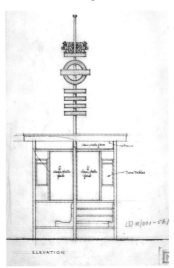

ELEVATION

increasing the seating capacity by twelve.

◑ LGOC S-type bus
1920

This side view of the S-type bus shows little change from the earliest motor bus designs, apart from the position of the driver alongside the engine. The extra length of the S, compared with the K-type, was achieved by inserting the additional short bay, which can be seen here as a narrow, central saloon window.

◑ Aldwych
1935

By 1935 the one-way traffic scheme has been put in place at Aldwych. Traffic is light enough, however, for the two policemen on point duty to safely stand and engage in conversation. No bus in this photograph is older than five years. There are three LTs, one with an open staircase, surrounding a recently delivered STL-type on the 77A route.

◐ Interior of a K-type bus

◑ LGOC K-type bus
1919

Before the First World War all drivers sat behind the engine ('normal control'), but in 1919 the LGOC unveiled the K-type, the first design to place the driver alongside the engine ('forward control'). This enabled the downstairs saloon to be increased in length. The body was also widened so that the lower-deck seats could be arranged in transverse pairs,

◑ Model of a Leyland LB-type bus
1923

A typical 'pirate' bus of the early 1920s, owned by one of the small independent operators that competed with the LGOC.

Cover of brochure celebrating Chiswick Works by Edward McKnight Kauffer
1932

In August 1921 the LGOC opened its new works at Chiswick to centralise the overhaul and repair of its buses and also to provide facilities for the construction of new vehicles.

Chiswick Works canteen
1922

The canteen at Chiswick Works was capable of seating over 1000 people, and staff could purchase meals at reasonable prices.

Body shop, Chiswick Works
1947

Long lines of bus bodies removed from their chassis and mounted on special trolleys receive attention. Most of the bus bodies in this picture belong to STL-type buses.

TILES DESIGNED BY HAROLD STABLER

Harold Stabler (1872–1945) was an associate of Carter, Stabler and Adams Pottery of Poole. He worked on many projects for the Underground Group, including the design of the first official seal of the LPTB; many of the tiles used in Underground stations from the 1920s onwards; a uniform cap badge for its staff; decorative station tiles; and a rabbit mascot to adorn the radiators of the Country Buses.

Around 1938 Stabler was commissioned to design a series of relief tiles for some of the plain tiled walls of the Underground's stations. Stabler designed 18 different patterns representing, among others, symbols of London Transport such as the roundel, heraldic devices of the Home Counties served by London Transport, and London icons such as St Paul's Cathedral.

55 Broadway, London Transport's headquarters

Buckinghamshire's heraldic device

London Transport roundel

St Paul's Cathedral

⬤ Charles Henry Holden FRIBA, 1875–1960

As consulting architect to the Underground Group and later London Transport, Charles Holden was to design some of the most outstanding and memorable inter-war buildings in Europe. Working closely with Frank Pick, whom he met in 1915, Holden worked on many commissions, including 55 Broadway, the Underground Group's headquarters; the Morden extension of the Northern line; the stations of the Piccadilly line extension; and the rebuilding of stations such as Leicester Square and Piccadilly Circus. He also designed street furniture for London Transport.

◑ Bond Street station, redesigned by Holden
1924

Holden chose to use Portland stone for the redeisnged frontage of Bond Street station.

Many of the features which he was to use in later projects are in evidence here. The projecting canopy bearing the station name in Johnston lettering, the projecting Underground signs and the positioning of Underground posters at the entrance to the station were all to become Holden trademarks.

◑ Tooting Bec station
1926

Holden's Northern line stations for the Morden extensions were his first wholly new designs for the Underground. Tooting Bec station is a typical example. The three-panel screen design was easily adapted to suit a variety of awkward locations. The Portland stone façade, large window incorporating a stained glass roundel and wide entrance canopy were common features of all the stations on the extension. Tooting Bec is seen here after renovation in the late 1990s.

🎧 **Globe light at Sudbury Town designed by Charles Holden**

🎧 **Passimeter at Chiswick Park station**
August 1933

Passimeters – free-standing ticket kiosks situated in booking halls – were first introduced in the early 1920s. This one at Chiswick Park was designed by Adams, Holden and Pearson and became standard at all the new stations built in the 1930s. The early examples had real travertine marble sides.

🎧 **Exterior of Sudbury Town station**

Sudbury Town station was the prototype for Holden's 1930s station architecture for the Piccadilly line. The brick-box design utilised load-bearing mass brick walls to support a flat reinforced concrete roof; the large steel-framed windows provided natural light for the booking hall and advertised the station's presence at night. The exposed brickwork echoed the surrounding suburban houses and reflected the functional nature of the building. The station opened on 19 July 1931, in readiness for the transfer of services from the District to Piccadilly line in 1932.

Holden was not only concerned with Tube railway buildings. Increasingly the details of stations, signage and street furniture also fell into his remit.

🎧 **To Sudbury Town or South Harrow by Harold Williamson**
1922

Before stringent legislation in the 1960s forced industry and householders to drastically reduce smoke emission, London was a dirty city, famed for its fogs and smogs. The countryside and fresh air were constant advertising themes.

🎧 **Sudbury Hill station**
c. 1931

This drawing is taken from the architect's submission.

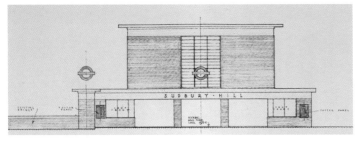

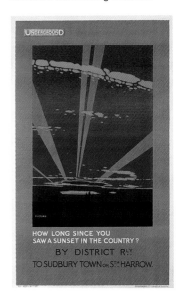

🎧 **Arnos Grove station exterior**

Of all the stations on the northern extension of the Piccadilly line from Finsbury Park to Cockfosters, Arnos Grove continues to be one of Holden's most admired. It features a large brick drum ticket hall with high windows to let in natural light.

🔌 **Arnos Grove station interior**

The central pillar of the ticket hall reaches up into the high ceiling, producing a spacious, light and airy atmosphere. The passimeter had fallen out of use and into a state of disrepair in 1988 but was restored to its former glory in 1990 to become a small museum and art gallery.

🎧 **Restored escalators at Turnpike Lane station, which opened in 1932**

Uplighters on the balustrades of escalators and on the station concourses were a feature of Holden designed stations.

🔌 **Wood Green station by night**
March 1933

Holden designed stations to be prominent not only by day, but also by night. With large-scale use of floodlighting, the curved façade of the station truly stands out. The large windows of the ticket halls were also designed to let in light during the day and to project light from inside the station at night. Some of the stations had search lights mounted on the roof to attract additional attention – and passengers.

style Holden developed for the Morden extension. A seven-sided Portland stone ticket hall features large clerestory windows displaying stained glass roundels. Exterior surfaces were clad in durable Aberdeen grey granite to door height and Portland stone above.

◖ Southgate station
1933

Southgate is considered to be Charles Holden's finest piece of work on the Piccadilly line extension. It is also one of his most unusual as it was designed as an integral development, incorporating a bus station and shopping centre. The curves of the bus station echo the circular construction of the station which is topped by an illuminated filial.

◖ Exterior of Hounslow West station
2000

Hounslow West station on the District line was rebuilt by Holden and Heaps in 1931. Piccadilly line services commenced in 1933. The station represents the final stage of the

◗ Hounslow West station ticket hall

Hounslow West's ticket hall has retained its original wooden passimeter. The tiled frieze was commissioned from the noted theatre designer, Basil Ionides.

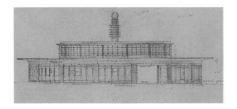

◖ Holden's elevation of Southgate station
c. 1931

◗ Escalators at Southgate station
1990s

When the escalators were replaced in the late 1980s, Holden's balustrade uplighters were retained and the metal panels given a bronzed finish in keeping with the rest of the station.

⟳ Leicester Square station escalators after reconstruction of the station
early 1930s

The station was reconstructed in the early 1930s. At the time the Piccadilly line escalators were the longest on the system. The original bronze pedestal uplighters, designed by Holden, no longer exist.

⟳ Tiling at Leicester Square station
1935

These brightly coloured tiled bands, consisting of the repeated initials of London Transport, were placed at the entrances to Leicester Square station.

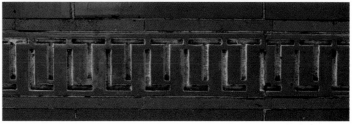

⟲ Train shed, Uxbridge station

The long train shed at Uxbridge was based on Holden's design for Cockfosters and designed to

accommodate the Metropolitan line trains by raising the height of the roof to give it almost nave-like qualities.

⟲ Uxbridge station
opened December 1938

Uxbridge station was completely re-sited, on a new alignment, that gave it a prominent position on the main street. The main entrance is crowned by winged rail wheels, symbolising the power and speed of the Underground.

⟲ *Uxbridge* by Charles Paine
Poster
1921

PICCADILLY CIRCUS STATION

Piccadilly Circus first opened in 1906, but by the early 1920s it was no longer coping with the millions of people using it each year. It was not possible to enlarge the buildings at street level, so it was decided to excavate a new ticket hall underneath the road. Work began in 1925, and the statue of Eros was moved to the Embankment until the work was completed. The architect Charles Holden produced a magnificent circular tiled hall using bronze fittings and travertine marble cladding to create a warm and welcoming environment. Holden referred to this circular walkway as an 'ambulatory'. In the centre were the new escalators, which replaced the original lifts, and banks of automatic ticket machines. The curve of the booking hall incorporated an arcade of display windows for shops such as Swan and Edgar, whilst specially designed lamps hung from ceiling columns. Five subways connected the booking hall with the surface.

When it was opened on 10 December 1928 by the Mayor of Westminster it became an immediate success and received international recognition. The Moscow Metro incorporated many of the features at Piccadilly Circus, including escalators with uplighters, when it opened in 1935. The booking hall was given a Grade II listing in 1983.

Night life at Piccadilly Circus
1926

This front cover of *T.O.T.*, the company's staff magazine, shows contemporary night life at Piccadilly Circus.

Opening of the new Piccadilly Circus Underground station
10 December 1928

The Mayor of Westminster, Major Vivian B. Rogers, sets the escalators in motion to declare the newly reconstructed station open. Lord Ashfield, Chairman of the Underground Group, stands on his right.

Art Deco lamp presented to the Mayor at the opening ceremony
1928

This lamp, called the 'Verriers d'Art Light' is now part of London's Transport Museum Collection.

A New Heart for London by **Charles W. Baker**
Poster
1928

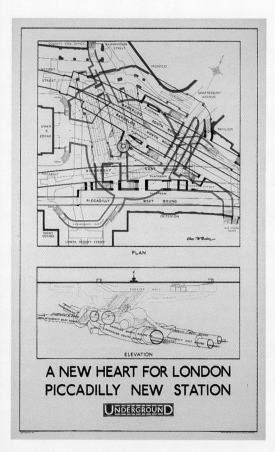

Piccadilly Circus station booking hall
1928

Lower escalator landing at Piccadilly Circus station
1929

Drawing of the restored entrance to Piccadilly Circus station
1990s

The ironwork overhead sign is one of only a few that retain their original lanterns.

LONDON TRANSPORT-

◖◗ **Front and reverse of LPTB gold medallion pass no. 1**
1933

Staff in railway companies normally carried a free travel pass in the form of a medallion. The majority were minted from bronze. Managers were normally issued silver medallions and those for the most senior staff were struck in gold. This medallion was issued to Lord Ashfield as Chairman of the London Passenger Transport Board.

◖ *London Transport* by **Man Ray**
1938

This is one of a matching pair of memorable posters that Man Ray produced for London Transport. Man Ray, born and trained in the USA, moved to Paris in 1921 and spent much of his working life there at the forefront of Dada and Surrealism, the new artistic movements of the time.

⟳ Lord Ashfield, 1874–1948

Albert Henry Stanley was born in Derby, but grew up in America. Working on the Detroit Street Railway, he rose from odd-job man to General Superintendent by the age of 28. In 1907 he returned to London to become Manager of the Underground Group. As the first Chairman of London Transport, he combined firm commercial management with public accountability and an awareness of the social benefits of an integrated public transport system.

◖ **Frank Pick, 1878–1941**

Frank Pick came to the Underground in 1906, and by 1928 had risen to the position of Managing Director. In 1933 he was appointed Vice Chairman and Chief Executive of London Transport. Reputedly a shy and humourless man, he was a skilled administrator and incisive in action. A founder of the Design Industries Association, he brought London Transport an international reputation for its graphic art, public architecture and design.

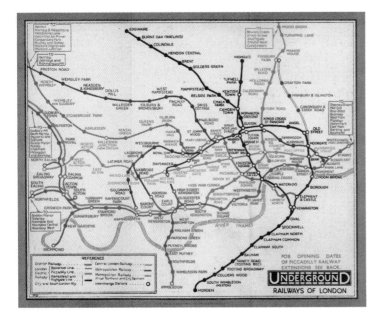

than the conventional geographical format. However, the concept was eagerly accepted by the travelling public. Beck's Underground map is still used today, and much emulated by transport companies around the world.

◑ *London Transport at London's Service* by **Abram Games**
Poster
1947

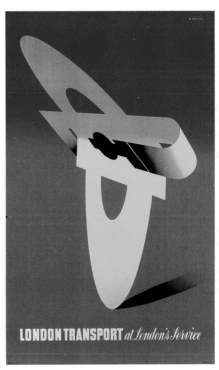

◔ F. H. Stingemore's last card folder map
1932

This was the last map to be designed for the Underground by Stingemore. By 1932 the expansion of the network made it increasingly difficult to represent the complexity of the lines in the traditional geographic map. However, this problem was to be resolved in 1933.

◑ Beck's map of the Underground
1933

After much development work, Henry (Harry) C. Beck, a junior draughtsman, devised a map of the Underground, which he said was inspired by electrical diagrams. London Transport was reluctant to adopt the idea, which was based on a diagrammatic principal rather

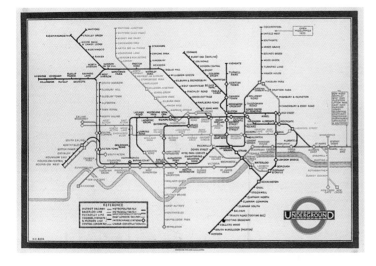

T.O.T. Philharmonic Society Programme
1921

The Underground Group was a paternalistic employer, and a number of social activities were organised and promoted by the company for the benefit of its employees. These were usually graced by the Chairman Lord Ashfield, who was also the president of T.O.T.

T.O.T. staff sports day
1931

Events ranged from serious athletics and team sports to light-hearted fun, such as this busmen's sack race.

◗ **LPTB Certificate of Service**
1936

London Transport was one of the capital's largest employers in the 1930s. All long-service staff were presented with special certificates when they retired.

◖ ***T.O.T. staff magazine* cover**
March 1927

T.O.T. (Train - Omnibus - Tram) was the Underground Group's staff magazine from 1913 until 1934, when it became known as *Pennyfare*. This cover depicts the Group's vehicles alongside Mercury, fleet-footed messenger of the Roman gods.

55 BROADWAY

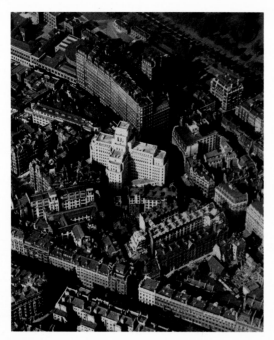

Aerial view of 55 Broadway
c. 1930

Electric Railway House, the headquarters of the Underground Group, had been built above St James's Park station. By the 1920s these premises had become too cramped, and Charles Holden was commissioned to design a new building on the same site above the station. The result was a design masterpiece, which rose to all the challenges of constructing a multi-storey building on a triangular site, whilst at the same time incorporating a busy Underground station into the plan. The building, faced in Portland stone, had nine floors and a tower rising above it, though the London Building Act prevented the ninth floor and tower from being occupied. Adams, Holden and Pearson were awarded the London Architectural medal for their design in 1929.

Holden had always had an interest in decorating the exterior of his buildings with sculptures, and seven sculptors, representing a cross-section of contemporary sculpture, were asked to produce bas-reliefs representing night, day and the four winds. These were to be carved straight on to the building. The sculptors were Jacob Epstein, Eric Gill, Henry Moore, Eric Aumonier, A.H. Gerrard, Samuel Rabinovich and Allan Wynon. Although the results caused some controversy at the time, the Epstein works in particular are now regarded as being amongst the most important British public sculptures of the twentieth century.

The building was opened on 1 December 1929 and named after its postal address, 55 Broadway.

Exterior view of 55 Broadway
1930

Epstein's sculpture of *Day* can just be seen on the left above the ground floor.

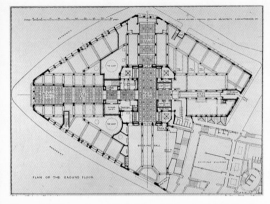

Ground-floor plan of 55 Broadway, by architects Adams, Holden & Pearson
c. 1928

Night view of 55 Broadway
January 1930

East Wind **by Eric Gill**

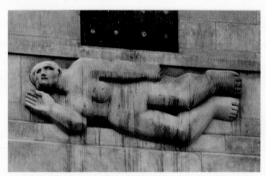

West Wind **by Henry Moore**

Henry Moore at work on *West Wind*

Night **by Jacob Epstein**

🎧 **Stanley Arthur Heaps
FRIBA, 1880–1962**

Stanley Heaps worked for the
Underground Group from 1903
to 1943. Initially assistant to
Leslie Green, he was appointed
architect to the company in
1910. His most notable designs
were the stations on the 1915
Bakerloo extension and the
Edgware extension in 1924.
Thereafter he worked closely
with Charles Holden on many
aspects of both new and
reconstructed stations and was
responsible for major depots
such as Aldenham and Hainault.
Additionally he was responsible
for work on numerous bus and
trolleybus garages.

➲ **Edgware station**
1927

Edgware station was built as
part of the final phase of the
extension of the Hampstead
Railway (later the Northern line)
in 1924. Designed by Stanley
Heaps in the style of an Italian
villa, the station was quite
elaborate with a neo-Georgian
facade, Portland stone Doric
columns and an Italian tiled roof.

🎧 *New Works* **by Fred Taylor**
1923

In this poster the suburban
development is depicted taking
place around a brand new
station on the Edgware
extension.

➲ **Ticket hall, Brent station**
1939

The booking hall of Brent station
has an air of spaciousness
typical of the stations on the
Edgware extension.

⋂ **Restored Underground roundel at Rayners Lane station**

☾ **Park Royal station, a view from the platform**

Architects Welch and Lander were obviously influenced by Holden when they designed Park Royal with its circular ticket hall and square tower in the 1930s.

⋂ **East Finchley station, viewed from platform level**
c. 1990
Photograph: Isolde Barrington

East Finchley was designed by Holden in association with L.H. Bucknell in July 1939. It is best known for its lead-coated archer sculpted by Eric Aumonier.

⟳ **Bounds Green station exterior as restored**
c. 1996

Designed in collaboration with the architectural firm James and Bywaters, Bounds Green can be compared with Holden's Sudbury box style. However, here the structure takes on an octagonal form, with the glazing occupying the corners rather than remaining within the main façade.

∩ **Detail of mosaic tiling at Farringdon station**

∩ **Willesden Green station**

Designed for the Metropolitan in 1925 by C.W. Clark to replace the original brick structure of 1879, the station is faced entirely with cream terracotta tiling. Both entrances are covered by a large cantilevered canopy, and the recently refurbished ticket hall retains many of its original finishes and fittings.

⊃ **Farringdon station entrance**

A detail from the facade of C.W. Clark's 1923 station. The red diamonds are a reference to the Metropolitan's logo of the time.

↻ **Croxley station**
opened 1925

Called Croxley Green until 1949, Croxley station was designed by Clark for the Metropolitan Railway's new branch line to Watford and is representative of the stations on that branch. Apart from the glazed canopy and two cast-iron columns, it looks for all the world like a large suburban house.

CHILTERN COURT

The Metropolitan Railway built a total of nine housing estates in Metro-Land. It also commissioned a block of 180 high class residential flats of varying size to be built above Baker Street station. The site of this imposing building extended along Marylebone Road from Baker Street to Allsop Place, with frontages on all three sides. Among its more famous residents were authors H.G. Wells and Arnold Bennett.

In addition to its luxurious flats, Chiltern Court boasted a restaurant, capable of accommodating 250 guests; a special unit of 30 separate bedrooms for the use of maids; and an elaborate hairdressing salon.

The Metropolitan Railway Estate Agents made great play of the site being within easy reach of the country, the City, Regent's Park, shopping centres and theatres in the West End. To use their phrase, 'It stands at the gateway to Metro-Land – London's nearest countryside.'

The Chiltern Court Restaurant
Poster
1931

Euston Road façade of Chiltern Court and Baker Street station

Main elevation of Chiltern Court
c. 1928

This illustration is from the Metropolitan Railway Estate Agent's handbook to Chiltern Court.

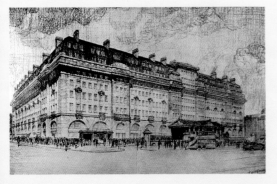

Main entrance to Chiltern Court

🎧 *For Tram Travel North to South*
Poster
1933

🎧 **Kingsway tram subway, Holborn station**
1933

When the Kingsway Subway was rebuilt to take double deck cars, the old 'G' class single deckers were all replaced by the 'E/3' class, seen here. Based on the common 'E/1' type, the main difference between the two was that the 'E/3' had an all-metal body, which was safer for operating through the Subway.

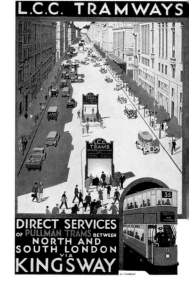

💧 **Opening of rebuilt Kingsway Subway**
1931

➲ **Kingsway tram Subway brochure**
1931

In 1929 the London County Council decided to enlarge the Kingsway Subway so that it could take double deck trams. Construction started in February 1930 and was completed within a year. The Chairman of the Council reopened the subway by driving a specially painted 'E/3' class tram along the new route. Brochures were produced giving a guide to services, together with a history of the Subway and the area.

NS-TYPE BUS

In 1923 an important new type of bus appeared in London. Called the 'NS', Nulli Secundus (second to none), it was the first bus to have a cranked chassis frame, allowing a lower floor and a single entrance step.

The first NS-type was submitted to the police for licensing with a temporary covered top, but this feature was not accepted. Deliveries went ahead, therefore, with open tops. Eventually in 1925 the police allowed an experiment with covered top NS buses, which were placed in service on Route 100 from Elephant and Castle to Loughton. This trial was successful, and so covered tops were fitted on NS buses from 1926 onwards.

Open top NS bus en route to St Albans for a day out of town
1926

Closed top NS bus in Epping Forest
1926

Fully developed NS-type bus

This has not only a covered top but also the pneumatic tyres that replaced the solid tyres of the earlier versions. The driver has also gained the protection of a windscreen.

The last NS-type bus
1937

The very last London Transport passenger service by an NS-type bus took place on 30 November 1937 on Route 166 from Aldwych to Bank via Holborn.

◐ **Record of Service – Underground 1931** by Maurice Beck
1932

This poster is one of the earliest examples of the use of photographic collage by the Underground. It was also unusual for real staff to be featured in this way.

◑ **Signal frame, Ealing Common**
1925

From 1905 signalling on the Underground was automated as far as possible. At junctions, though, signalmen were retained to switch the trains between routes as necessary. This photograph shows the signalman at Ealing Common operating the signal and point levers, which were mechanically interlocked to prevent conflicting moves occurring. The diagram showed the position of the trains and allowed large track layouts to be controlled safely even when the trains could be seen physically.

◐ **Signal frame, Loughton**

Loughton signal box opened in 1948. This 1990s picture (taken shortly before its closure) clearly shows the levers used to operate the signals (red levers) and points (black levers). The points were physically moved by compressed air, but the air-valves were electrically actuated by the point levers.

◑ **Chancery Lane**
1934

This poster was published to explain the modernisation work taking place at Chancery Lane in 1934. Work included a new booking hall and new escalators connecting platforms with stairs leading to four new station entrances on Holborn.

STANDARD STOCK

New trains were introduced in 1923 in response to the need for additional trains on the combined Hampstead & Highgate and City line services. Six experimental cars were built by different manufacturers and a standard design was developed from these. All new Tube stock built between 1923 and 1934 conformed to this basic pattern, known as Standard Stock. The total fleet eventually amounted to 1460 cars. Standard Stock incorporated many of the characteristics of modern Tube trains, including air-powered doors which replaced manual end gates, and comfortable seats covered in woollen moquette fabric. By 1930 all the original gate stock trains had been modernised or replaced with Standard stock which reduced stopping times. They were also cheaper to run because they only required one guard to do the work of four gatemen.

↻ **Keep Pace with Time by Frederick Charles Herrick**
1927

Posters featuring Tube trains were not common but here a Standard Stock train is used to emphasise the punctual and efficient service made possible with the new sliding air-powered doors.

↻ **Quickly Away, Thanks to Pneumatic Doors by Laszlo Moholy-Nagy**
Poster
1937

Air-operated carriage doors were remotely controlled by one or two guards and considerably speeded up loading and unloading at stations, as well as reducing staff costs.

🎧 **Standard Stock Piccadilly train at Hammersmith station**
1925

↻ **Value for Money**
Poster detail
1926

This poster extols the modern Tube features of the time, including a spacious and light booking hall, stylish wooden booking offices (passimeters) and the efficient Standard Stock train.

∩ **Safety Underground by Alan Rogers**
1930

∩ **O stock train at Ealing Common depot**
1937

This simple but effective Art Deco poster, using the Underground roundel as a shield, promotes safe travel when travelling Underground.

Three classes of new surface stock were ordered from Gloucester and Birmingham car builders as part of the 1935/40 New Works Programme. These were the O stock (replacement cars for Hammersmith and City), P stock (replacement for Metropolitan) and Q stock (replacement for District). A new design of car was produced, with a smooth, all-steel exterior, distinctive flared sides and pneumatically operated doors. O and P stock cars employed a new form of electrical traction control, the Metadyne sytem.

rubber hand grabs for standing passengers were common features of the new surface stock.

⊃ **P stock car interior**

Woollen moquette seating, single sheet glass draught screens and flexible moulded

1938 TUBE STOCK

A massive expansion of the Underground in the late 1930s produced a need for over a thousand new Tube stock carriages. To test a whole host of new ideas it was decided to order four prototype cars embodying various elements of the proposed new features. They entered service in 1937. Following prevailing fashion, some of these striking vehicles had streamlined ends. Streamlining was not found beneficial at the low speeds at which Tube trains ran, and the cars were later rebuilt without them.

Following experience with the experimental cars, a new design was adopted, known as 1938 Tube stock. It was to become the standard London Tube train for the next 50 years and came to be regarded as a classic. Over 1100 cars of the new design were ordered, and the first 1938 stock train entered service on the Northern line in June 1938. All cars were of air-smoothed design and, for the first time on Tube stock, had all equipment mounted under the floor, releasing valuable

space for additional passengers. They contained a wealth of new features, including automatic couplers at the end of each three- or four-car unit, making it easier to run shorter trains outside rush hours. The interiors featured varnished wood which, combined with red and green finishes, gave a warm appearance. The fittings were functional, and the lampshades were inspired by the Art Deco style.

The last 1938 Tube stock ran until 1988, its Golden Jubilee year, and some are still in use on the Isle of Wight.

Detail of cab front design of the 1938 stock

The classic 1938 Tube stock at Acton Town

Experimental streamlined train 1936

1938 TUBE STOCK

1938 stock car interior

Interior of a restored car of 1938 stock at London's Transport Museum. The control panels used by the guard are at the end of the car.

1938 stock at Piccadilly Circus station

The 1938 stock operated mainly on the Northern and Bakerloo lines.

Elegant 'shovel shade' light fixtures and moulded rubber hand-grips

Restored 1938 stock unit

The last 1938 stock train operated on the Northern line in 1988. One four-car unit of that train has been preserved and is seen here, after restoration, at London's Transport Museum's Depot.

William Sebastian Graff-Baker, 1889–1952

W. S. Graff-Baker came to the Underground as a junior electrical fitter in 1910, working his way up to Chief Mechanical Engineer in 1935. He was responsible for innumerable innovations and particularly the development of the 1938 Tube stock.

Unusual view of a 1938 stock motor car

Underside view of a 1938 stock driving motor car showing traction and auxiliary equipment beneath. At the front the wedglock automatic coupler enabled the electrical and pneumatic connections to be made automatically when joining up with another car.

1938 Tube stock during overhaul at Acton Works

Until quite recently all cars periodically went to Acton Works for a complete overhaul and repaint. Modern trains need considerably less heavy maintenance, and most of the work is now undertaken at depots, with major refurbishment contracted out.

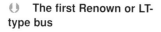

N.S.E.W. Safety First by Charles Paine
1926

This unusually shaped poster, one of two produced by Charles Paine, was probably posted in vehicle interiors. Until the formation of London Transport, artists were often employed directly by poster printers in their studios, and technically, Baynard Press were commissioned to produce this artwork.

The first Renown or LT-type bus

The Associated Equipment Co. built the chassis of the Renown, a three-axle petrol-engined vehicle with an LGOC-designed body. The LT-type was the first standard design to be built from scratch with a covered top, although the first 150 had an open staircase, unlike the later models which were enclosed.

Enamel licence badge for PSV driver

This is typical of the type issued between 1931 and 1935.

The single-deck LT-type

The LGOC also chose the AEC Renown chassis for its single-deck fleet renewal in 1931, and 199 were ordered. The police requirement that the passenger doorway should be at the rear was lifted, and these were the first to be built with a front entrance. The extra length resulting from this design enabled the LTs to have 35 seats, five more than previous types.

➲ Inter-station Leyland Cub

In 1936 London Transport purchased eight of these for the new inter-station service. Their distinctive feature was the raised saloon at the rear, under which was a capacious luggage compartment. When they were withdrawn in 1950, they were the last petrol-engined buses operated by London Transport.

◑ Hammersmith
August 1934

London Transport took over responsibility for all of London's public transport in 1933. Its founding principle was to avoid 'wasteful competition' by ensuring that buses, trams and the Underground operated in harmony. Seen here in 1934 are the former Underground Group's Hammersmith station, a 'General' LT-type bus in its final design and a former London County Council 'E/1' tram.

◐ Cover of LGOC booklet by Bip Pares
1932

Before the London Passenger Transport Board Act prohibited operations outside a roughly 30-mile radius of central London, the LGOC was able to advertise destinations like Canterbury and Oxford in its tour programme.

STL-TYPE BUS

The Associated Equipment Company (AEC) was born out of the LGOC's bus building and repair works and was hived off as a separate concern in 1912. It continued to be the main source of London buses. The AEC Regent chassis was the basis of the 'ST' class introduced in 1930, a petrol-engined 25-feet long four-wheeler. The 49-seat standard ST was the first type designed to be fully enclosed, although the driver's cab remained open until 1931 when police restrictions were lifted. It had a large full-width rear platform and a straight staircase. The STL-type, a petrol-engined 60-seat bus, longer than the ST was introduced by the LGOC in 1932. Over the next seven years the body design was improved, diesel engines were fitted in new buses from 1935 and pre-selective gearboxes became standard. In its way it was a design classic, and over 2000 were built.

A special version of the STL with a rounded roof profile was introduced in 1937 for routes running through the two tunnels under the Thames at Blackwall and Rotherhithe. Because of the sloped sides to the upper deck, the staircase turned through 180 degrees. STLs built for use on Country Area routes had a front entrance and staircase and seating for 48 passengers. It was not until 1939 that the standard rear entrance type served the country routes.

ST-type bus

**STL-type bus
1939**

This is one of the last STLs, dating from 1939, and it paved the way for the standard bus of the post-war years, the RT.

AEC letter
1932
Public Record Office

In this letter the AEC seeks police authorisation for the longer length of buses ordered in 1932 by the LGOC.

Special curved roof STL

This type of bus was built to serve the routes using the Rotherhithe and Blackwall tunnels.

LT badges

London Transport placed their own badge in the shape of a triangle at the top of the radiator grilles of AEC vehicles. Central Buses used the blue and red version, while the green was fitted on Country Area buses.

STL built for Country Area routes

🎧 *Signs that Signify Service* by H. A. Rothholz
1946

The formation of London Transport in 1933 brought together the majority of London's public transport under one organisation, with the intention of providing an integrated, high quality service. A new logo was designed, but it was quickly replaced by the familiar 'roundel' symbol, which was adapted to suit all the constituent parts of the organisation, as illustrated in this poster.

🎧 **Gillespie Road football crowd**
1922

Football fans outside Gillespie Road Underground station. The station was rebuilt and enlarged in the 1930s because of overcrowding, and renamed Arsenal.

🎧 **Private hire buses en route to the F.A. Cup Final**
1923

Hiring an LGOC double-deck bus to travel to large sporting events was common in the 1920s. Here fans are on their way to the first Cup Final to be held at the new Wembley Stadium. On this occasion West Ham lost 2-nil to Bolton Wanderers.

🔁 *Private Hire,* **brochure illustrated by Reinganum**
1935

The hire of buses and coaches was another activity vigorously promoted to increase revenue. Brochures like this one, which was illustrated by Reinganum, were regularly produced to encourage group travel.

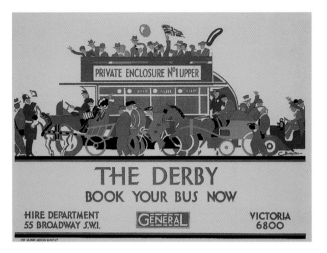

🎧 *The Derby – Book Your Bus Now*
Poster
1930

For decades the biggest single event in the 'Private Hire' calendar was the Derby at Epsom.

🎧 **Derby Day**
1933

Open top double deck buses provide a viewing platform as well as a means of transport.

🎧 **The Zoo, booklet cover by Moira and Robert Gibbings**
1923

London Transport and its predecessors produced copious publicity for Regent's Park Zoo, and later Whipsnade Zoo, to encourage Londoners to see exotic creatures for themselves and of course to use public transport to get there.

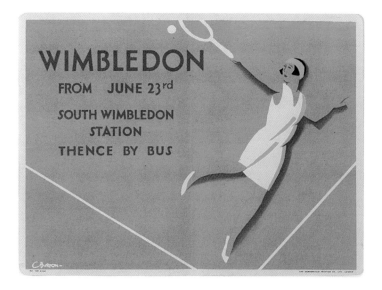

♫ *Wimbledon* by Charles Burton
1930

Wimbledon's tennis fortnight, then as now, was a key sporting event in London's calendar. Numerous stylish posters were produced during the interwar years, not least to explain that there was a bus connection to the tennis courts situated some distance from the Underground.

⤳ *Motor Show* by Dorothy Paton
1929

Today it would not be permissible to use the Underground symbol in the way it is used in this poster to promote the Motor Show.

⤳ *Boat Race*
1921

The annual Boat Race between Oxford and Cambridge Universities was a major sporting occasion for Londoners between the wars. The Underground, bus and tram companies all provided lavish and stylish publicity, such as this anonymous poster, for the event.

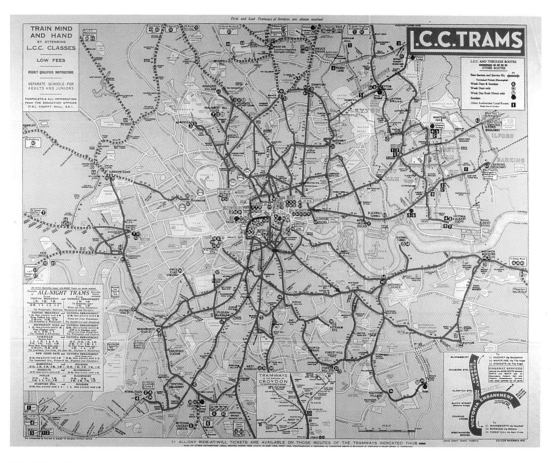

○ **London County Council Tramway Network map**
1932

○ *London's Tramways to the West End,* **leaflet**
1928

Although their trams never ran right into the heart of the West End, the London County Council was keen to promote its services along the Kingsway and the Victoria Embankment for shoppers and theatregoers. On many services cars ran until 12.30 am, and on some routes they ran throughout the night.

○ *Midday Fare,* **leaflet**
1928

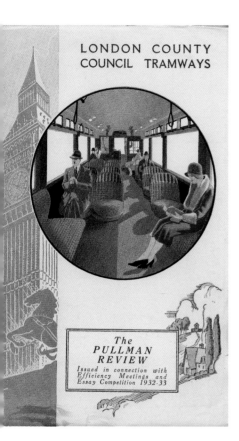

LONDON COUNTY
COUNCIL TRAMWAYS

The
PULLMAN
REVIEW

Issued in connection with
Efficiency Meetings and
Essay Competition 1932-33

The Pullman Review
May 1932

This stylish booklet was issued by London County Council Tramways to describe aspects of the tram network and its operations. The cover shows the plush interior of the new Pullman tramcar.

LCC Tramways map and timetable
May 1932

The cover of this LCC Tramways map illustrates the use of eye-catching design to advertise its services.

The Pullman Year Calendar, leaflet
1930

LCC Tramways detail the scope of their 24-hour services in this attractive leaflet.

BIG BEN &
BOADICEA

MAY, 1932   ISSUED FREE

Tramways Map
and Timetable

L.C.C.TRAMS

L.C.C. TRAMWAYS   T. E. THOMAS.
23, Belvedere Road, S.E.1.   General Manager.

Southwark Bridge by Oliver Burridge
1925

This poster, showing a tramcar on Southwark Bridge, was issued to promote the LCC's new tram services to the City. Trams had previously terminated on the south side of the river.

NIGHT CARS
ALL DAY 1/-
WORK MAN FARES
CHEAP RETURNS
CHEAP MIDDAY FARES

P.M.   A.M.

A PULLMAN SERVICE
ALL ROUND THE CLOCK
ALL THE YEAR ROUND

Transfer Facilities

apply, where practicable, to all tramway
journeys between suburban & Central
London points for these fares—

5D   ORDINARY SINGLE
     Child under 14 2d
2D   CHEAP MIDDAY
     SINGLE
     Child under 14 1d
5D 6D 8D ORDINARY
         RETURN
4D 6D WORKMAN
        RETURN

—whether there are direct services
or not for such journeys. Transfers

Save Money & Time

THE
PULLMAN YEAR

Calendar

for
1930

LONDON COUNTY COUNCIL TRAMWAYS

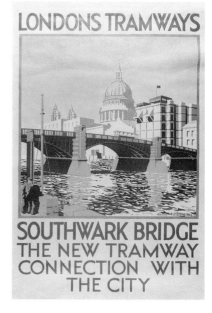

LONDONS TRAMWAYS

SOUTHWARK BRIDGE
THE NEW TRAMWAY
CONNECTION WITH
THE CITY

LCC Tramways map and timetable
November 1931

Until the absorption of LCC Tramway routes by London Transport in 1933, these maps were issued twice a year. Their colourful covers, often based on poster designs, were among some of the most distinctive transport maps published in London.

Class HR/2 tram

When the LPTB was formed in 1933, it inherited 2630 trams from the London area municipalities and the Underground Group companies. This is one of the high-powered cars built in 1930-31 with special braking equipment. They were used on hilly routes such as Highgate Hill and Dog Kennel Hill, near Dulwich.

Trams on Westminster Bridge in their heyday
1930s

This classic view of Westminster Bridge in the early 1930s shows a procession of trams interspersed with buses and coaches. The trams are a 1908 class E/1 and a 1931 class E/3, both much taller than the LT-type bus following. The tram tracks ran close to the footpath on this side of the bridge, running as they did from the reserved track along the Victoria Embankment.

🌀 *The Thames at Hammersmith and Putney,* **leaflet**
1920s

Although the LCC's steamboat service (with joint ticketing on its trams) had not run since 1907, the River Thames remained a popular image, often appearing on the front of LCC Tramways' publicity material. This publicity leaflet also promoted leisure trips as far afield as Epping Forest, Hampstead and Eltham.

🌀 **Tramway network map published by the Underground Group**
1932

🌀 *Record of Service – Tramways* by Maurice Beck, **poster**
1931

🌀 *Barnet by Tram* by **Charles Paine**
1922

Barnet was famous for its horse fair, and was used in this poster to promote travel to the furthest northern point reached by Metropolitan Electric Tramways.

◐ **Charlton Works Paint Shop**

The Central Repair Depot for trams was situated off Woolwich Road in Charlton and was opened in March 1909. The paint shop, with permanent scaffolding, enabled the painters to carry out their work. Most of the work was done by hand and very labour intensive.

◑ **The Plough Shop at Charlton Works**

In the Plough Shop renovation work was carried out on the ploughs that were fitted under the tramcars to pick up the current from the conduit system. Being dragged along by the tram, they suffered heavy wear in everyday use.

◐ *London's Tramways – Travel Quickly – Read in Comfort,* leaflet
1928

The cover of this LCC Tramways leaflet effectively employs Pegasus, the winged horse of Greek mythology, to extol the speed of its services.

National Tramway Museum at Crich in Derbyshire. This original model shows its pleasing but functional lines.

☺ A MET Feltham tram at Gray's Inn Road terminus, Holborn

The last new tramcars to be built in numbers for the London area in the 1930s were the 'Felthams', so-called because they were built in Feltham, Middlesex, by the Union Construction & Finance Co. Ltd for the LUT and MET companies.

☺ 'Poppy' passing the gates of its birthplace

'Poppy' was the only tramcar ever built by the LGOC at Chiswick Works. Originally built for the MET in 1926, it passed to the LUT after modifications in the following year, and, as shown here, worked on the Hounslow to Shepherd's Bush route. The similarity to the LGOC NS-type bus behind it is evident in this photograph.

☺ Picking up the current at Mile End

When the LCC electrified its trams it was forced to use the expensive 'conduit' system of current collection. In later years on new routes the overhead wire method, already used by other operators in London, was chosen instead. At Mile End the 'plough' is being inserted under the tram to enable it to pick up current from the conduit for the rest of its journey into Aldgate. On returning, the reverse operation took place.

☺ Bluebird Tram No. 1

In 1932 the LCC built 'Bluebird', which was intended to be the prototype for a new fleet. However, London Transport, formed in 1933, stopped further tramway development. Bluebird worked in London until 1951 when it was sold to Leeds Corporation. Today it is in the

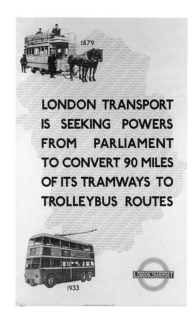

🔊 Trams to trolleybuses

The first tram to trolleybus conversions by London Transport dealt with the run-down municipal systems in Bexley, Erith and Dartford and the company services between Sutton, Croydon and Crystal Palace. The first standard 70-seaters appeared in west London. These were AEC vehicles of the 'C' classes, some of which had distinctive deep metal mudguards over the rear wheels.

Tram to trolleybus leaflet
1936

Conversion from tram to trolleybus
1939

Considerable work had to be carried out to effect the transition from tram to trolleybus, not least the erection of overhead wiring. Even in the areas where trams used this system of current collection, new wires had to be erected since two – positive and negative – were required for the trolleybuses. Much work, particularly at busy junctions, was done during the night, as here at the Lea Bridge Road intersection with Markhouse Road. The specialist tower wagons were constructed using old bus chassis.

Drawings of the first trolleybuses

These sketches are of the first trolleybuses introduced into the London area by the London United Tramways in south-west London. Built by the Union Construction & Finance Co. at Feltham, they bore some resemblance to the Feltham tramcars. They were always known as 'Diddlers', though the origin of this name is unknown.

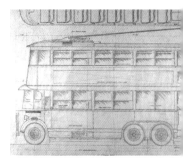

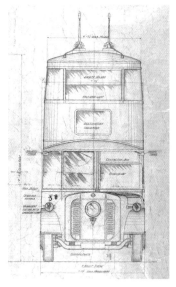

Trolleybus Route 660
1936

On and from April 5
Tram route 89
will be withdrawn

TROLLEYBUS ROUTE 660
will operate
between
HAMMERSMITH and
ACTON (Market Place)
Times of first and last trolleybuses

London United trolleybus at Twickenham
1931

Trolleybus No. 2 stands at the terminus in King Street, Twickenham in May 1931. This must have been a trial run, since at this date it was not possible for the trolleybuses to reach Surbiton, as shown on the destination blind.

Trolleybus passing Smithfield Market
1938

The majority of London trolleybuses were built to a standard design and looked very similar. To the discerning eye, however, there were differences associated with various manufacturers, such as AEC and Leyland Trolleybus 976, a class 'J2' AEC vehicle turns from Farringdon Street into Charterhouse Street at the Holborn loop terminus in 1938. In the background is the bustling activity of Smithfield market.

Smithfield Club Show by Compton Bennet
1928

This humorous poster advertises a show at the old Agricultural Hall at Angel, Islington.

Bexleyheath trolleybus depot
1936

Although much of the architectural focus of the 1930s was on the Underground, the work of the road services division, particularly with regard to new county area bus garages, should not be forgotten. When trolleybuses began to replace

trams, many existing facilities had to be reconstructed to house the new contender. Oddly, only one purpose-built trolleybus depot was ever commissioned. Here at Bexleyheath the architects produced a depot of sleek, clean lines that echo the modernity of the vehicles it housed.

To Fields everywhere quickly by GENERAL

◑ **To Fields Everywhere Quickly By General by Walter Spradbery**
1929

With over 80 posters and panels to his credit, Walter Spradbery was a prolific artist for the Underground Group, and later London Transport. This panel is representative of his love of rural subjects presented in a fresh and simple style.

CHILTERN STROLLS · & RAMBLES

◑ **Chiltern Strolls & Rambles, booklet cover**
1934

Londoners are fortunate to be surrounded by some beautiful countryside, and by 1934, London Transport was able to provide better access than ever to the country's simple pleasures by Underground, Green Line Coach or Country Bus .

◑ **The Q-type bus**

The LPTB chose the Q-type as its first standard bus for Country Bus services. At first Country Buses standardised on centre entrances, which allowed sliding platform doors to be fitted.

◑ **Leyland Cub in Richmond Park**

London Transport's operating area included light traffic routes operated by small capacity buses without a conductor. London Transport's first attempt at vehicle standardization saw the purchase of Leyland Cub buses in 1935 for driver-only operation. This Cub hurries through the open spaces of Richmond Park on the route which ran from Richmond Park Golf Club to Barnes.

◑ **Wilfred the Bunny**

This drawing by Harold Stabler most closely resembles the aluminium rabbits he designed to adorn the radiators of the buses on routes into the country. Early in 1923 they were fitted at Chiswick Works. Originally it was proposed they be a mere 4" high, but it was finally decided that 8" would have more impact.

Holiday Outings August Bank Holiday leaflet
1922

In the early 1920s mascots on motor vehicles were very much in vogue. This leaflet advertising Bank Holiday outings to the country, published in 1922 by the Underground Group, may have been a foretaste of the LGOC's intention to use rabbit mascots on its country services

Rabbit mascot by Harold Stabler

The Carter, Stabler and Adams Pottery of Poole took an order for pottery versions of the rabbit mascot to be made, and many of these were sent to directors and other notables, such as Lady Ashfield. Coan, the company who produced the aluminium versions, cast just two in bronze. This one was presented to George Shave, the LGOC's Operating Manager and Chief Engineer.

TF-type Green Line coach

The last new coaches added to the Green Line fleet immediately prior to the outbreak of the Second World War were the TF-type. These Leyland vehicles were revolutionary in having the first flat horizontally mounted engines, a commonplace feature today. Most were fitted as ambulances during the war but returned to Green Line service afterwards.

Green Line radiator badge

The bus operating companies always imposed their own identity on the vehicles they owned, suppressing the name of the manufacturer. This special Green Line version of the triangle occupied the place on the radiator shell where the AEC blue triangle would otherwise have been carried.

The 10T10-type Green Line coach
1938

A classic Green Line coach design, which reached new heights of passenger comfort, while continuing the move towards cleaner uncluttered external lines. Developed by AEC in association with Leyland Motors Ltd, whose basic design was adopted for the first RTs, they had quieter, more powerful engines.

The Open Gate to the Country. School & Pleasure Parties leaflet
1925

This leaflet was designed to capture the group travel market. Escaping to the fresh air of the country from the grime and pollution of London was seen as a social necessity, as well as generating revenue for the transport companies.

School Picnics & Pleasure Parties, leaflet
1930

The same theme is still relevant five years later. This attractive leaflet advertises the cheap travel arrangements available for school parties and groups travelling to sports events.

Whose Land?, booklet by Jessie M. King
1923

This illustration for a children's booklet was a relatively late rendition of whimsical Art Nouveau, owing much to the artist's background in the Glasgow school. King pictures the country as calm and magical, leaving the noisy town far behind.

⮑ **Map for leaflet** *School Picnics & Pleasure Parties*
1930

The brightly illustrated map shows the extent of possible trips, from Southend in the east, to Uxbridge in the west.

◑ *Outings,* **booklet illustrated by Shep (Capt. Charles Shepherd)**
1929

The London General Omnibus Company was keen to promote excursions by coach which were both popular and profitable. In the days before the mass use of the motor car, this represented an affordable means of escape for many Londoners.

⮑ **Children's outing to South Harrow**
1921

The Underground organised special recreational trips to suburban beauty spots for inner city children throughout the 1920s.

◑ *Whitsun Country Motor-Buses*, **poster**
1921

Bank Holidays provided transport operators with unrivalled opportunities to earn revenue by encouraging use of their services to far flung parts of their empire through imaginative publicity.

THE TIMES SHOWN ARE FOR SUNDAY AND WHIT-MONDAY.

A World at War

To Shelter and
to Serve
1939–1945

Back Room Boys: Car Maintenance
1942

Poster from the series *They Also Serve* by Fred
Taylor, 1942.

A World at War
To Shelter and to Serve, 1939–1945

We travelled fantastically through the bowels of the earth with all the others. They were
thronging, laughing, lusting, looking sad. We saw strange old women sleeping in the
bunks that lined the wall. 'They have to sleep in their bunks', Helen said, 'to keep their
claim on them if the raids begin again.' One bunk was draped in sacking, but I could just
see sticking out a delicate child's leg.

From *Denton Welch's Journals* ,1942, edited by Jocelyn Brooke

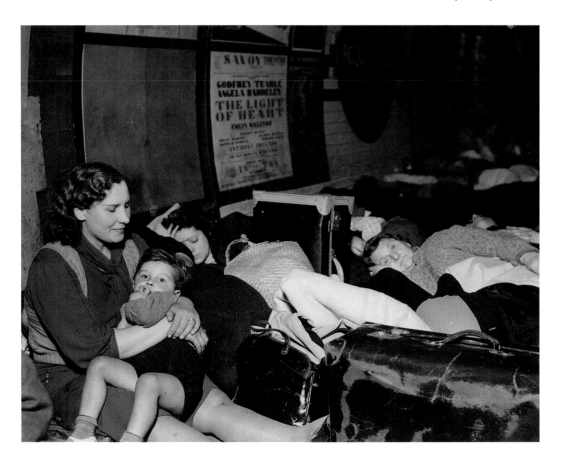

When a second war with Germany seemed
increasingly likely in the late 1930s, there
was a general fear of more immediate and
devastating bombing raids. London Transport
set up an Air Raid Precautions Committee
(ARP) in 1937, and by September 1938,
when the Munich crisis arose, detailed

**Shelterers at Piccadilly Circus Underground
station**
1940

Evacuation of children from the East End of London
September 1939

defence plans had been drawn up, which would allow the system to remain operational under aerial attack, with the safety of passengers and staff secured as far as possible. Floodgates were installed in Tube tunnels, and emergency control centres were prepared. A year later ARP arrangements came into effect on 1 September 1939, two days before the official declaration of war.

The mass evacuation of London's children, hospital patients and expectant mothers took place in the first few days of September 1939. In four days more than

550,000 evacuees were conveyed out of the danger zone by London Transport vehicles, either to mainline termini for transfer to trains or direct to the country. Some buses travelled as far afield as Northampton and Weston-super-Mare. Hospital patients were removed by Green Line coaches, which had been withdrawn on 31 August and converted within hours into ambulances.

Blackout restrictions were applied immediately, and bus services were restricted or withdrawn altogether to save fuel and limit blackout working. Within four months more than 800 central buses were lying idle. Underground, tram and trolleybus services also had to be reduced, but fortunately there was a considerable drop in passenger traffic because of the effect of the war on business and the evacuation of many offices.

THE PROUD CITY

ST. THOMAS'S HOSPITAL AND THE HOUSES OF PARLIAMENT

"Dull would he be of soul who could pass by
A sight so touching in its majesty."

William Wordsworth "Upon Westminster Bridge"

The Proud City: St Thomas's
Hospital and the Houses of
Parliament by Water Spradbery
Poster
1944

Disused platforms and passageways at a number of Tube stations were converted for various special uses. At Down Street station, closed since 1932, an emergency headquarters was prepared for London Transport and the wartime Railway Executive Committee, which was later used for meetings of the War Cabinet during the Blitz. An Operations Room for London's Anti-Aircraft Command was established deep in another disused station at Brompton Road, South Kensington, within a few feet of passing trains. Treasures from the British Museum, including the Elgin Marbles, were stored in the tunnels of the Aldwych branch.

London Transport staff had been receiving regular ARP training in rescue, fire fighting and first aid since before the war, but in May 1940 the Board also formed its own Home Guard unit, in which nearly 30,000 employees served. As growing numbers of male staff were called up for service in the Forces, the Board began to recruit more female staff to replace them, but on a much larger scale than in the First World War. Women now took on virtually every job previously carried out by men, including labouring and heavy engineering work, though they were not allowed to become drivers. During the six years of war more than 22,000 male staff were called up for military service and were replaced by 16,000 additional female staff and men over the call up age.

The long expected air raids finally began in the summer of 1940. The first bombs to damage London Transport equipment hit New Malden on 16 August and immediately demonstrated the vulnerability of the trolleybus system to aerial attack by bringing down a section of overhead wiring. Heavy bombing started on 7 September with a daylight raid on the docks and East End. London was then bombed every night until 2 November, after which the Blitz continued intermittently until May 1941. Nearly 50,000 high explosive bombs and millions of incendiaries fell on the capital, killing more than 15,000 civilians. For every person killed, another 35 were made homeless.

Amazingly, despite the disruption caused by bombing, a service of some kind was nearly always maintained, though this was more difficult with the trams and the Underground when trackwork and tunnels were hit. Buses could always be diverted, and this was possible even with trolleybuses. Wherever necessary, maintenance crews

Underground tunnels being used by the Plessey aircraft components factory during the Second World War
c. 1941

erected new traction poles and overhead wiring quickly and efficiently, often working on their tower wagons while the Blitz raged around them. The average time taken to reinstate the trolleybus service after an 'incident' was only four hours.

As soon as the Blitz started, thousands of Londoners took to the Tubes for shelter. At first this was not officially encouraged, and as no special facilities had been installed, there were chaotic scenes. Gradually sheltering arrangements became properly organised with special admission tickets, bunk beds on the platforms, refreshments and, at some stations, libraries, music and live entertainment. At one there was even a newsletter, 'The Swiss Cottager', produced by the local shelterers' committee. The Underground tunnels were not entirely safe from attack, however. Shelterers were killed in six separate bomb incidents when Tube stations were hit. London Transport began building eight new tunnels at a deeper level in 1940. These were to act as more secure public shelters while the war continued, and there were long-term plans to use them as the basis for new express Tube lines. In fact the tunnels were used exclusively for military purposes from their completion in 1942 until the flying bomb attacks in 1944, when five were opened up as public shelters. The express Tube idea was never implemented, and today some of the tunnels are used for archival storage.

London Transport not only transported and sheltered both civilians and military personnel, it also made an important contribution to the war effort through its workshops and facilities. In the safety of the newly completed Central line extension tunnels between Leytonstone and Gants Hill, the Plessey Company manufactured aircraft components. The London Aircraft Production (LAP) group was set up in 1941 in association with four motor companies to build Halifax heavy bombers. Over a four-year period 710 were built by a workforce of whom 80 per cent had no previous engineering experience. Over half were women. London Transport's building department made parts for trestle bridges, landing craft, pontoon floats and aircraft turntables. The engineering shops at Charlton tram and trolleybus works were turned over to the manufacture of ammunition and gun parts, while the bus and coach department at Chiswick built nearly a thousand lorries, overhauled War Department vehicles and made parts for tanks. At Acton railway works London Transport overhauled landing craft motors, and repaired and converted tanks and bren gun carriers. This work reached a peak in the months leading up to the Allied invasion of Europe in June 1944. As D-Day approached, London Transport buses carried six infantry divisions to their ships and assault craft in the Channel ports. Over the next few weeks many of them were needed again to transfer returning army casualties from trains to hospitals.

By this time London was under attack from a sinister new weapon, the 'V1' flying bomb. The heaviest 'V1' assaults were between June and August 1944, but from 8 September the Germans began using the more powerful 'V2' rocket bombs as well and continued to hit London until the end of March 1945. Damage was much less serious than during the Blitz of 1940–41, but the final months of bombing prompted another wave of evacuation and contributed to a new reduction in London Transport's passenger-carrying levels, which had increased again in 1942–3 with greater mobilisation for war work and the arrival of US Forces in London.

The final toll of injury and damage to London Transport's staff and property was high. 699 members of staff were killed on active military service. In the air attacks on London 426 staff were killed and nearly 3000 injured. 241 road vehicles and 19 railway cars were totally destroyed by enemy action and many others badly damaged. The backlog of repair, replacement and renewal of property, which started in 1945, was huge.

LEAVE THIS TO US
SONNY—YOU OUGHT
TO BE OUT OF LONDON

MINISTRY OF HEALTH EVACUATION SCHEME

↺ *Leave this to us, Sonny* by
Dudley Cowes
1940

London Transport took a leading role in evacuating children from London. The organisational effort was enormous. Many thousands of signs, special instructions and posters, such as this one by Dudley Cowes, were produced and distributed. In just four days more than 550,000 children – some excited, many bewildered – travelled by bus, tram and Tube to mainline railway stations, and onward to safe destinations around Britain.

⟳ **Evacuating hospital patients**
September 1939

Anticipating severe air raids, Green Line services were withdrawn on 31 August 1939 and the coaches converted into ambulances. Their first task was to help evacuate patients and staff from London hospitals to safer areas. This coach, which had been operating its usual service to Windsor only the day before, is evacuating patients from Westminster Hospital.

TUBE SHELTERERS

◷ **Shelterers on escalators at Piccadilly Circus station**
1940

No fewer than 177,000 people took shelter during the night of 27 September 1940.

> **SHELTERERS' BEDDING**
>
> The practice of shaking bedding over the platforms, tracks and in the subways is strictly forbidden
>
> ⊖

◷ **Public information poster**
1941

◑ **Shelterers at Highgate Underground station**
1941

At night time, Tube stations were filled to bursting with Londoners seeking a safe haven. At first they came armed with food, blankets and all manner of possessions. They squatted wherever they could – on the platforms, the escalators, and, once the power was safely off, even on the tracks. As the Blitz proceeded throughout 1940 and 1941, London Transport recognised a public need and opted for regulation. White lines were painted on some platforms to mark sleeping areas; bunk beds for up to 22,000 people were built in others.

A total of 79 deep Tube stations were employed as shelters, whilst a number of disused stations were modified to provide high quality shelters. A refreshment service was set up, and medical aid posts were established at every station. Libraries, play centres and classrooms were even set up at some.

⌒ **Constructing a shelter at British Museum station**
June 1941

A wall was built along the former platform edge of British Museum station (on the Central line), which had closed in 1933.

⌒ **Medical aid post, Notting Hill Gate station**
1940

The Tube provided shelter not just for the fit, but also the elderly, ill and infirm. Medical aid posts were quickly established in every Tube station, staffed by a total of 30 doctors and 200 nurses.

THIS STATION WILL NOW REMAIN OPEN DURING AIR RAID ALERTS

LONDON ⌒ TRANSPORT

TUBE REFRESHMENTS

This Depot supplies
Service Points
Stations and Feeds
People

They rely on us for food and drink night and morning

We must not let them down

⊖

⌒ **Feeding the shelterers**
December 1940

⌒ **Public information poster**
1940

⌒ **Public information poster**

Up to seven tons of food and 2400 gallons of tea and cocoa were served nightly to shelterers.

🌀 **Station shelter ticket**

In the early days of the Blitz, people obtained access to stations by buying platform tickets. As London Transport recognised the need for regulation, special shelter tickets were introduced, not least to try to limit overcrowding. Nevertheless, it was not unheard of for racketeers to reserve spaces and sell them on at up to half a crown each.

This notice to staff underlines London Transport's commitment to maintaining Londoners' spirits.

⟳ **Shelterers**
1941

Serving refreshments to shelterers at Holland Park station, 1941.

Although Tube stations made highly effective shelters, they could not offer complete protection. This colossal crater is the result of a single bomb, which caused the road to collapse into the concourse of Bank station. The escalators were destroyed in the blast, and passengers waiting on the platform were blown into the path of an oncoming train. Survivors had to make their way out along the tunnels, as there was no other way out.

🔘 **Moorgate station**
December 1940

This train caught fire. The heat was so intense that the glass windows and aluminium doors melted.

🔘 **Balham station**
October 1941

In terms of casualties, this direct hit on Balham Underground station was the worst single incident of the war. About 600 people were sheltering in the

station when a bomb penetrated the northbound station tunnel. The whole length of the platform was buried in gravel, and water from burst mains flooded in to a depth of three feet. One hundred and eleven were killed. The driver of the bus, however, managed to scramble to safety before his vehicle toppled into the crater.

↪ **Clapham tram depot**
April 1941

This hit on Clapham depot damaged many trams. Both trams and trolleybuses were particularly vulnerable during air raids. Tracks and overhead wires were easily damaged, bringing services along whole sections to a halt.

◑ Sloane Square station
November 1940

Sloane Square was the site of one of the worst incidents during the winter of 1940. A direct hit on the station at 10 pm caught a crowded train as it was leaving the station. There were 79 casualties.

◑ Air raid damage, Harrington Square
September 1940

During the Blitz many buses were damaged or destroyed. Fortunately the passengers and crew of this bus decided to take refuge in a garden shelter during this raid. They emerged unscathed to find the bus upended against the façade of a nearby house.

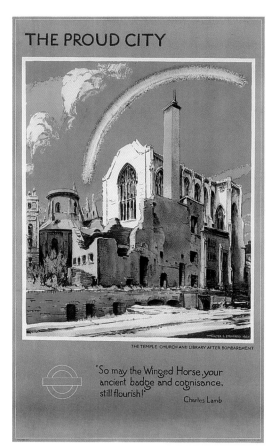

THE PROUD CITY

THE TEMPLE CHURCH AND LIBRARY AFTER BOMBARDMENT

"So may the Winged Horse, your
ancient badge and cognisance,
still flourish!"
Charles Lamb

⟳ **The Temple Church and
Library after Bombardment**
1944

This example from the series of
six posters, *The Proud City* by
Walter Spradbery, celebrated
London's survival of the Blitz. In
the artist's own words, it was
intended to convey 'the sense
that havoc is itself passing and
with new days come new
hopes'.

THE PROUD CITY

A NEW VIEW OF ST PAUL'S CATHEDRAL FROM BREAD STREET

"...the principal Ornament of our royal City,
to the Honour of our Government, and
of this our Realm...."
Letters Patent under the Great Seal of England the 12th day Nov.1673.

⟲ **St Paul's Cathedral**
1944

Poster from the series
The Proud City by Walter
Spradbery.

Protected windows on a Tube train
1941

Netting was glued on to the windows of buses and trains to reduce the risk of injury from flying glass in the event of a bomb-blast. The clear opening in the middle was to enable passengers to read the station names.

Fixing blast netting on to a bus window
1943

'I'll Trust You'll Pardon My Correction'
1941

David Langdon's sanctimonious 'Billy Brown' character figured

BILLY BROWN *of* LONDON TOWN

"I trust you'll pardon my correction

that stuff is there for your protection."

Printed for London Transport

throughout the war, dispensing all manner of advice and information in verse. In this poster he makes an appearance to remind a thoughtless passenger of the importance of blast netting.

Flood gate at Strand station
January 1940

A major concern for London Transport was the risk of flooding, should a bomb breach one of the tunnels under the Thames. Flood gates were installed at strategic points, and hydrophones placed on the bed of the river to detect the fall of delayed-action bombs. Track layouts were modified so that the trains could still run a reduced service when the doors were closed. It was an expensive precaution, but without its reassurance the Underground would have been brought to a standstill during air raid alerts.

reduce ticket length. On shorter routes with few stages the otherwise blank backs were used for timely reminders, such as these, about wartime travel.

◑ *Rehabilitation – It Takes Time* by Fred Taylor
1945

Rehabilitation started soon after VE day (Victory in Europe).

Tooting was the first of 75 stations to have its entrance restored, and the rest followed at the rate of about three per day. London Transport published posters urging patience, but in fact an extraordinary amount was achieved in very short order, to the great satisfaction of Londoners.

◑ Staff shelter, St James's Park station
July 1939

To enable key staff to remain at their posts during raids, tiny shelters – designed to accommodate one or two people – were installed at stations throughout the Underground.

◑ Wartime paper economy
1941

The layout of fare sections on bus tickets was simplified to

VISITING ?
2
Leave rush-hour seats
for workers; please
START HOME EARLY
A0624

Don't leave
10
your GAS MASK
on the bus
A0201

REHABILITATION

For the protection of passengers 137 anti-blast walls were placed at the entrances to 75 stations. These walls are being demolished as quickly as possible – but

IT TAKES TIME

◐ Moorgate station
1944

Anti-blast wall in front of the entrance
at Moorgate station, August 1944.

◑ River bus
1940

As docks and factories were
damaged during the bombing,
workers had to be relocated,
and the Government asked
London Transport to provide a
boat service between
Westminster and Woolwich.
Fifteen boats loaned by the Port
of London operated the service.
Its introduction was timely as the
day before services started
almost all of south-east London
was without trams and
trolleybuses. However, the
service was withdrawn after six
weeks as the journey took more
than two hours.

Underground map
1941

New editions of the Underground map were produced throughout the war, although paper shortages restricted the number that were printed. Coloured inks were in short supply, and later editions were printed in black and white only. In this 1941 edition, designer Harry Beck experimented with a new symbol for interchange stations, and drew the sloping lines at 60 degrees rather than the usual 45 degrees. It also shows a number of Tube extension projects on the Northern and Central lines that had been curtailed by the war.

Make Sure it is the Platform Side by Bruce Angrave
1942

During the war, many trains on the Underground still had hand-operated doors. A particular hazard of the blackout was the risk of getting out on the wrong side of the train. This poster warns passengers of the danger.

Before Alighting, Look for Platform
Poster
1942

**Billy Brown
of London Town**

The safest travelling in town
Is not too good for Billy Brown
He's much too sensible and knowing
To jump down off a bus that's going,
Especially in blackout hours
Or when the kerb is wet with showers.
On these occasions Billy B
Goes by the slogan 'Wait and See'.

*Printed for
London ⊖ Transport*

⟨⟩ Billy Brown of London Town by David Langdon
1940

This is one of Billy Brown's first appearances, in a London Transport poster.

⟨⟩ Stand on the Right by Fougasse
1944

A fougasse was a small landmine, an appropriate pseudonym for cartoonist Cyril Bird, who adopted it when he was a Royal Engineer in the First World War. His humorous public information posters, such as this, are some of the best-remembered images of the Second World War.

⟨⟩ In the Blackout by Zero (Hans Schleger)
1943

The feeble glow emitted by shaded bus headlamps provided no illumination for the driver. Consequently it was easy to miss people waiting for the bus. The advice was to carry a torch, which could be shone on to the passenger's outstretched hand, as shown in this poster.

PLEASE STAND ON THE RIGHT
OF THE ESCALATOR

IN THE **BLACKOUT**

To hail a bus or tram shine a torch on to your hand

LONDON AIRCRAFT PRODUCTION

During the war, London Transport turned over many of its maintenance facilities to a wide range of manufacturing and repair tasks. The single biggest operation was London Aircraft Production (LAP), which undertook the manufacture, assembly and test flying of four-engined Handley-Page Halifax bombers. The organisation was centred on London Transport's Chiswick Works, but included factories owned by Duple, Chrysler, Express Body Works and Park Royal coach works. The LAP group of factories utilised a new building at Aldenham

London Aircraft Production (LAP) pamphlet
1944

LAP's logo features a graphic of the Halifax bomber in flight.

that had been built before the outbreak of war as a new depot for a planned extension to the Northern line. This site produced the Halifax fuselage fronts and the centre section of the wings, including the bomb bay.

The technology required for the production of Halifax bombers was in advance of anything London Transport had ever attempted. Skills, machine tools and materials were all in short supply. The complete production process involved not just the eight factories of the LAP group, but also sub-contracting to more than 500 other firms. Most extraordinary of all is that an army of hitherto untrained women swiftly adapted to the task and carried out the majority of the work.

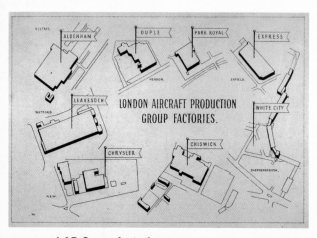

LAP Group factories
1944

Factory Number 2

Diagram showing the work carried out at Aldenham, known as Factory Number 2 in the LAP group. After the war, Aldenham became London Transport's main bus overhaul works.

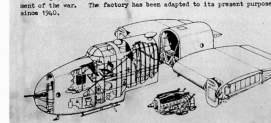

★ L.P.T.B. Factory Nº 2 ★

The assembly and installation of the Centre Section, and the in ation of the Front Fuselage and Engines are carried out in this factory The No. 2 factory was intended for the housing and maintenance of Underground trains and was in course of construction at the commence ment of the war. The factory has been adapted to its present purpose since 1940.

Halifax fuselages
1942–5

Halifax front fuselages constructed at the Aldenham factory.

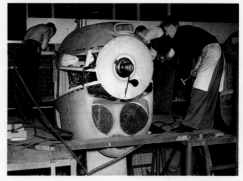

🔵 **Assembling an engine Nacelle, White City factory**
1942–5

Engine cowlings for Halifax bombers were produced at White City, in buildings built for exhibition purposes and converted by London Transport in 1942.

🔵 *Our Machine is a Halifax* by D. Vesper
1942

This poster urged workers not to leave tools, equipment and other unwanted parts in the aircraft they were building. The play on 'junk' refers to the enemy aircraft manufactured by the German Junkers company.

LONDON AIRCRAFT PRODUCTION

Halifax bomber construction

A woman greases the main undercarriage arch of a Halifax bomber.

Aircraft construction
1943

Fitting bomb steadies during aircraft construction.

Halifax bomber construction

The young woman in this photograph is putting the finishing touches to a Halifax bomber in one of the London Transport workshops converted to aircraft production at Leavesden, near Watford.

Ashtray in the form of a Halifax bomber
1945

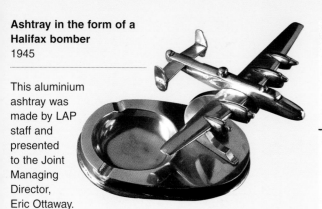

This aluminium ashtray was made by LAP staff and presented to the Joint Managing Director, Eric Ottaway.

LAP's last Halifax Bomber
1945

Invitation to the handing-over ceremony at Leavesden Aerodrome on 16 April 1945 of 'London Pride', the last Halifax bomber to be manufactured by LAP. The RAF took delivery of the aircraft during the ceremony, which was attended by both Lord Ashfield, who served as Chairman of LAP, and Sir Frederick Handley Page, together with hundreds of aircraft workers.

Completed Halifax bomber

This aeroplane is at LAP's Leavesden aerodrome, where final assembly and test flying was undertaken.

LEAVESDEN AERODROME.

16th. April 1945.

On the Occasion of
the delivery to the
Royal Air Force
of the last Halifax
Bomber manufactured
by the
London Aircraft Production
Group

London Passenger Transport Board,
Chrysler Motors Ltd,
Duple Bodies and Motors Ltd,
Express Motor and Body Works Ltd,
Park Royal Coach Works Ltd.

◑ Bus with 'producer gas' trailer
November 1939

Petrol shortages during the war restricted bus services. 151 buses were converted to run on 'producer gas', made by injecting water into burning coal. This took place in a trailer, towed behind the bus, which had to be stoked with anthracite about every 80 miles.

◑ STL-type bus
November 1941

One of the war's first effects on the public was the imposition of the blackout. From 1 September 1939 buses had to run with reduced lighting, so headlights and interior lights were covered with cowls. To help people see buses in the dark, mudguards were painted white. As the war progressed, shortages of materials for repairs led to glass windows being replaced with wood or metal panels.

◑ Interior of Guy 'Utility' bus
December 1943

The shaded lamps and wooden-slatted seats were typical features of the wartime Guy 'Utility' bus. This woman conductor is one of 5000 who had been taken on by the middle of 1942.

Buses at war

An LT-type bus in Second World War condition, with blast netting on the windows and masked headlamps for blackout operation.

Guy 'Utility' bus, Golders Green
August 1943

Production of new buses was curtailed at the outbreak of war. By the end of 1940 so many buses had been blitzed that a plea for assistance was sent to the Ministry of War Transport. Soon, buses from the provinces started to appear on London's streets. In 1941 the Government allowed the resumption of bus building on a limited scale.

Economy of materials and skilled labour were essential: the result was the Guy 'Utility' bus, of which London Transport received 435.

U.S. Army on-duty travel pass
1945

A single journey ticket for U.S. Army Personnel travelling on duty in the London Area.

Wartime off-peak travel pass
1940

A popular facility for His Majesty's and Allied Forces in

Uniform was a one-day rover ticket, valid after 10.30am for travel on all Central Bus routes, trams and trolleybuses and the majority of the L.P.T.B. Railways.

Green Line coaches on military service

Ninety-four former Green Line coaches were seconded to service with the American armed forces from 1943 onwards. Some were used as transports, but 55 were converted into mobile canteens called 'Clubmobiles'.

Upper deck of D-type bus
June 1944

In 1943 the Ministry of Supply decreed that all new buses would have wooden seats to economise on scarce materials. This bus is one of nine special 'low bridge' Daimlers, which had a sunken gangway on the offside of the upper deck, allowing the height of the bus to be reduced.

The London Transport Spitfire Fund
1942

LT staff contributed to a fund dedicated to paying for the production of vital Spitfire fighters. A cheque for the first was handed to the Minister of Aircraft Production in 1942, and a second followed nine months later. Both aircraft bore the familiar London Transport roundel sign.

Spitfire fund commemorative plaque

London Transport Spitfire Fund
1942

Poster issued to raise money for the LT Spitfire Fund.

LONDON TRANSPORT

SPITFIRE FUND

SUBSCRIPTION FORMS ARE NOW OBTAINABLE FROM THE PAYMASTER

GET YOURS, GIVE WHAT YOU CAN AND KEEP GIVING

One Spitfire = £5,000
Nine Spitfires = 40 Messerschmitts
Give as many penny units as you can afford

IN THE HOUR OF PERIL THE MEN AND WOMEN OF THE LONDON PASSENGER TRANSPORT BOARD EARNED THE GRATITUDE OF THE BRITISH NATIONS SUSTAINING THE VALOUR OF THE ROYAL AIR FORCE AND FORTIFYING THE CAUSE OF FREEDOM BY THE GIFT OF SPITFIRE AIRCRAFT
They shall mount up with wings as eagles
Issued by the Ministry of Aircraft Production
1942

LT anti-aircraft unit in training
August 1939

The 84th (London Transport) Heavy Anti-Aircraft Regiment was formed in 1938. Seen here training at Cleave Camp near Bude, they went on to serve in Norway, North Africa and Italy.

Plessey's underground factory
1942

Plans in the 1930s to extend the Central line to the east from Liverpool Street were held up by the war. However, a five-mile length of tunnel constructed between Leytonstone and Gants Hill was used as a factory for the Plessey aircraft components factory in 1942 and became known as the 'Plessey Tunnel'. To avoid long walks for the staff, intermediate entry points were constructed to supplement the existing stations. A miniature railway was installed to carry materials and completed parts to and from the men and women who operated the machinery, such as this pillar drill operator.

Anti-aircraft operations room, Brompton Road
c. 1942

London's anti-aircraft guns were all controlled from the Anti-Aircraft Command operations room. This was located within a few feet of passing trains at Brompton Road, a Piccadilly line station that closed in 1934.

Home Guard at Chiswick Works
March 1941

Many of LT's workers were called up for service. Many more joined LT's own Home Guard units. Within a few weeks of the start of the war, more than 4000 staff had volunteered for service in six battalions.

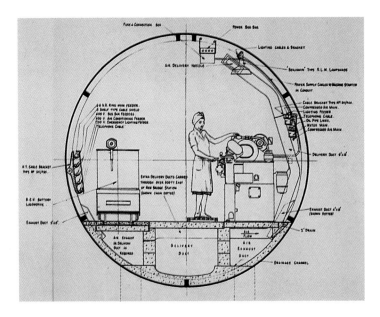

⋒ London Transport farm at Bushey
September 1944

At the outbreak of war, LT turned some 125 acres of its land over to agriculture, supplying fresh vegetables for its own canteens. Pictured are Mary Howe, formerly an art student, and Gwen Seale, an ex-employee of the Post Office on the right.

⋒ The 'Plessey Tunnel'

Sectional drawing of the cast-iron tunnel that housed the Plessey factory during the war.

◷ *Back Room Boys: Cable Maintenance* by Fred Taylor
1942

A series of posters, *They Also Serve* by Fred Taylor, highlighted the role of staff from behind the scenes – many of them women – which lent the series title a certain irony.

◷ Emergency kitchen
1940s

London Transport was well known for looking after the welfare of its staff, and a square meal was very much part of a worker's benefits. This open-air oven probably took over from some canteen facility damaged in the bombing.

⊃ Despatch riders at Camberwell garage
April 1940

Motorcycles provided a fast and economic means of carrying essential documents and other supplies between garages, depots and LT's headquarters.

'THEY ALSO SERVE'

↺ **Seeing It Through: Bus Conductor by Eric Kennington** 1944

The characters depicted in Eric Kennington's *Seeing It Through* poster series were actual members of LT staff. Featured on this poster is clippie Mrs M. J. Morgan from Poplar, who saved four children during an air raid.

↻ **Seeing It Through: Station Woman by Eric Kennington** 1944

Station woman Elsie Birrel of Stockwell station was one of the first woman porters.

◔ **Women workers** 1941

The many women recruited to London Transport undertook a wide range of jobs, many of which had always been seen as men's exclusive preserve. Below left, Mrs Simpson is working on a bus chassis at Chiswick Works. Below, female machine workers operate a lathe at Acton Works, 1942.

➦ *Back Room Boys: Bus Maintenance* **by Fred Taylor** 1942

Poster from the series *They Also Serve* by Fred Taylor.

◑ **Training with anti-gas equipment** March 1940

London Transport permanent way staff practise changing a rail wearing gas masks, capes and steel helmets at Neasden Depot. Fortunately, the threat of gas attack never materialised.

🎧 **Victory procession, The Mall**
1946

LT vehicles took part in a massive victory parade during a day of celebrations on 8 June 1946. Nearly 9000 incidents of damage to vehicles and property had been recorded. Even so, thanks to the extraordinary efforts of staff and Londoners in general, LT had 'carried on'.

➲ **Victory procession, The Mall**
June 1946

London Transport buses taking the victory salute from the royal family during the Victory procession on 8 June 1946.

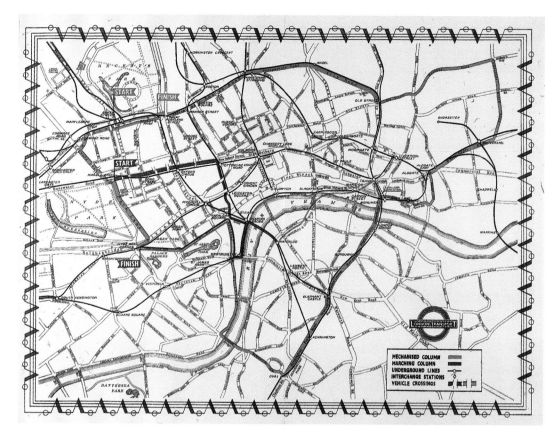

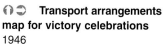 **Transport arrangements map for victory celebrations**
1946

After the Herculean efforts of the war, arranging special transport services for the London-wide victory celebrations must have seemed a straightforward task.

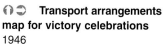 **Programme for staff reunion victory dinner**
1946

This dinner was held to honour those who served in the armed forces – no fewer than 22,580 had been called up – and those who kept the system operating at home.

VICTORY
CELEBRATIONS

TRANSPORT
ARRANGEMENTS

*LONDON TRANSPORT
AT LONDON'S SERVICE*

50th Anniversary
1995

This commemorative 'journey planner' was produced for the 50th anniversary celebrations of Victory in Europe.

VE Celebrations
6 - 8 May 1995
Commemorative journey planner

VE Day Celebrations in Whitehall
8 May 1945

Huge crowds bring traffic to a halt in Whitehall and throng the entrance to Downing Street, celebrating the end of the war in Europe.

Commemorative Travelcard
1995

Issued in May 1995 to mark the 50th anniversary of Victory in Europe.

Seven Battalions, booklet cover
1947

A commemorative publication celebrating the history of London Transport's Home Guard, 1940–46.

Public Transport in Decline

The Car is King
1945–1970

**Traffic outside the National Gallery,
Trafalgar Square**
1960

Public Transport in Decline
The Car is King, 1945–1970

One in every two Londoners was worried by the noise of traffic penetrating his home. The din on some pavements, when measured, reached eighty decibels, which was equivalent to an alarm clock ringing two feet away from the ear... motor cycles, sports cars and 'hotted up' engines added to the noise; while over the streets hung the heavy smell of diesel oil from thousands of taxi-cabs and buses. 'A noisy exhaust,' said a Member of Parliament, 'is the modern mating call.'... To own a car was the principal target in life for a substantial slice of the working classes.

The Fifties by John Montgomery, Allen & Unwin, 1965

After the Second World War transport in London did not get 'back to normal'. It was impossible for London Transport to reinstate services at their pre-war level as soon as the war ended. Many vehicles had been completely destroyed by enemy action, and

In a jam

A typical 1960s congested traffic scene at the Elephant and Castle.

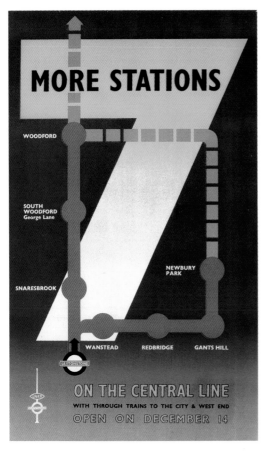

Seven More Stations on the Central Line by Beath (John M. Fleming)
1947

The third stage of the Central line eastern extension involved projection of trains from Leytonstone both over the mainline tracks to Woodford and through new tube tunnels to Newbury Park, both achieved in 1947.

hundreds more were either damaged or badly run down through lack of maintenance. New 'RT'-type buses were ordered almost immediately, but the rate of delivery was slow. By 1948 old vehicles were being withdrawn more quickly than new replacements could be introduced. It had already been decided to use diesel buses instead of trolleybuses to replace the remaining trams, and this took place between 1950 and 1952. On the evening of 5 July 1952 huge crowds turned out for an emotional farewell to a cheap and popular form of transport that had served Londoners well for over 80 years.

Plans to resume the interrupted New Works Programme on the Underground were reviewed in the light of post-war financial difficulties. London Transport was authorised to proceed with the unfinished eastern and western extensions of the Central line (completed in 1946–9). With the application of new Green Belt planning regulations there seemed little prospect of substantial traffic on the proposed Northern line extension north of Edgware to Bushey Heath. This was abandoned in 1950, and it was decided to make the unfinished railway depot at Aldenham, which had been used to build aircraft during the war, the basis of a large new bus overhaul works. The bus fleet had more than doubled since the 1920s when Chiswick Works was opened by the LGOC. By the 1950s it was essential to provide more spacious and better equipped facilities for the overhaul of the massive standardised post-war bus fleet. Conversion and extension work at Aldenham was completed in 1956.

In 1948 London Transport was nationalised by the Labour government along with the four mainline railway companies. Priority for capital investment was given to other essential areas of the economy such as house building and electricity generation, while within the public transport field the needs of the badly run down British Railways network took precedence. London Transport had also lost the two leaders who had set its direction before the war. Frank Pick had left in 1940, and died the following year. Lord Ashfield retired as Chairman in 1947, and also died within months of his departure. This 'formidable pair', as Herbert Morrison had called them, were not succeeded by anyone with comparable drive and ability to take London Transport forward.

In its technical and engineering development, London Transport was still

Royal opening

The first two sections of the Victoria line were officially opened by the Queen on 7 March 1969.

setting some of the highest standards of any urban transport organisation in the world in the 1950s and '60s. Particularly valuable lessons in standardisation of engineering parts, assembly methods and use of new materials had been gained during the war with aircraft production work, and were applied to the new overhaul procedures at Aldenham. The new Routemaster bus, developed in the 1950s, used lightweight aluminium alloy construction, and the same material was used for new Underground train bodies. Because aluminium does not rust and can be left unpainted, silver unpainted trains were introduced from the 1950s. In the 1960s London Transport experimented with automatic driving equipment for trains and first applied this newly developed technology on the Victoria line.

However, this continued progress in research and development was taking place in a period of rapid social and economic change, to which London Transport could not easily respond. Years of increasing demand for bus services peaked in the late 1940s, after which passenger numbers began to decline for reasons largely outside London Transport's control. Between 1950 and 1965 the number of private cars licensed in the London Transport area rose from 480,000 to 1,920,000. As more people had access to personal transport, they used public transport less, particularly for leisure travel. Meanwhile television sets appeared in a growing number of homes, particularly after the introduction of a commercial channel in 1955, and Londoners made fewer trips out for entertainment at the cinema and football matches.

The new Routemasters introduced from 1959 to replace first the trolleybuses and then many of the older diesel buses were as comfortable as most private cars, but they could not provide a reliable service on increasingly congested streets. The various traffic management schemes introduced in London at this time – one way streets, fly-overs, underpasses and parking meters – did little other than to shift the jams from one pinch point to another. Congestion both in central London and the busier suburbs slowed buses down to speeds little better than those in horse bus days.

The public lost confidence in bus services. The number of passengers carried by London Transport's road services fell from 3955 million in 1948 to 2485 million in 1962. Ever since the merger of the LGOC and the Underground Group in 1912 it had always been the buses that produced most of the profit. This deterioration therefore struck a mortal blow at the financial viability of the whole undertaking. With operating costs rising and revenue falling, bus services were about to start losing money in the 1960s.

A far more positive development at this time was the authorisation from government for the construction of the first completely new tube line under London since the burst

Routemasters undergoing overhaul at Aldenham Works
1978

The large modern flow-line factory was fully operational by 1955. This photograph shows the ability to move bus bodies along the line.

of activity in the Edwardian years. This was the Victoria line, originally proposed in 1948 but not begun until 1962 after cost-benefit surveys and experimental tunnelling finally persuaded the government to allocate funding. The 14-mile line was built at a cost of £91 million. It was opened in stages between 1968 and 1971 and contained railway interchanges at almost all of its 16 stations. The effect was to spread the traffic and speed up journeys, especially under central London. Passenger mileage as a whole increased. For a while this sleek new tube railway, with its automated trains and ticketing seemed the realisation, on one line at least, of a thoroughly modern and efficient urban public transport system.

➲ RT1 is launched
1939

The AEC-engined RT class of bus, with its Leyland counterparts the RTL and RTW became the standard London post-war bus spanning 40 years from 1939 to 1979.

RT1 was launched in August 1939, only weeks before the outbreak of the Second World War, which eventually brought a halt to new vehicle construction. Mechanically the vehicle was a further development of the well tried AEC Regent chassis, giving a smoother ride and better acceleration.

ꙩ RT on parade

This RT passing Horse Guards is wearing the new livery style introduced in 1950, The ultimate post-war design emerged in 1948 when the classic arrangement without a roof route-number box began to enter service.

∩ Features of the RT-type

High standards of design on the RT extended to such details as the elegant lifting handles on the bonnet side and the spring-mounted bonnet lock.

Interior of the RT

The interiors boasted large windows and light colours, which gave the saloons a fresh and airy feel, and the brown and green on the lower surrounds were echoed in the neat design of the moquette upholstery.

Coast-to-Coast American Goodwill Tour
March-July 1952

Such was the symbolic nature of the red London RTs, that they were used for overseas tours to promote tourism in the early 1950s. This publicity leaflet was designed by Emett, a popular cartoonist of the time.

Coast-to-Coast American Goodwill Tour
MARCH-JULY 1952

An RTW and RT compared

London's first eight-foot wide motor buses were 500 Leyland-built RTWs, first introduced in 1949. The Metropolitan Police opposed their use in central London until 1951. No more eight-feet wide buses went into service, however, until the Routemasters arrived.

The RT in Canada

The Royal Canadian Mountie leaves no doubt that this RT is on the Canadian part of the North America tour. The Route 11 blinds were authentic enough, although the via points were doctored to emphasise such places as Buckingham Palace Road and Westminster Abbey.

◐ Aldenham Overhaul Works

The highly standardised jig-built fleet of the post-war years provided the opportunity for bus overhauls to be based on flow-line factory principles. A large site became available at Aldenham, and this led to the development of a unit capable of handling the whole of the motor bus fleet, then expected to reach 10,000 vehicles. The new factory opened in 1955, but its usefulness declined over the years as the fleet diminished in size and the gap between overhauls widened. Increasingly uneconomic, it closed in 1986.

⮕ *Winter in The Country – Country Walks – Green Rover* by Harry Stevens
1965

Riding the green RTs through London's countryside was a popular attraction. In 1956 the Green Rover ticket appeared giving a day's travel on the green buses for 5/-. The Green Rover ticket was still in use when this attractive poster appeared in 1965.

◑ RTs in the country

London Transport buses serving the surrounding countryside were painted green instead of red.

Some of the original red liveried RTs were painted green in 1955 to give further service on a route from Hertford to Nazeing, where there was a weight restriction. These original vehicles were wooden framed and 15cwt. lighter than their post-war sisters.

◑ *Country Markets* by Philip Roberts
Poster
1960

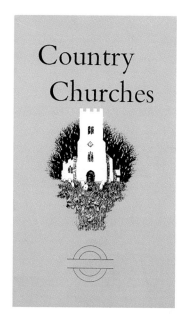

🔵 *Country Churches* leaflet 1967

🔵 **Gibson ticket machine**

In 1953 the Gibson ticket machine was introduced. Named after George Gibson, the Superintendent of the Stockwell punch works, these were able to print a range of different tickets onto a single roll of paper.

🔵 **An RF bus leaves Harrow Weald garage**

The standard single deck bus in post-war years was the RF class. 700 of these vehicles based on the AEC Regal IV chassis were built in Green Line coach, red bus and green bus versions. Originally the red buses had open doorways, but when one-person operated buses reached the Central Area, doors were fitted.

🔵 **Goodbye to the punch ticket**

For many years the conductor's rack of brightly coloured pre-printed tickets and the friendly 'ting' of his cancelling punch was a part of the London bus scene. Various experiments at mechanisation were carried out over the years, but eventually, starting in 1953, the racks began to disappear largely in favour of the Gibson ticket machine seen here.

🔵 *At your Service* by Leo P. Dowd 1947

In this poster a bus conductor uses a Bell Punch ticket machine and ticket rack.

AT YOUR SERVICE

He does a difficult job with patience and understanding. He is one of 22,000 conductors who issue nearly ten million tickets to travellers on London Transport road vehicles every day.

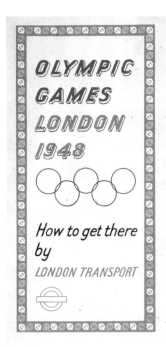

◑ **Olympic Games map**
1948

The first Olympic Games after the Second World War was the first major international event held in postwar London. The famous rings symbolising unity are prominent on this map produced to encourage travel to sporting venues during the Games.

◑ *Olympic Games – Welcome To London* by **Clement Dane Studio**
Poster
1948

◐ **Olympic Games decorations, Westminster station**
1948

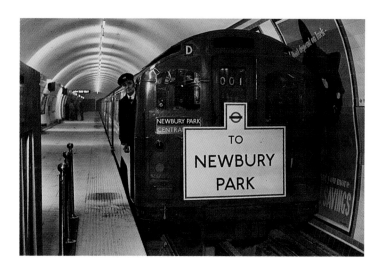

◖ **Open to Newbury Park**
1947

◖ *Extension Central Line*
by Zero (Hans Schleger)
1946

Before the Second World War the Underground embarked on a scheme of extensions on the Northern and Central lines, parts of which were to join and then run over sections of mainline railway. The Central line works stopped during the war and were resumed immediately afterwards. The first section, from the Central's 1912 terminus at Liverpool Street to Stratford, opened in 1946, as advertised in this poster. It included a new station at Bethnal Green and an interchange with the District line at Mile End.

➲ **Ceremony for the opening of the Stratford extension**
1946

Both London Transport and the Ministry of Transport were anxious to gain as much publicity as possible from the Underground's first post-war extension, and elaborate arrangements were made for the event. Here, the Minister, Alfred Barnes, is operating a special key that would give the green light to the first train.

The trains used on the Central line, and therefore on the new extensions, were second hand from the Northern line, but extensively refurbished. This view is taken at Wanstead on the occasion of the opening to Newbury Park.

◔ **Wanstead station entrance**
1950

Amongst Holden's last commissions for London Transport was Wanstead station on the Central line extension. It had to be remodelled for opening as a passenger station in 1947 as it had seen wartime use as an entrance to the underground factory which utilised the newly built Tube tunnels between Leytonstone and Newbury Park.

◔ **Ruislip Gardens station**
1950

Concrete butterfly-wing roofs were a characteristic of the stations on the western extensions of the Central line and were quite a feature at the time.

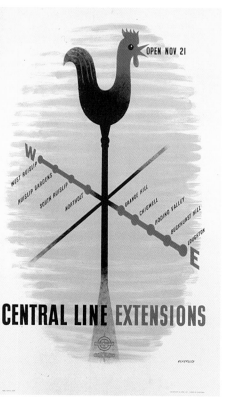

◔ *Central line extensions* by **Tom Eckersley**
Poster
1948

In 1948 the Central line was extended to Loughton in the east and West Ruislip in the west.

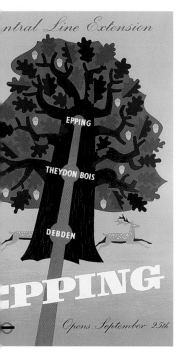

ⓘ *Epping – Central Line Extension* **by K.G. Chapman**
Poster
1949

The final section of the Central line extensions opened from Loughton to Epping in 1949, offering a reduced journey time to Liverpool Street and a vastly more frequent service.

ⓘ **Old and New at Epping**
1953

With electric trains from Epping now serving London, the old steam service from Ongar was cut back to operate as a shuttle service. It was not electrified until 1957.

ⓘ **White City station**
1950

Part of the Central line modernisation works involved replacement of Wood Lane station by White City, a little further west. The spacious ticket hall was built partly with visitors to the adjacent dog-racing stadium in mind. A separate exit to the stadium is just visible on the right. The station opened in 1947.

○ 'Moscow Concourse', Gants Hill
1954

The unique lower concourse at Gants Hill was said to be inspired by stations on the Moscow Metro and was often referred to as the 'Moscow Concourse'. The concourse intersected the platform tunnels forming a continuous opening between the two, separated only by the supporting columns. This ingenious arrangement effectively widened the platforms at the busiest point and removed the usual constrictions in passenger flow caused by the small connecting passages common to most stations.

○ Underground concourse, Moscow Metro
c. 1936

Whilst the Underground Group's top engineers provided valuable consultancy work and recommendations to the builders of the Moscow Metro in the early 1930s, Russian architects provided the inspiration for Gants Hill's broad subterranean concourse, as this station on the Moscow system illustrates.

○ White City, sign and seating

An attractive feature at platform level was the station name sign, designed to form an integral part of the seating.

○ Gants Hill, platform detail

Attention to detail produced this attractive clockface design, only used on platforms on this section of line. The name frieze, however, was an enduring feature of the extensions of this period. It was soon replicated at nearly all other Underground stations, initially on paper and then using enamelled-iron name plates forming a continuous frieze.

Bethnal Green station
1946

Built in the late 1930s, this station, like others on this section of the Central line, was not completed until after the war. On many of these stations fluorescent lighting was used for the first time.

Hanger Lane station
1949

Hanger Lane ticket hall is actually underground, but the circular street-level building, housing one of the entrances, acts as a light well. It is a distinctive structure designed by Dr F. F. Curtis, Great Western Railway's Chief Architect, and built in 1949.

Gants Hill refurbishment
1994

The refurbishment of Gants Hill was completed in early 1994. The 'Moscow Concourse' is seen here after modernisation with fittings sympathetic to the original design.

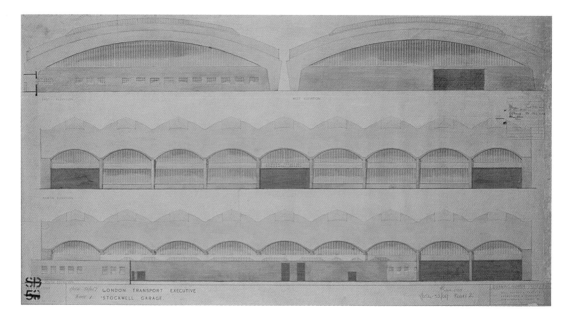

◑ Stockwell garage elevation
1952

◑ Stockwell garage
1953

Stockwell garage was built in 1952 to replace Norwood tram depot, although delays in clearing the site caused a change of plan, and it only partly fulfilled its original purpose. Post-war shortages of steel led to the choice of reinforced concrete for the structure, which fortuitously inspired the construction of a massive barrel-vault roof, illustrated in this drawing, to give a completely clear parking area.

This photograph taken in 1953, a year after the garage opened, shows the substantial roof supports and the barrel vault rising above them.

Victoria bus station
1970

Victoria bus station was equipped with a canopy, built using cantilevered beams of reinforced concrete, supported on a relatively small number of columns. Shallow 'valleys' provided for drainage. The resulting structure was inexpensive but gave a very large covered space for the comfort of passengers.

Newbury Park bus station
1949

Situated on the eastern extension of the Central line, Newbury Park station was carefully designed to include an integrated bus stand and shops. The design by J.D.M. Harvey was very much in line with London Transport's philosophy – modern, practical and fit for purpose. Sadly, construction was interrupted by the war, and the full scheme was never realised. The dramatic bus station was built in concrete, with a salmon pink ceiling and roof clad in copper.

Hounslow bus station
1970

Designed at the same time as Victoria bus station, this one at Hounslow also gave improved weather protection for waiting passengers.

GREEN LINE

On 17 July 1930 the Green Line started operating with three routes and some borrowed vehicles. It was a time when motor coaches were becoming acceptable as a comfortable alternative to rail travel, which in the days of steam could be a dirty experience.

The services proved popular with the public, and by 1960 they were carrying 36 million passengers a year. Vehicles used were initially single deck, the AEC Regal RF-type serving Green Line for over 20 years after its introduction in 1951. London Transport had long wished to improve the financial performance of Green Line by using double-deck vehicles. The stability and riding qualities of the Routemaster met the requirements. Two batches were built: 68 RMCs in 1962 and 43 longer RCLs in 1965.

In the later years of Green Line history, traffic congestion played a large part in defeating its principle of a cross-London coach service. Nowadays Green Line still exists, but the network is very different with few, if any, cross-London routes, and the coaches reaching destinations well outside the area of the map on the right.

⇨ **Green Line RF26**

In this photograph Green Line crews admire the first new arrival, RF 26, at Windsor garage. The Green Line RFs used the new underfloor-engined AEC Regal IV chassis with 39-seat bodies by Metro-Cammell.

☞ *The Country by Green Line*
by Barnett Freedman
Poster
1936

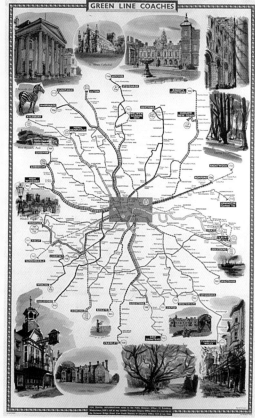

Golden Jubilee 1930–1980
1980

This poster, produced to celebrate the Golden Jubilee of Green Line in 1980, shows the development of the types of vehicles.

Green Line Coaches Map by B.G. Lewis
1961

This poster map shows the traditional Green Line network in 1961 at its zenith before subsequent decline.

Routemaster Green Line coach
1960s

An RMC at Harlow, ready to give passengers a very comfortable ride to Windsor.

◑ Locking up
1952

◑ Car cleaning
1954

Undergound stationman and British Transport Police officer locking up for the night, January 1952.

While most routine maintenance is done by depot staff during the night, train washing takes place during the day, although now it is fully automated.

◑ Overhead wire maintenance
1952

Maintenance work on trolleybus overhead wires was undertaken at night to minimise disruption to traffic and services. The inflexibility of overhead wires, and the expense and inconvenience of upkeep were major factors in the decision to scrap the trolleybus system in 1954.

↻ **Underground billposter**
1957

Advertising has been an important source of income for the Underground since its inception. While large posters can only be changed at night, smaller ones can be put up at any time.

◑ *A Secure and Interesting Job* **by Victor Galbraith**
1957

As attracting recruits became more difficult, recruitment posters, such as this one started to appeal to women as well as men, and to list the advantages of working for LT – although women were still not allowed to drive buses, and had no pension scheme at that time.

➲ *Men Conductors Required*
1951

The 1950s saw labour shortages in London, and a succession of LT recruitment campaigns. This poster shows a conductor still working with a ticket rack and Bell Punch machine. These were to be replaced by the first of the famous Gibson ticket machines in 1953.

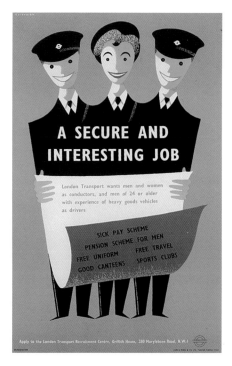

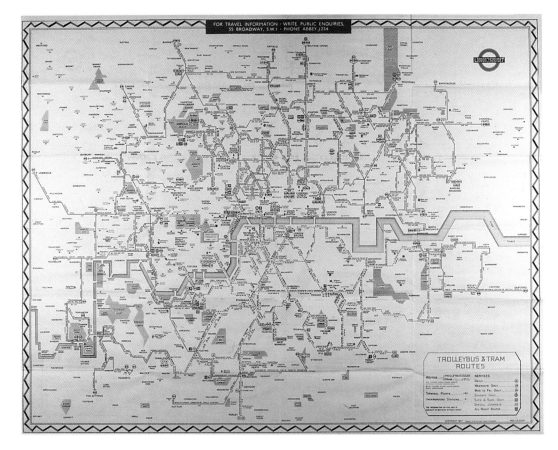

TROLLEYBUS & TRAM ROUTES

〇 Trolleybus and tram routes map
1947

This diagrammatic map shows the extent of the tram and trolleybus network in London in 1947. Conversion of the tram routes to trolleybuses had been halted by the Second World War at the point where all the north London routes, except those running through the Kingsway Subway, and a few in south London had been converted.

↪ Trams crossing Westminster Bridge, postcard
1947

In 1947 little had changed on Westminster Bridge for a decade. This postcard shows trams still crossing in numbers, while an LT bus travels towards Big Ben. At peak times 138 trams an hour would cross in each direction between Victoria Embankment and Westminster Bridge Road.

⌒ London's Last Tram Week

The tram routes that remained after the Second World War were converted to motor bus operation from October 1950. On this poster the funeral rites of the London tram system are officially announced for 5 July 1952.

⟳ Last week for Car 100

Car 100, which had been new to the East Ham Corporation in 1928, passes Eltham Church on its last week in service. Most of the trams carried 'Last Tram Week' posters, which proved a good publicity exercise since unprecedented loads were carried as Londoners took the opportunity of a last ride.

⌒ Crowds at Westminster as the last trams pass
1952

On the last night of tram operation, 5–6 July 1952, many crowds turned out at various places between London, New Cross, Woolwich and Abbey Wood to witness the last cars passing. Class E/3 car 1904 ends an era at Westminster. Those lucky enough to get on board crowd the interiors, and pennies are placed on the line to be bent by the tram to provide souvenirs.

Trolleybus at Holborn Circus

Class L/3 chassisless trolleybuses were originally concentrated mainly in east London, particularly on the routes serving Commercial Road. When those routes were converted to motor bus, the L/3s replaced older vehicles elsewhere. Here 1521 is seen at Holborn Circus after its transfer to Finchley Depot. This particular vehicle was significant in that, after its subsequent further transfer to Fulwell Depot in south-west London, it became the very last in service. It is now preserved at the East Anglia Transport Museum near Lowestoft.

Destruction of London's last tram at Charlton
1953

The 'tramatorium', as it became known, was at Penhall Road, Charlton, where most of south London's tramcars met a fiery end. The very last tram to be burnt was dealt with on 29 January 1953. In this photograph workmen watch the final funeral pyre in the otherwise deserted yard.

Last Tram Week tickets
July 1952

These tickets were issued on cars serving the remaining routes.

'Last of London's trams and trolleybuses'
1961

The Eagle comic of 9 September 1961 mourns the end of the trams and the forthcoming departure of trolleybuses from London streets.

LAST OF LONDON'S TRAMS AND TROLLEYBUSES

Farewell to London's Trolleybuses ticket
1962

Commemorative tickets were issued to mark the last day of trolleybus services in London, 8 May 1962.

Q1-class trolleybus, postcard
Photograph: J. S. Laker

127 trolleybuses were purchased by London Transport after the Second World War. Mostly they replaced the vehicles from 1931 that had opened the system in south-west London. They were the first standard vehicles in London to be eight feet wide, and special dispensation was obtained for their operation. They were renowned for the smoothness and quietness of their ride.

Trolleybuses waiting to be broken up at Colindale Depot
1962

A large number of London's trolleybuses were scrapped by the same firm as dealt with the tramcars, but this time at Colindale. This batch of trolleybuses came from the penultimate stage of withdrawal. In the snows of January 1962 they present a bizarre sight, as their booms seem to search for the wires that are no longer there.

CANTEENS AND CATERING

The idea of welfare services for staff is not new. The London General Omnibus Company provided basic, but for the time, welcome facilities for their staff. Before the Second World War 113 canteens served 42,000 meals daily; by 1949 180 canteens were serving more than the equivalent of 50 million meals a year, spread over the London Transport area of 2000 square miles.

Women provided much of the canteen workforce during and after the Second World War, and, together with clerical workers, these were the two dominant areas for female labour.

When the Baker Street Canteen and Training Centre opened in 1949, it was the first centre of its kind run by an industrial organisation. Until then training had been undertaken by the individual canteens, but it was now centralised at Baker Street, and 1200 catering staff were trained each year.

LT supplied mobile as well as static canteens for its staff. In the 1930s these took various forms, including converted NS-type buses and refreshment tricycles. LT's Food Production Centre was located at Purley Way, Croydon, and provided most of the food consumed at staff canteens. By the late 1970s this type of operation was under threat, with cheaper provision of more varied services from private contractors becoming increasingly attractive to a financially pressured management.

Cricklewood Bus Garage canteen
c. 1911

Staff canteen at Vauxhall
1951

The cantilevered canteen seating in this photograph was originally devised by London Transport's welfare office and redesigned by Douglas Scott with Roy Perkins *c.* 1950. It was designed to withstand heavy usage.

Turnpike Lane canteen
1933

The clean, elegant design of this 1930s canteen would not look out of place today.

Fulwell trolleybus depot canteen
1947

It was unusual to see an all-female staff in a canteen at this time. The depot cat also poses. London Transport 'employed' cats at many sites to control vermin, although staff canteens must have been an attractive distraction to duty.

CANTEENS AND CATERING

🎧 **Serving hot dinners to Permanent Way staff during the Second World War**
June 1943

🎧 **Interior of a mobile staff canteen**
1937–8

Interior of an NS-type bus which has been converted into a mobile staff canteen.

🎧 **Mobile staff canteen**
1937–8

Following the withdrawal of the NS-type buses in 1937, twelve were converted to staff canteens for use at sites where permanent facilities were unavailable.

🎧 **Catering Department tricycle**
1936

The refreshment tricycle has here been adapted by London Transport to provide sustenance to staff at a special event at Epsom, where more sophisticated facilities could not be justified.

⊙ *Diana, Goddess of the Harvest*

This sculpture by Edward Bainbridge-Copnall adorned the new Baker Street Training Centre and Canteen and symbolised the part played by women in the preparation of food.

⊙ **Baker Street Canteen and Training Centre**
1949

The Baker Street Training Centre provided ideal working conditions for training staff in all branches of canteen catering. The Training Centre and Staff Canteen overlooked Baker Street station.

⊙ **Catering staff making sausages, Food Production Centre at Croydon**
late 1970s

⊙ **Icing a cake at the Food Production Centre**
late 1970s

⌒ London from a Bus Top
1958

London Transport once took a distant interest in the provision of special sightseeing services, preferring visitors to use its normal bus and Tube services. Today its sightseeing services are used by most visitors to London.

⤴ 'Hop on a Bus' Map
1958

After the long strike in 1958 over bus staff pay and conditions, the famous 'Hop on a Bus' slogan was used for a two-year publicity campaign. Unfortunately, the effect of the industrial action was the withdrawal of many lesser-used services.

⌒ Sightseeing Bus Tours – Enjoy London Transport's Twenty Miles by Dobson (Clement Dane Studio)
Poster
1963

⤴ For Your Own Comfort Avoid Rush Hour Travel by Victor Galbraith
1958

London Transport issued posters with this message from the late 1930s onwards. It also encouraged passengers to 'stagger working hours'.

The traffic grows, and the Londoner's dependence on his public transport grows, too ⊖ New circumstances need new techniques, new methods ⊖ New automatically-driven trains for the Victoria Line ⊖ New buses for London's Red Arrow and flat-fare routes ⊖ New machines for automatic fare collection to save staff on road and rail ⊖ More station car parks ⊖ London Transport must change to keep pace with the constantly changing pattern of London on the move ⊖

Queuing at Charing Cross
1962

A very orderly bus queue by today's standards, outside the Charing Cross mainline terminus.

London Transport Must Change To Keep Pace
by William Fenton
1969

The end of the 1960s saw radical changes in London's transport system. Flat fare buses, increased station car parking and the new Victoria line are all part of the message of this poster.

These Vehicles Are Carrying ...
by Heinz Zinram
1965

A simple pro-bus message in a poster, using three dramatic photographs taken from a fire engine tower, at a time of falling passenger numbers and increasing congestion.

The 'Red Arrow' route
1966

In 1966 a new bus service was introduced. The 500 'Red Arrow' route between Victoria and Marble Arch or Oxford Street used single-deck buses with the emphasis on standing room. Flat fares and coin machines were used to speed loading.

◄RED ARROW►

ROUTE 500
**VICTORIA STATION-
MARBLE ARCH**

This is London's new limited-stop flat-fare bus service—specially designed buses with room for 48 standing and 25 seated, running every 3 - 4 minutes to clear quickly the rush-hour crowds over this short and heavily used route. Outside the rush hours the Red Arrows provide a circular service ideal for Oxford Street shoppers.

FESTIVAL OF BRITAIN

A 'Tonic to the Nation' was the slogan coined for the Festival of Britain in 1951 when the country was still recovering from the Second World War. The Festival's origins dated from 1947 when the Government decided that there should be displays to mark the centenary of the Great Exhibition of 1851. It was to focus on the arts, architecture, science, technology and industrial design. Early in 1950 Road Services Inspector, Edwin Bonny visited eight European countries to plan the route for a travelling exhibition by four LT buses to advertise the Festival. Seven members of staff were specially selected to accompany the buses, and the promotional 4000 mile tour proved a great success.

The South Bank site in the heart of London was to house the main exhibitions, but there were other sites throughout the country and a travelling exhibition. Selected by the Council of Industrial Design, the South Bank site featured one of London Transport's new aluminium-bodied Underground cars.

The tone of the exhibition was modern and forward-looking, reflected in structures such as the Festival Hall, the Dome of Discovery and the futuristic Skylon. The large crowds visiting the Festival posed a challenge for the services and staff of LT, which responded with special buses, trains and travel publicity.

◑ **London Transport buses being shipped to the Continent**

◔ **London Transport bus drivers in Belgium, promoting the Festival of Britain**
1950

◑ **Plaque describing the Underground car on display at the South Bank Exhibition**
1951

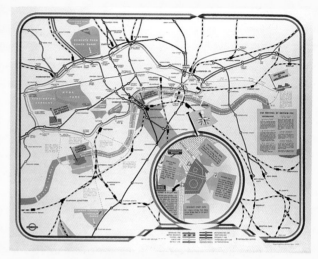

⊙ *Festival of Britain – Transport Information*
by Abram Games
1951

⊙ **The Festival of Britain Map showing**
special travel information
1951

The Festival of Britain ran from May to September
1951.

⊙ **New Underground car arrives at the**
Festival of Britain site
1951

London Transport's new aluminium bodied
Underground car was exhibited for the first time at
the Festival.

⊙ *Go by Green Line to the Festival* by Hans Unger
Poster
1950

⊍ **Tickets for special bus services for the Festival of Britain**
1951

⋒ **Scale model of the main South Bank Exhibition at the Festival of Britain**

⊍ **South Bank Exhibition by night**
1951

◠ **Robert Dell, 1900–1992**

Robert Dell worked in the Underground's signalling section from 1940 until 1969, rising to the position of Chief Signalling Engineer. He was a strong character in a powerful position, and had a major influence on both signalling and operating practice. The programme-machine method of controlling the signals was his invention, and his life's work culminated in the introduction of automatic signals and trains on the Victoria line in 1969.

◠ **Removing a programme-machine roll**
1962

The programme-machine method of controlling signals was devised by Dell. These unmanned machines ran the timetable on a punched roll, and feelers detected what had to be signalled and then did so.

◔ **Ealing Broadway signal cabin**
1951

Robert Dell was involved throughout his career with the modernisation of the Underground's signalling systems, which were frequently in advance of mainline railway practice. The first stage saw the move from traditional mechanically operated signals, exemplified by the large levers seen here on the left, to the miniature powered equipment, visible in the background. Later, steps were taken to automate the entire system and eliminate signal cabins completely.

SILVER TRAINS

In the 1950s the introduction of lightweight aluminium alloy in the construction of car bodies and underframes set a precedent for all subsequent surface and Tube rolling stock. Aluminium alloys are corrosive resistant which means that the bodies no longer have to be painted to protect them from the weather.

These unpainted aluminium cars were often referred to as 'silver' trains. As well as being more spacious and lighter in weight, the new trains featured rubber suspension and fluorescent lighting throughout.

One of the aluminium cars was exhibited at the Festival of Britain in 1951.

Aluminium train at South Kensington
1953

Aluminium was first used extensively on 90 new 'R' stock cars built by Metro-Cammell for the District line.

'Silver' train at Piccadilly Circus
1957

The first three 'silver' Tube trains were built in 1956 and entered experimental service on the Piccadilly line in 1957.

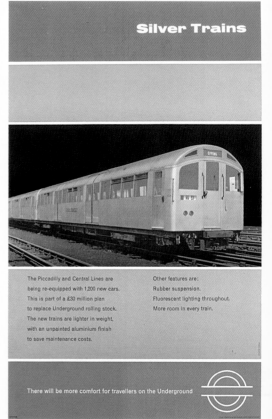

Silver Trains by Frank Overton
Poster
1960

In 1959, after the successful trials on the Piccadilly line, full scale production of the new aluminium Tube stock commenced. 1200 new cars were ordered for the Piccadilly and Central lines.

A60 stock leaving Rickmansworth in the snow
1962

All the old rolling stock on the Watford, Chesham and Amersham services was replaced between 1961 and 1962 with new aluminium 'A' (Amersham) stock.

Guard on Metropolitan line 'A60' stock

Air-operated doors on the A60 stock could be operated by passengers as well as the guard. Many aluminium stock trains were converted to one-person operation.

Silver stock interior

The interiors of 'silver' trains were lit by a fluorescent tube lighting system in the centre of the ceiling panels – a new innovation for Tube stock.

Interior of an A60 stock carriage

The new aluminium trains had spacious open saloons, in contrast with the old Metropolitan compartment stock.

Interior of a traditional Metropolitan carriage

The Metropolitan operated compartment stock before the introduction of the 'A' stock.

Your New MET by William Fenton
Poster
1960

This poster illustrates the planned improvements for the Metropolitan line. By 1960 the line had been electrified beyond Rickmansworth to Amersham and Chesham. New rolling stock was due to replace the old compartment stock and plans for the implementation of a four track system between Harrow and Watford were well underway, leading to improved stations, signals and rail bridges.

Commemorative ticket for the electrification of the Chesham branch line to Chalfont & Latimer
1960

A ticket to commemorate the operation of a special train to mark completion of the electrification of the Chesham branch, 10 September 1960.

Commemorative ticket for the end of steam shuttle operation
1960

Special tickets were issued for the commemorative run on the last day of steam operations between Chesham and Chalfont & Latimer, 11 September 1960.

Special train ticket
15 June 1962

The fast, impressive 'A' stock trains not only improved services but swept away the last traces of the regular use of steam traction for passenger services on the London Underground.

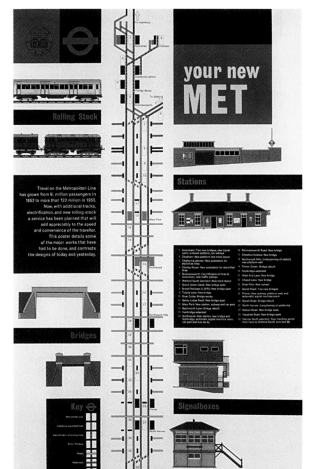

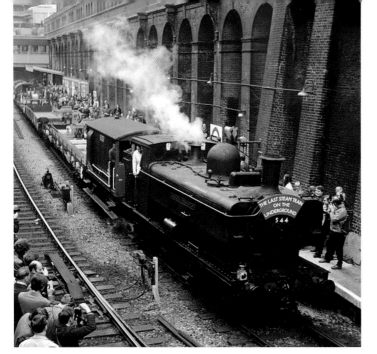

⟳ **End of the steam era**
1971

London Transport's steam passenger trains operated for the last time in September 1961, but a small fleet of steam locomotives was retained for hauling engineer's trains and for shunting in depots. These were finally withdrawn in June 1971 and the occasion was marked by a commemorative run from Barbican to Neasden depot and an exhibition of railway vehicles.

🎧 **'C69' stock at Euston Square**
1971

New 'C' stock cars were introduced on the Circle and Hammersmith and City lines from 1970 onwards. Four pairs of double doors per car greatly assisted the passenger flow on the busy Circle line.

⟳ **Commemorative ticket marking the end of steam**
1971

🎧 **Circle line train**
mid 1970s

Unpainted aluminium bodied 'C' stock on the Circle line.

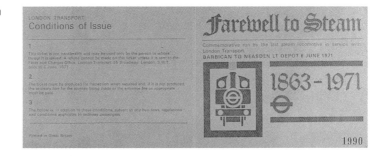

THE CORONATION

On 28 April 1952 it was announced that the Coronation of Her Majesty Queen Elizabeth II would take place on Tuesday 2 June 1953. London Transport immediately began planning its Coronation services. At the request of the Metropolitan Police, London Transport undertook to produce a special folder map for free issue in unprecedented numbers. In all, 32 press notices were issued on Coronation arrangements. To keep staff informed, supplements to the weekly road and rail traffic circulars detailed the arrangements for working stations, trains and buses.

An extension of the first part of the route, to enable parties of schoolchildren to view the procession, was announced on 8 December 1952. 33,000 children were selected from schools in and around London to line the Victoria Embankment, the last section of the Queen's route to Westminster, arriving on a network of special bus and train services between 6 and 8 am.

The Metropolitan Police requested that four central Underground stations be closed until after the procession and use of another seven be restricted. Ten minor stations were to be closed all day. Throughout central London, Underground stations were decorated in honour of the new Queen.

Normal bus services across the procession route ceased at midnight the night before, and from 3 to 7 am, special services carried people to termini near the route.

● ○ ***Long Live The Queen***
1953

This anonymous design was printed up in various formats, to be placed in bus stop timetable frames and inside and outside all London Transport vehicles, alongside information about Coronation day services.

○ **Coronation route map, cover**
1953

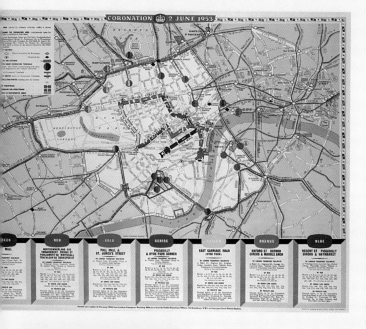

Special folder map, showing
Coronation procession route
1953

**Coronation day VIP
Underground ticket**
1953

The only train stopping at
Westminster on Coronation day was
a special service from South
Kensington for VIPs attending the
service at Westminster Abbey.

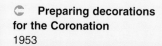

**Children arriving at Temple
Underground station for the
procession**
1953

**Preparing decorations
for the Coronation**
1953

**Installing a decorative
facia at Charing Cross station**
1953

THE ROUTEMASTER BUS

The Routemaster, introduced in 1959, was the culmination of more than 50 years of bus development in London Transport. Despite its traditional appearance, it was rigorously designed and contained much that was radically new.

The Routemaster was conceived in 1947, as the replacement for London's huge fleet of trolleybuses. Building on wartime experience of aircraft manufacture, it was designed around a monocoque aluminium alloy body, without a chassis. It would need to carry more people than existing buses, so that it could take over from the high-capacity trolleybuses. Above all, it was to be as light as possible, with high performance and low maintenance.

The first prototype took to the roads in 1956, and London Transport placed orders for some 800 Routemasters that same year. The first was ready in 1958, and full production finally started in 1959. In the end, AEC and their associate, Park Royal Vehicles, built a total of 2756.

Despite its success, production of the Routemaster ceased in 1968, in favour of rear engine one-person operated buses. Many were withdrawn during the 1970s and 1980s, but for busy routes the RMs had many advantages. In the early 1990s, 710 Routemasters were refurbished with new engines, lighting, upholstery and paintwork, to give the buses another 10 years working life. Many are still in service at the start of the new millennium.

🎧 **London's First Routemaster**
1956

Industrial designer, Douglas Scott, soon remodelled the rather bland bonnet and 'nose' of the first prototype Routemaster.

↻ **Notice displayed in the saloons of RM1**

> **THIS BUS** is the forerunner of the future London bus and is on trial to test its general performance and suitability.
> It is of lightweight construction, embodying special features contributing to your riding comfort.
> If you would like to make any comments on the 'Routemaster,' please send them to the Public Relations Officer, 55 Broadway, S.W.I.

➲ **Overhaul at Aldenham**

Routemasters were routinely overhauled at Aldenham works. Here, an RM body is being dismounted from its running units.

The Eagle **reveals all**
1956

Cutaway drawing from *The Eagle* comic revealing the Routemaster's technical details.

The tilt test

All double deck buses are tested for stability, with the top deck loaded with sand bags. The lightweight Routemaster easily passes the minimum requirement of 28 degrees.

Poplar garage
November 1959

The first fleet of new Routemasters stands ready to take over from trolleybuses.

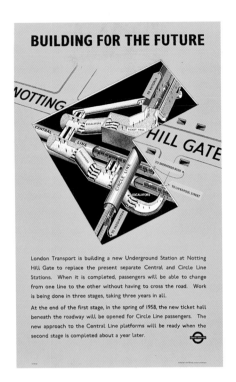

BUILDING FOR THE FUTURE

London Transport is building a new Underground Station at Notting Hill Gate to replace the present separate Central and Circle Line Stations. When it is completed, passengers will be able to change from one line to the other without having to cross the road. Work is being done in three stages, taking three years in all.

At the end of the first stage, in the spring of 1958, the new ticket hall beneath the roadway will be opened for Circle Line passengers. The new approach to the Central Line platforms will be ready when the second stage is completed about a year later.

◐ *Building for the Future* by Clement Dane Studio
Poster
1957

In 1957 an LCC road widening scheme at Notting Hill Gate necessitated the demolition of the existing Central and District line street-level stations. A combined sub-surface ticket hall was built beneath the road with an interchange link between platforms. Passengers could now avoid crossing a busy road between stations.

◐ **New Escalators at Notting Hill Gate**

The reconstruction of Notting Hill Gate station took place between 1957 and 1960 led by London Transport architects A. V. Elliott and A. D. McGill. The new escalators were the first to be fitted with aluminium side panels. Hard-wearing laminates were used on the suspended ceilings, and lightweight tiles on subway and platform walls. All these features would later be used on the Victorial line.

◐ **Improved facilities at Notting Hill Gate**

The new Notting Hill Gate ticket hall served Central, District and Circle line passengers. The light blue and maroon colour scheme extended across wall tiles, ticket booths and entrance barriers, maintaining a visual harmony throughout. The ticket hall also incorporated new concealed ceiling lighting behind 'egg-crate' grilles.

◖◗ Hammersmith station clock

The Hammersmith & City line station was rebuilt in 1907–9 to the design of GWR architect, P.E. Culverhouse. This fine clock is set in the stonework at the apex of the central gable. The man seen winding the clock (below) gives an idea of its size.

◗ Platform clock, North Acton station
1923

Typical of the early timber-cased clocks on the Underground system, this example survives on the platform at North Acton station.

◗ Sudbury Town station clock
early 1930s

By 1932, architect Charles Holden's brief was extended to incorporate station furniture in order to create a uniform style. An example is this clock at Sudbury Town station.

↻ Bar and diamond logo clock, Willesden Green station

The Metropolitan Railway clock outside Willesden Green station is based on the Metropolitan's bar and diamond logo. It dates from 1925 when the present concourse and booking hall, designed by C.W. Clark, were opened. The clock face is not the original.

↻ The World Clock, Piccadilly Circus station
1928

The World Clock was a feature of the new circular station ticket hall when it was opened in 1928. It is still in use, indicating the time of day in major cities throughout the world.

↻ Hammersmith station clock
1990s

When the District and Piccadilly Hammersmith station reconstruction was completed in 1994, attention had been paid to the smallest details. This included the station clock, which reflects the colours of the lines that serve the station.

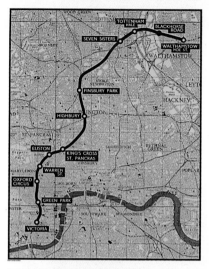

VICTORIA LINE

NOW UNDER CONSTRUCTION

🎧 *The Victoria Line Now Under Construction*
1962

🎧 **Victoria Line pick and shovel tunnelling at Highbury**
1964

This poster shows the route of the Victoria line, which cut across central London, joining the mainline termini at Victoria, Euston and King's Cross, and providing new interchanges with several other tube and mainline routes. Little changed from plans made originally in 1946.

a total of eight rotary diggers was needed, plus nine Greathead-type shields for running tunnels, and fifteen more for station tunnels.

Short lengths of tunnel were dug by hand under a shield no more sophisticated than Greathead's 1880s model. For long straight tunnels a mechanized digger was used.

🔄 **Victoria Line tunnel breakthrough**
1966

Tunnel workers pose on the cutting face of a rotary drum digger, at a running tunnel breakthrough point. Because work progressed simultaneously at various sites along the route,

🎧 Platform roundel at Victoria

Platform roundels on the Victoria line were screen-printed on glass and backlit to increase visibility

🎧 Platform view at Victoria
1969

The Victoria line stations were designed 'in-house' by the London Transport Design Panel, including LT Chief Architect Kenneth J. H. Seymour and design consultant Misha Black of the Design Research Unit. At

platform level, the predominant use of grey tiles was enlivened by the inclusion of colourful designs in the seat recesses, inspired by the station name or location. The Victoria station motif was designed by Edward Bawden.

🎧 Oxford Circus booking hall with AFC (Automatic Fare Collection) gates
1969

After two years of trials, it was decided to use automatic entrance gates activated by magnetically coded tickets at all Victoria line stations, to speed

passenger flow and improve the efficiency and economy of fare collection.

🎧 Control Centre at Cobourg Street
1969

Operation of Victoria line trains was automated for the first time. Signals and the coded electronic impulses in the track were co-ordinated from the central control room at Cobourg Street.

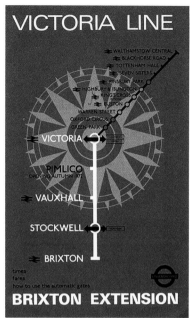

VICTORIA LINE

WALTHAMSTOW CENTRAL
BLACKHORSE ROAD
TOTTENHAM HALE
SEVEN SISTERS
FINSBURY PARK
HIGHBURY & ISLINGTON
KING'S CROSS
EUSTON
WARREN STREET
OXFORD CIRCUS
GREEN PARK

VICTORIA

PIMLICO
OPENING AUTUMN 1972

VAUXHALL

STOCKWELL

BRIXTON

times
fares
how to use the automatic gates

BRIXTON EXTENSION

1967 Tube stock, Victoria line

The Victoria line's major technical innovation was the introduction of automatic train operation (ATO). The driver has only to press two buttons to start the train and operate the doors, although he can override the system in case of emergency.

Brixton extension booklet

Part of the original plan for the line in the 1940s, the extension from Victoria to Brixton was finally authorised in October 1965, and opened in July 1971.

Platform tile motif at Stockwell station
1969

This tile motif by Abram Games at Stockwell recalls the name of a local landmark, the famous Swan pub.

Platform tile motif at Brixton station
1969

Staff enjoying Hans Unger's playful 'ton of bricks' visual pun on the platform at Brixton.

🎧 **Pimlico station ticket hall**

Aluminium panelling was used throughout on Victoria line escalators. In contrast to the uniform grey colour scheme of the platforms, the Victoria line ticket halls were enlivened by a variety of colours. The Pimlico ticket hall combined brown tiling with orange wall and door panels.

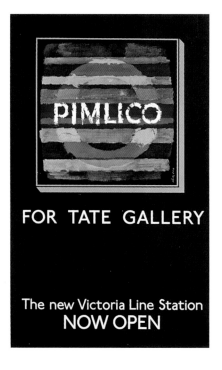

↻ *Pimlico for Tate Gallery* **by Hans Unger**
Poster
1972

Pimlico was a late addition to the Victoria line's extension to Brixton, and so was not completed until September 1972. Championed by the local council and residents, it was opened by the Mayor of Westminster.

🎧 **Platform tile motif at Pimlico**

The abstract Op Art design reflects the influence of British artist Bridget Riley, and signifies the station's proximity to the modern art collection at the nearby Tate Gallery (now Tate Britain).

**Blackhorse Road
Underground station
exterior**
1969

Blackhorse Road was the
only completely new surface
station on the line, designed
by in-house architects under
the direction of London
Transport's Design Panel
and Misha Black's Design
Research Unit.

**Sculpture at
Blackhorse Road station**
1969

The exterior to Blackhorse
Road was decorated by a
fibreglass relief by David
McFall, with a mosaic
surround by Trata Drescha.

CARIBBEAN RECRUITMENT

The 1950s saw labour shortages in London, and London Transport simply did not have enough staff to do the necessary jobs on the buses and Underground. A series of recruitment campaigns was launched, including a direct recruitment drive in the Caribbean. In 1956 London Transport opened up a recruiting office in Barbados. The Barbadian recruits were met on arrival in England and given welfare assistance and advice from a government official.

Similar offices were set up in Trinidad and Jamaica in 1966. Recruitment continued until 1970, by which time several thousand recruits had been lent the fare to travel to Britain by their governments. Many more made their own way from the Caribbean to find work with London Transport.

The West Indian culture has had an enormous impact on London, and the children of LT's West Indian recruits are part of a new generation of black Londoners active in all areas of the capital's life.

Recruiting in Barbados
1956

Charles Gomm, LT Recruitment Officer, with the first batch of applicants for London Transport's direct recruitment drive in the Caribbean.

Conductor and driver at Crystal Palace
Museum of London
1962

Platform guard, White City station
c. 1970

Driver and conductor
c. 1970

London Transport canteen assistant
1965

***Dancing in the Street* by Paula Cox**
1994

This poster was published to coincide with the Notting Hill Carnival, a celebration of Afro-Caribbean culture that is now a major event in London's calendar and reputedly the biggest street festival in Europe.

Dancing in the street

Enjoy open-air London by Tube

Carnival by Paula Cox
A new work of art commissioned by London Underground

Art on the Underground

© London Underground Limited

From Decline to Renaissance

A New Beginning
1970–2000

**Concourse of Southwark station on the
extended Jubilee line**
1999

From Decline to Renaissance
A New Beginning, 1970–2000

That's why the architecture is assertive, why the Extension stations' heroic aesthetics match fitness-for-purpose, why, in short, they are a great expression of confidence in the future. Our stations are big enough to accommodate the needs of Londoners for the next 100 years.

Denis Tunnicliffe, Chief Executive, London Transport, speaking about the Jubilee line extension in 'Delivering the JLE', *NCE Jubilee Line Supplement,* October 1999

Fly the Tube to Paris by Ian Southwood
Poster
1990

From 1 January 1970 financial and broad policy control of London Transport was transferred to the Greater London Council (GLC). It was logical to put London's public transport under the authority responsible for broader strategic planning in the metropolis, but control of major capital funding still rested with central government, which weakened the GLC's ability to make major changes from the start.

London Transport had always been expected to cover its operating costs through fares revenue and contribute to new capital expenditure met by loans or direct support from the Government. By the late 1960s this funding formula was no longer working as the fall in revenue income had begun to require an annual subsidy for London Transport. The GLC was soon looking for ways to minimise its need to subsidise London Transport and at the same time deal with the capital's growing transport problems. In the late 1970s and 1980s finding a solution to London's traffic problems that was acceptable to politicians, ratepayers and the travelling public became the major political issue in the capital and the subject of almost daily debate in the London evening papers.

It often seemed to Londoners that more effort went into argument over the control and funding of transport in London than its effective operation. The consensus over the best way forward which had enabled the

creation of London Transport to take place in the 1930s no longer existed fifty years later and the clear sense of direction had been lost. The transport body which had started life as a dynamic and forward looking organisation had become slow and reactive, no longer setting the pace in urban transport management.

Even before the political battles of the early 1980s over fares subsidy led to London Transport's removal from GLC control and private sector involvement in operations, there were moves to break down the monolithic structure of the organisation. Bus operation was split into geographical districts, which in turn became separate subsidiaries of London Buses when this was set up in 1984. When competition from the private sector was introduced a year later, and routes were put out to competitive tender, the London Buses' companies had to bid for the contracts against outside operators. By 1994 all the London Buses' companies had themselves been privatised, though regulation of services continued through the tendering process. The operation of all bus services in London is now undertaken by private companies, a complete reversal of the arrangements established in 1933.

London Transport's huge bus engineering operations were also wound down over this period with the eventual closure of both Chiswick and Aldenham works. Purchase and maintenance of vehicles is no longer undertaken centrally but is carried out by the individual bus operating companies. The idea of an increasingly standardised bus fleet for the whole of London has gone, although a large number of refurbished Routemasters are still in operation on central area routes over 40 years after their introduction. Over most of London the traditional open platform double-deckers with conductors have been replaced by a variety of driver-only vehicles ranging from double-deckers to midibuses and minibuses. The first generation of new buses bought 'off the peg' from manufacturers in the 1970s did not measure up to London Transport's traditional high standards, but by the 1990s the quality and reliability of new buses had improved considerably. By the turn of the century service changes, such as the use of frequent midibuses on new local routes instead of infrequent double-deckers, had contributed to the first sustained upturn in passenger numbers since the 1940s.

The Underground followed the completion of the Victoria line with two further

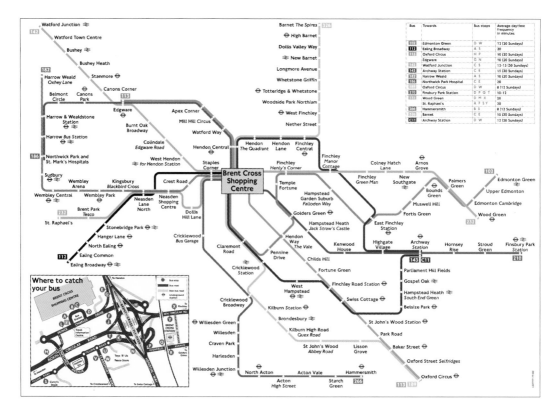

'Spider map', Brent Cross shopping centre
June 2000

Local bus maps, popularly known as 'spider maps', help to guide passengers at locations where service provision is complicated. The similarity of style to the Underground map is a tribute to that design's enduring simplicity.

capital projects in the 1970s. The Heathrow extension opened in 1977 and the first stage of the Jubilee line in 1979. There were also deliveries of new rolling stock to enable the last pre-war underground trains to be replaced. In the 1980s, however, as passenger numbers grew, new capital funding was limited to station refurbishment. The only completely new rail project was the Docklands Light Railway, much cheaper than a new underground line in the short term, but requiring upgrading and extension almost as soon as it was opened.

The London Underground was not included in the Conservative government's privatisation programme for British Rail in the 1990s, but a financial input from the private sector became a requirement for all major capital expenditure, from the acquisition of new trains to the construction of new lines. Public-private partnerships of this kind have been slow to develop but the Jubilee Line Extension, completed in time to serve the Millennium Dome's inauguration at the very end of the twentieth century, is an impressive demonstration of what can be achieved. The Croydon Tramlink project, London's second light rail scheme, which opened a few months later, is another example of this new approach to transport planning.

From 3 July 2000 planning and delivering the provision of transport facilities in London, and ensuring their integration, have been the responsibility of Transport *for* London (T*f*L). T*f*L is directed by a board of members appointed by the new Mayor of London, who chairs this successor body to London Transport. In the run-up to the first mayoral election, transport became one of the key issues, and immediately after his election Mayor Ken Livingstone confirmed that his top priority was 'breaking London's transport log jam. Provision of better and more reliable transport facilities heads Londoners' list for improving the quality of life in the capital.'

London Transport's final annual report, published as it handed over to Transport *for* London, showed clearly why this is so. Despite the information technology revolution, which may yet reduce the need for daily commuting to an office, travel demand in London is growing again, both for work and leisure. During the morning peak 85% of people travelling into central London use public transport. Underground journeys are at record levels and bus journeys the highest since the late 1970s. The number of passenger journeys overall in 1999/2000 by bus and Underground had reached more than 2.2 billion.

Clearly, continued investment in, and commitment, to improving London's

transport is essential. It means securing the resources to implement projects already on the drawing board, such as the major east-west CrossRail scheme, new improved interchange facilities at key points such as Vauxhall and Tottenham Court Road, and better quality bus travel with easy access vehicles and more bus priority measures to speed up journeys. An integrated transport strategy must also include better provision for pedestrians and cyclists, effective arrangements for taxi services and appropriate regulation of private cars which enables public transport to be an attractive, rather than an enforced, alternative.

There can be no certainties about future outcomes, but keeping the metropolis moving is in everybody's interest. Strategies that can help provide workable solutions to London's many transport issues must be a concern for all of us. There are good reasons for taking pride in the achievements of the past and for optimism over London's transport future.

The Millennium Bridge
2000
Architects: Foster and Partners
Engineers: Ove Arup & Partners

Formed by a single sweeping arc, the suspension bridge that links the City with the south bank of the Thames relies on the latest developments in structural technology to support its delicate design.

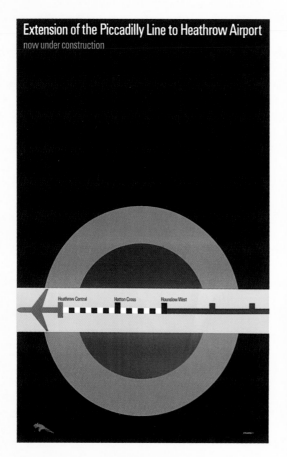

◑ *Extension of the Piccadilly Line to Heathrow* by Tom Eckersley
Poster
1971

◑ *Hatton Cross Station Now Open* by Walter Brian
Poster
1975

After years of planning, and more than six years' construction, the Piccadilly line's three and a half mile extension from Hounslow West to Heathrow Airport was opened by the Queen in December 1977. The first section, opened in 1975, went as far as Hatton Cross, which serves the airport's engineering and maintenance areas on the south-east edge of the airport.

For the Heathrow extension Sydney Hardy, London Transport's Chief Architect, set out to provide for a station identity that marked a departure from the neutral grey colour scheme of the Victoria line built ten years earlier. The platforms of the new Hatton Cross station incorporated motif designs of the former Imperial Airways 'Speedbird' emblem in a striking blue mosaic. This theme of flight was continued on the platforms of Heathrow Terminals 1, 2, 3 (previously Heathrow Central), for which Tom Eckersley produced graphics depicting the tail section of Concorde for the platform walls.

Heathrow Terminal 4, designed by London Transport Architect David Taylor, which opened on 12 April 1986, is in marked visual contrast to the earlier stations of the Heathrow extension. The walls and floors are finished in random marble panels, which incorporate restrained motifs. A stylised figure '4' is etched into the walls at regular intervals, in complete contrast to the colourful graphics provided at Hatton Cross and Heathrow Terminals 1, 2, 3, during the preceding decade.

'Speedbird' emblem incorporated into the mosaics on the platform at Hatton Cross station

Programme for the opening ceremony of the Heathrow Airport extension
1977

Platform at Hatton Cross station

Piccadilly line 1973 Tube stock

The Piccadilly line's new 1973 stock trains were designed with the Heathrow extension in mind.

Souvenir ticket
1977

Ticket for the opening of the extension by the Queen on Friday 16 December 1977.

Interior of a Piccadilly line 1973 stock train

The new cars serving the Heathrow extension incorporated additional luggage space for air travellers.

HEATHROW EXTENSION

Platform detail at Heathrow Terminals 1, 2, 3 station

Blue platform seating and fixtures reflect the Piccadilly line colours.

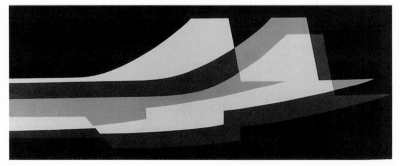

Design based on tail section of Concorde by Tom Eckersley

Platform at Heathrow Terminal 4 station

A figure '4' is etched into the cream-coloured marble walls.

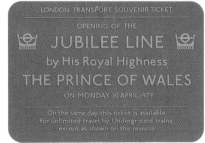

◯ Prince Charles opens the Jubilee line
1979

◔ Jubilee line platform at Baker Street station
1979

◯ Jubilee line souvenir ticket
1979

The long-awaited Fleet Line was renamed the Jubilee line in honour of the Queen's Silver Jubilee in 1977, and opened by her eldest son two years later.

The Jubilee line platforms utilised illuminated roundels and recessed lighting, with yellow bands across the platforms to accentuate the exits.

A souvenir ticket for the opening of the Jubilee line by the Prince of Wales on Monday 30 April 1979.

○ Charing Cross Underground station platform motif

David Gentleman took a graphic approach to the platform motif theme, using grainy black and white photographic images of Nelson's Column to emphasise the station's close proximity to Trafalgar Square.

○ Bond Street station platform motif

The Jubilee line followed the Victoria line stylistically in the use of tiled platform wall motifs at several stations. The design at Bond Street refers to the West One shopping complex that encompasses the entire station.

○ Ticket hall at Charing Cross station

The Jubilee line's designers opted for bright contrasting colour schemes, moulded fibreglass ticket windows and suspended slat ceilings incorporating fluorescent lighting in the new booking hall.

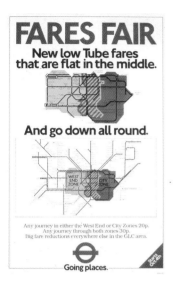

'Fares Fair'
1981

In 1970 control of London
Transport was passed to the
Greater London Council (GLC).
Fares were rising steeply, and in
1980 a radical Labour group
took control of the GLC under
the leadership of Ken
Livingstone, having campaigned
on the issue of cheap public
transport. Fares were slashed,
but only at the cost of subsidy
from the rates. Conservative
controlled Bromley Borough
Council successfully challenged
the move in court, and in 1982
fares increased by 96%.

**London Regional
Transport logo**
1984

In 1984 control of London
Transport passed from the
former GLC to a new co-
ordinating authority – London
Regional Transport (LRT). The
Underground and buses were set
up as operating subsidiaries.
Reflecting the new structure, the
operators carried on using their

**Catch these 'air-lines'
to update our lines**

Every weekday morning live broadcasts are made from our studio to these
radio stations with up-to-the-minute information concerning your journey.
So catch the latest tube news before you catch your train.

own version of the 'roundel' sign,
and LRT adopted its own logo.
After the 1987 King's Cross fire,
however, such a 'hands off'
relationship was felt to be
unacceptable. The LRT logo was
dropped, and LRT re-adopted

the red roundel, symbolising its
responsibility for the operational
side of the business.

*Catch These 'Air-lines' to
Update Our Lines*
1993

Commercial radio was tightly
regulated until the late 1980s.
London Transport was swift to
see the opportunities to be
gained by operating its own
studio and broadcasting through
existing radio stations, as
advertised in this poster.

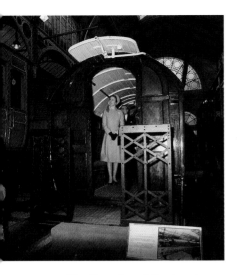

⌒ Opening of the London Transport Museum
1980

When London Transport was nationalised in 1948, the British Transport Commission (BTC) undertook a study of its inherited historical material. This led to the opening of the Museum of British Transport at Clapham in 1961. By 1968, however, the BTC had been abolished and the collections dispersed. After a few years on display at Syon Park in west London, the London Transport Collection found a new home in the former flower market at Covent Garden. The new London Transport Museum was opened on Friday 28 March 1980 by Princess Anne.

⟳ London's Transport Museum
1999

In 1993 the London Transport Museum was closed for nine months for a major refurbishment. New mezzanine floors were constructed to maximise the display space within the historic flower market building, which was refurbished at the same time. New thematic displays were installed, based on the collections, with a particular focus on the social history of London. The Museum re-opened on 12 December 1993. In 2000 the Museum became part of Transport *for* London and was renamed London's Transport Museum.

⟳ 'Mind the Gap'

The safety message 'Mind the Gap' has become as strongly associated with London Transport as the red double-deck bus. The poster seen here on the trackside wall at Bank station, cleverly positioned opposite a 'Mind the Gap' sign on the platform, was part of a major Underground safety campaign in 1987.

⟳ Dot matrix system at St James's Park station

A dot matrix train information system was trialled at St James's Park station in 1981. The first production model was installed on the Northern line at Euston in 1983.

Countdown

Countdown is an electronic system that provides 'real-time' information regarding the expected arrival of buses. The system has been progressively installed since 1992.

Accessible buses for the visually impaired

The LT Unit for Disabled Passengers develops improvements in accessibilty for disabled passengers. These include high contrast handrails for people with visual impairments.

Wheelchair access

One of the low-floor buses introduced experimentally in 1993.

Improvements for visually impaired passengers

The specially raised tactile strip seen here near the platform edge assists blind passengers. New Tube trains and stations on the extended Jubilee line have introduced audio announcements for visually impaired users and display screens for hard-of-hearing customers.

Dial-a-Ride

Among London Transport's many statutory responsibilities is the operation of Dial-a-Ride services for the disabled and elderly. The small midibus vehicles are equipped to carry wheelchairs and are available by appointment.

'Getting around London' leaflet

Published in Gujarati, this leaflet was designed to encourage the non-English speaking Asian community to make greater use of public transport.

Shepherd's Bush station platform
1986

The interior redesign of Shepherd's Bush on the Central line, by Chapman Lisle Associates, was based on a rural theme, reinforced by a booking hall mural by Julia King.

Central line platform at Bond Street station
1982

The Central line platforms at Bond Street station were the first to be redecorated as part of a large-scale programme of station modernisation undertaken by London Underground in the 1980s. Several designers and artists were commissioned to redesign the platforms and public circulation areas of central London stations according to themes. The platform name frieze photographed here at Bond Street hides a plethora of cabling and wiring.

Circle line and Hammersmith and City line platforms at Baker Street station
1990

This platform formed part of the world's first underground railway in 1863. The station platforms were cosmetically restored in the 1980s following over a century of extensive alterations. The walls have been stripped back to the original brickwork, and the ventilation recesses have been exposed. The addition of replica platform furniture and the installation of lighting that mimics daylight create an impression of what London's earliest underground stations were like – minus the steam and smoke.

Charing Cross Underground station platform
c. 1980

David Gentleman was responsible for the decoration of the platforms of two of the three lines serving Charing Cross station. The Northern line platforms are decorated with unusual, platform-length murals showing the construction of the mediaeval Eleanor Cross, which gives the station its name. The images were derived from original wood blocks engraved by the artist, which were then photographically enlarged on to laminate sheets.

○ Bakerloo line platform at Charing Cross
1983

A montage of images from the nearby National Gallery and the National Portrait Gallery were selected by Richard Dragun and June Fraser of the Design Research Unit.

◐ Refurbished Northern line platforms at Embankment station
c. 1988

Designed by Robyn Denny, the theme of multi-coloured streamers was inspired by the idea of celebration associated with the proximity of the river and the site of the 1951 Festival of Britain. The colours of the streamers represent the four lines served by the station, whilst the curved streamer represents the river.

○ Holborn station refurbishment
1985–9
Allan Drummond designed large vitreous enamel panels with images from the nearby British Museum's collections for both the Central and Piccadilly line platforms at Holborn.

UNDERGROUND DECORATION

**Motifs on the theme of an arch by Annabel Grey
on Marble Arch station platforms**
1985

Piccadilly line platforms at Finsbury Park station
1986

Annabel Grey designed these mosaics for the Finsbury Park station platforms, which had been in use since 1906.

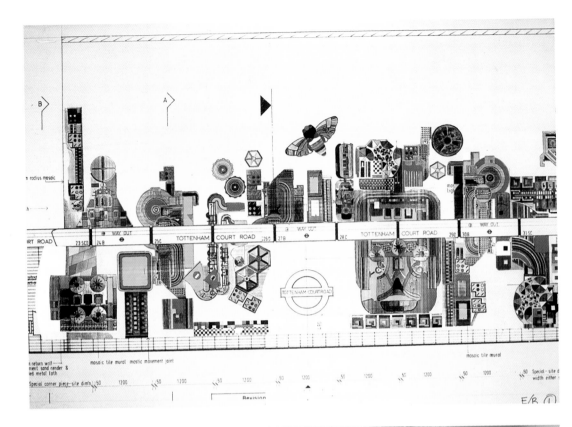

Tottenham Court Road station, designs by Eduardo Paolozzi
1983–5

Of all the artworks designed as part of the station refurbishment programme, the works at Tottenham Court Road, commissioned from the artist Eduardo Paolozzi, excite most comment – they are either loved or loathed. The artist's design conception is continued through passageways, up the escalators and into the ticket hall.

Wapping station
1998

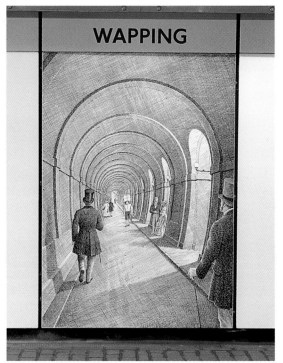

During the extended closure of the East London line from 1995, to allow for essential engineering works, the stations were extensively refurbished. Wapping was treated to platform murals showing the original Thames Tunnel and an archive illustration of the station, taken when freight traffic shared the line with Underground passenger trains.

🎧 **Sherlock Holmes statue**
1999

A statue of Conan Doyle's fictional detective, Sherlock Holmes, was commissioned by the Abbey National Building Society, whose London offices are on the site of his mythical home, 221b Baker Street. It was unveiled outside Baker Street station in September 1999. The statue is seen here with the Metropolitan Railway monogram on the wall behind it.

🔄🎧 **Sherlock Holmes motifs**

The image of Sherlock Holmes dominates Baker Street Underground station. The tiled silhouette motif on the Bakerloo line platforms and in passageways was designed by Michael Douglas and printed on to tiles by Pamela Moreton. The Jubilee line platforms at Baker Street feature murals illustrating famous Holmes stories.

⊙ Hammersmith, Piccadilly and District line platforms
1993

The rebuilding of Hammersmith station, serving the District and Piccadilly lines, was part of the Hammersmith Centre West development. The project included a new bus station and huge shopping complex. A second booking hall and platform canopies were designed by Minale Tattersfield & Partners.

⊙ Roundel platform seat at Hammersmith station

The new station design includes elaborate modern steel and glass platform canopies, but retains elements from the 1930s such as the clerestory booking hall windows, glazed rounded waiting rooms and this original platform seat from 1932.

⊙ Platform waiting room at Hammersmith station

The design was inspired by the earlier work of architect Charles Holden.

◑ Monument station concourse
1996

As part of the extension of the Docklands Light Railway to Bank, London Underground embarked on a major refurbishment project which involved a major reconstruction of the ticket hall and concourse areas at Monument.

◑ Travolator, Bank station
1960

The original exit from the Waterloo & City line at Bank station had long proved inadequate. The solution was to build a moving walkway paralleling the existing tunnel. It opened on 27 September 1960.

◑ The longest escalator, Angel station
1992

Angel station was completely rebuilt in 1992. The old lifts were replaced by six new escalators. Using the most up-to-date technology, these escalators were the longest in Britain and considerably speeded up passenger flow at this deep-level station.

↻ Hillingdon station platform canopies
1994

Similar to those at Hammersmith, the steel and glass canopies at Hillingdon, by Cassidy Taggart, are designed to let in as much natural light as possible on the platforms. A whole new surface level station was required at Hillingdon due to the realignment of Western Avenue (A40). It was completed in 1994.

⌒ Shadwell station
1983

A completely new station entrance and ticket hall were built in Cable Street to replace the existing East London line ticket hall in Watney Street. The new building was designed by London Transport Architects Department and built in 1983. The ticket hall, clad in sloping anti-sun glazing, forms a punctuation mark at the end of Dellow Street, whereas the side cheeks and rear are completed in brickwork to match the adjacent buildings.

↻ Hillingdon platform canopy detail

Aldersgate and Barbican station
1950s

Artist's impression of the station with original platforms and glass and iron roof, which somehow survived the heavy bombing of the City during the Blitz. The roof was removed in 1955 at the start of major works leading to the redevelopment of the station and surrounding area, known as the Barbican.

Electricity substation, Elephant and Castle

London Transport always aimed to ensure that even mundane buildings made a positive contribution to their environment. This electricity sub-station was given an unusual finish as part of a programme of improvements to the Elephant and Castle area.

Platforms at Barbican station
c. 1972

The original walls of the 1865 station are all that remain of Aldersgate and Barbican station following the massive redevelopment of the area in the late 1950s and '60s. The station was renamed Barbican in 1968 following realignment of the Circle line to introduce a more direct path between Moorgate and Aldersgate stations.

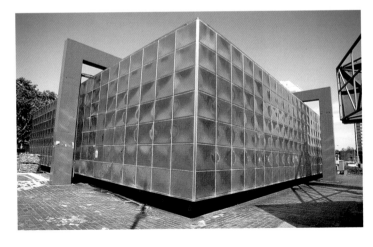

⌒ **Underground car covered in graffiti**

⮌ **Removing graffiti**

Weathering of the unpainted aluminium panels, combined with damage from graffiti vandals led to a marked deterioration in the appearance of many trains. Also, cleaning off graffiti caused damage to the bodywork of unpainted aluminium trains and was expensive. Therefore, in the 1990s, it was decided to revert to painting all Underground stock as part of a major train refurbishment programme.

◐ Refurbished 'C' stock train

The development and application of a corporate livery led to a sustained improvement in the appearance of the Underground's trains, as this view of a refurbished 'C' stock train at Hammersmith shows.

◑ Refurbished car interior

Two welcome features resulting from the refurbishment of the Metropolitan line fleet have been the addition of windows in the car ends and the use of removable seat covers, which minimises the risk of a train being cancelled if seats are soiled or damaged.

◑ Refurbished Piccadilly line train

An intensive programme of train refurbishment has improved customer satisfaction on the lines. Here a refurbished 1973 stock train is seen ready for use on the Piccadilly line.

◐ New seating

The new, brighter seat moquette used on the Piccadilly line trains reinforces the line's corporate identity and has proved to be durable as well as attractive.

Interior of refurbished 1972 stock on the Bakerloo line

Improvements to the refurbished 1972 stock cars included elegant draught screens, newly designed seat covers, decor in the 'line' colours and fixed grab rails.

Car interior refurbishment

The 1969 and 1977 trains used on the Circle, Hammersmith and City and District lines have all been refurbished. Internally, improved lighting, seating and support for those standing has been matched by the addition of windows at the trailing end of driving motor cars and at both ends of trailer cars. Like other refurbished stocks, grab rails have been finished in a contrasting colour to assist the partially sighted.

MOQUETTE

London Transport has always believed in providing passengers with comfortable seating on both its trains and buses, with seat coverings made in hard-wearing woollen moquette. Originally fabric designs were 'off the peg' from standard ranges, but in the 1930s Frank Pick began commissioning artists such as Enid Marx to design fabrics for London Transport's vehicles. This tradition has continued in the refurbishments of the 1990s, in which the colours of the seating moquettes reflect the line colours, thus reinforcing the identity of the line. Each moquette pattern forms an integral part of the car's colour scheme, uniting interior panel work, arm rests, grab poles and hand rails. The bold and colourful designs of the refurbished trains are intended to be bright and welcoming, replacing the ageing grey and blue interiors of the 1960s and '70s.

Central line 1992 Tube stock

Bakerloo line refurbished 1972 Tube stock

Jubilee line 1996 Tube stock

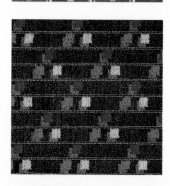

Circle and Hammersmith and City lines refurbished 1969 and 1977 stock

Victoria line refurbished 1967 Tube stock

Metropolitan line refurbished 1962 surface stock

◔ Waterloo and City line trains

The links between London Underground and the British Rail 'Network South East' operation were strengthened with the delivery of a new fleet of trains for the Waterloo and City line in 1993. The stock utilised the 1992 Tube stock design, and management by the Central line team was a natural development when London Underground assumed control of the line in April 1994.

◔ D78 stock at Earl's Court station

The arrival of the new 'D78' stock on the District line introduced to the Underground the concept of wide single-leaf doors throughout the train. These provided improved reliability over the more common double-door designs.

◔ New Jubilee line stock at Green Park station
1980s

The Jubilee line to Charing Cross was initially operated with 1972 stock trains. These were progressively replaced by the 1983 Tube stock, which displayed a number of features introduced on the District line, including the single-leaf doors and new interior colour schemes.

⌒ ⌒ New Central line trains

Now a familiar sight for Central line travellers, the 1992 stock introduced a number of features new to the Tube fleet. These included externally mounted doors equipped with customer open and close buttons, in-cab closed-circuit television for coverage of platform areas and wider communicating doors between cars. These trains were a development of the best features of the 1986 prototypes.

⌒ Poster heralding three prototype trains
1988

The experience gained from the operation of three 1986 prototype Tube trains led to the final design adopted for the current Central line fleet. The prototypes were built by two manufacturers and operated on the Jubilee line between May 1988 and August 1989.

 UNDERGROUND

Take a brand new car to work tomorrow

A prototype 1990s Underground train is now making trial runs on the Jubilee Line. It's quicker, smoother and offers many new features. Lighter, brighter cars, interior signs indicating next station and destination, even a communications link with the driver. Take a test drive towards tomorrow's Underground.

Contract cleaner at Gloucester Road station
14 May 1996

London Transport's first woman bus driver
1974

Jill Viner became London Transport's first female bus driver in 1974.

London Transport recruitment poster
1980

Legislation in 1974 gave women the right to occupy jobs previously done by men. By 1975 London Transport employed 20 women drivers and 8 women inspectors.

Group Station Manager at Hammersmith station
1999

Bus conductor
1994

This conductor is wearing the new uniform and using the 'Clipper' ticket machine introduced in 1993.

London Transport's first woman bus engineer
1984

Helen Clifford, London Transport's first woman bus engineer, working at Holloway Garage.

⟲ London Underground's first woman Tube driver
1978

Hannah Dadds, London Underground's first woman Tube driver climbs into the driver's cab. Women guards were also employed by London Transport in the late 1970s.

⟳ *More Cops Less Robbers*
1993
Photograph: Tapestry

The British Transport Police, from a poster assuring the public that more police than ever were patrolling the Tube system.

⟲ Underground staff pose in their new uniforms at Westminster station
21 January 2000

⟳ British Transport Police officer with a police dog
1994

○ **Bus driver and Inspector at Cricklewood Garage**
1984

○ **Remembrance Sunday at the Cenotaph**
1991

Until 1998 London Transport was the only non-military organisation to march at the Cenotaph. Many London Transport employees were called up during the First and Second World Wars. Quite a number served in the 84th (London Transport) Heavy Anti-Aircraft Regiment, Royal Artillery.

○ **The Emergency Response Unit**

Emergency Response Unit (ERU) team and ER Manager Joan Saunders-Reece at the ERU Training Centre at Acton. The ERU provides highly trained fast-response teams, capable of dealing with all manner of problems on the Underground, from train collisions to suicides.

○ **The Pit Cleaner**

Pit cleaner Eugene Abiona clears rubbish from the tunnel entrance at Vauxhall station, 1998.

THE RIVER

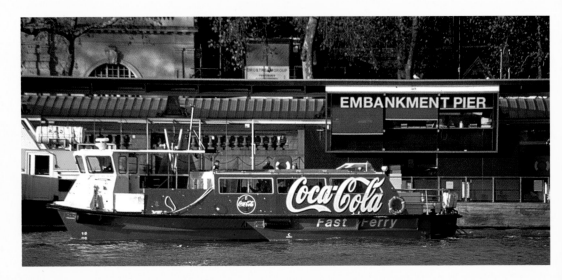

The River Thames is one of London's greatest assets, varying in character from gentle and pastoral in the west, defining London's great monuments at its centre, and a mature waterway that was once a key commercial centre, in the east.

London River Services, a new division of London Transport, assumed responsibility for licensing boats, river services and piers from the Port of London Authority in 1998. However, provision of river services was not new to London Transport. An emergency riverboat service was provided in 1940 when there was severe disruption to tram and trolleybus power supplies caused by bombing during the war. These river services operated between Woolwich and Westminster for a short time. LT also organised coach tours to places of interest, which included combined river and road tours that took in the delights of the Thames in the 1950s.

Now that London River Services has become part of Transport *for* London, new and refurbished piers are being provided, and operators are encouraged to introduce new boats and services.

🎧 **White Horse fast ferry at Embankment Pier**
1999

White Horse Ferries purchased two fast new boats for their service between the rebuilt Embankment Pier and Canary Wharf. These boats can carry 60 people.

Waterside London by **Hans Unger**
Poster
1972

Thames river services

Times and fares Spring/Summer 2000

See London from
a different point of view...

Leaflets for Thames River Services

Traditionally, marketing of the numerous river services was left to individual operators, but London River Services speedily introduced new comprehensive timetables and a map of services in 1999.

London Transport's Thames Passenger Service in operation on 14 September 1940

This photograph shows a conductor issuing tickets on board London Transport's passenger service. Train, bus and tram tickets were all valid for the appropriate journey on the river service.

a day by THE RIVER

A LONDON TRANSPORT PUBLICATION

***A Day by the River* leaflet**

London Transport always understood the popular appeal of the Thames, and numerous leaflets were produced to encourage passengers to enjoy its diversity.

***Simply River by Tube and bus* by John Miller**
July 2000

This is the very last art poster commissioned by London Transport. John Miller, famous for his striking treatments of sea, sky and landscape, was judged to be a fitting artist for this notable brief. The former power station, now transformed into the Tate Modern art gallery, is one of the most exciting additions to the life of a vibrant capital.

Simply River by Tube and bus

DOCKLANDS LIGHT RAILWAY

Docklands Light Railway (DLR) was opened in 1987 with the aim of revitalising the moribund Docklands. Tower Gateway station opened in 1987 as the original DLR City terminus, close to Fenchurch Street mainline station and Tower Hill Underground station. The first DLR extension to Bank in 1991 improved access to the City and the main Underground network. A further extension to Beckton followed in 1994.

The trains on the DLR were designed with easy access in mind and built to high engineering standards. The trains are driverless, and staffed by a 'train captain' whose main task is to operate the doors, check tickets and ensure the safety of the passengers.

London Transport operated the DLR from its inception until 1992 when it was transferred to the London Docklands Corporation. An extension to Beckton opened in 1994 and a further extension to Lewisham in 1999. The integrated station designs are light and modern, using durable materials. The DLR transferred to Transport *for* London in 2000.

DLR Route Map

🎧 ***Architecture in Docklands* by Neil Gower**
1990

In 1990 Docklands Light Railway commissioned several posters, such as this one by Neil Gower, celebrating features of interest in an area at that time little known by Londoners or visitors. The new railway was keen to promote this pumping station on the Isle of Dogs, as a 'post-modern' building worthy of a special journey.

↻ **Docklands Light Rail map**

Catch the Light

Docklands Light Railway.
Britain's newest railway will soon make
all the running in Docklands.

Docklands

🖝 *Catch the Light*
1987

🖝 **Canary Wharf DLR station**

Canary Wharf lies at the heart of
the Docklands Light Railway
network. The soaring tower
blocks of this major development
demanded special treatment for
the station, which is crowned by
a spectacular arched glass
canopy.

🖝🖝 **Tower Gateway DLR station**

A distinctive rotunda provides street-level
prominence to this elevated station, which is
reached via escalators and stairs. Many design
elements used on the station echo other DLR
stations, but on a larger scale.

**Train at Canary Wharf
DLR station**

**Leaflet promoting the DLR
extension to Beckton
1994**

Docklands Light Railway, South Quay

South Quay Plaza, seen here in the background, was the first
major new office development to be occupied on the Isle of
Dogs.

A new design for ticket gates

The slim supports on these modern gates at Whitechapel station allow extra width for the passage of buggies and trolleys, whilst the paddles prevent people from jumping over the gates.

Early ticket gates

This example of the early tripod gates at Dagenham Heathway station dates from the late 1960s. They were originally installed mainly on the Victoria line. They were soon replaced because it was discovered that the public could easily climb over them.

Think What You Save When You Buy a Ticket
1993

London Transport had for many years periodically exhorted its less honest customers to buy tickets or face fines and criminal

records. A shift in emphasis to more shocking tactics occurred in 1993, when a campaign loosely based on the work of the Norwegian artist Edvard Munch attempted to make fare dodgers nervous.

Travelcard
1983

Travelcards revolutionised people's attitude to public transport in London as passengers no longer had to buy separate tickets for each leg of the journey. They could also use them on both buses and the Underground. From 6 January 1985 Travelcards could also be used on the London suburban network.

Think what you save when you buy a ticket.

Take your Travelcard to the Pictures
1987

Travelcards were initially issued for seven days or longer, but one-day tickets were soon introduced, making a significant contribution to the increase in the number of people using public transport.

Smartcard Trials I
1992

The first trials of contactless Smartcards took place in 1992. Local bus route 212 from Walthamstow to Chingford was chosen for the first service trial of the new technology.

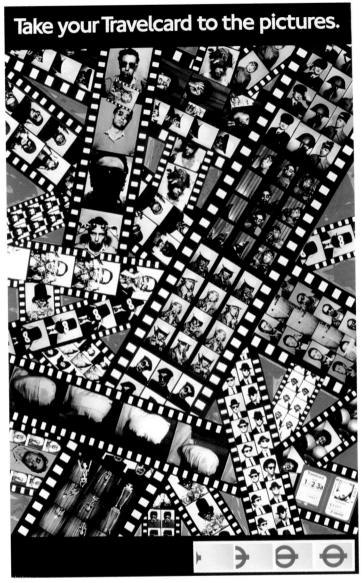

Take your Travelcard to the pictures.

Smartcard Trials II
1994

The Harrow bus network was chosen for an extended service trial of Smartcards. In February 1995 'stored value' tickets were introduced, known as Farecards. The trial ended in December 1995 and its success will lead to the introduction of Smartcards throughout the network.

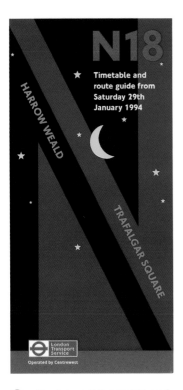

🎧 **Centrewest timetable and route guide for night buses**
January 1994

🎧 **Night bus number N26 at the Lloyds building in the City**
October 1992

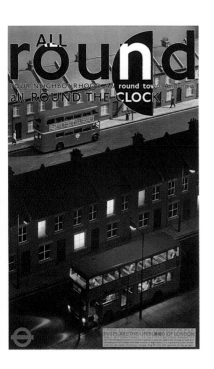

🔄 **London Buses poster promoting night and 'round the clock' buses**
1990

Night buses first ran in 1913 (and trams even earlier), but night bus services were greatly expanded from the mid-1980s for a new leisure market.

🔄 **Christmas and New Year travel leaflet**
1995

Christmas and New Year have now become an almost seamless holiday period, requiring special services and timetables for Tubes and buses.

Christmas and New Year travel

Travel around town with London Transport

Tube and Bus services
between Sunday 24 December 1995
and Monday 1 January 1996

↻ **Interchange sign, Stratford station**

This sign at Stratford station on the extended Jubilee line indicates an interchange with mainline railways, the Docklands Light Railway and the London Underground. In fact, it links several separate rail systems, including the North London line, the Central line, and part of the national rail system running parallel to it. The Channelsea river also runs under part of the site. The new Stratford bus station lies to the south-east of the station.

∩ **Booking hall at Liverpool Street Underground station**
1992

The large open space of the new booking hall at Liverpool Street Underground station, which was designed by London Underground Architects in 1992 when the mainline station was rebuilt.

↻ **Concourse of the newly reconstructed Liverpool Street mainline station**

↻ **LT roundel at Hammersmith interchange**

This sign is situated at the busy Hammersmith interchange between the District and Piccadilly lines, the Hammersmith and City line, and the new bus station.

How to get to the Dome by public transport

Buses • Underground • National Rail
Docklands Light Railway • River Boats

The Millennium Experience at the Dome, Greenwich

↻ *How to Get to the Dome* **leaflet**
2000

The Docklands Light Railway and the Jubilee Line Extension were both designed to improve transport infrastructure in the redeveloped docklands. As well as providing an important deadline for the completion of the Jubilee line, the Millennium Dome required close integration of new and existing transport options.

SIMPLY POSTERS

The Art on the Underground poster programme has gradually evolved since its inception in 1987, from a series designed to improve the Underground environment, to a comprehensive marketing campaign involving posters, leaflets and showcards. Poster subjects are decided up to two years in advance, and sophisticated campaigns are organised to encourage greater off-peak use of London's Transport and travel to a variety of venues and events. London Transport's marketing campaign for the last few years has been based around the 'Making London Simple' theme, which continues on into the new millennium.

Simply Flora & Fauna by Tube and bus by Peter Welton
Poster
1999

Simply Music by Tube and bus by Paul Waring
1999

This, the first art poster to be produced as a digital image, was commissioned from Paul Waring, now enjoying international acclaim as one of Britain's leading artists.

Simply Alfresco by Tube and bus by Glynn Boyd
Harte
Poster
1998

Simply Nightlife by Tube and bus by Dan Fern
Poster
1988

Simply Alfresco by Tube and bus

Painting commissioned by London Transport from Glynn Boyd Harte.

This poster is available from the London Transport Museum, Covent Garden Piazza.
For details of great places to eat out of doors visit us at http://www.londontransport.co.uk

Supported by
TDI

Simply Spring by Tube and bus by Reg Cartwright
Poster
1988

Simply Showbiz by Tube and bus by
Lesley Saddington
Poster
1998

◑ Fairways London taxi

There are around 14,000 Fairways operating in London. Many are no longer painted the traditional black. Some are red or blue, and others have all-over advertising, making them bold and colourful additions to London's streets.

◐ London taxis

London taxi cabs are famous all over the world. Most of the taxis in this photograph are Fairways, which have a distinguished ancestry. The Fairway is based on the FX4, which first appeared in London in 1959 and remained in production until 1997. The design has been modified over the years, and the latest models can accommodate five passengers.

ⓘ Bus in a traffic jam
1992

This bus is stuck in a traffic jam in Trafalgar Square, despite the exhortation on its side to 'Take one to relieve congestion'.

ⓒ London Buses poster promoting family bus travel
1990

This poster was produced to encourage families to travel by bus, to exploit the better views from the top deck and to avoid the traffic by using bus lanes.

🎧 **New bus lane at Piccadilly Circus**
1972

Bus-only lanes were introduced in 1968 to keep buses moving, thus reducing delays caused by traffic congestion. A contra-flow lane came into use in Piccadilly in April 1973. The number of bus lanes has increased considerably since then.

🎧 **Driver's eye view of the bus lane**
April 1993

🔄 **Traffic-free streets**

Transport developments have opened up cities for pedestrians and enabled café society to flourish. This elevated Docklands Light Railway bridge gives a futuristic feel to Docklands streets, whilst the traffic-free zoning makes the area more relaxed and informal.

CROYDON TRAMLINK

Originating in a joint British Rail/London Transport study, the 18-mile network known as Tramlink opened in 2000 using existing British Rail lines, a disused rail trackbed, newly built reserved track and new lines laid around the streets of central Croydon. The trams were built in Vienna by Bombardier Transportation, the vehicle manufacturing member of the consortium. The two-section articulated units are based on a design used in Cologne since 1995.

Rail-style tickets are sold via ticket vending machines, and passengers are expected to have a valid ticket on boarding. Vending machines are provided at each stop. The trams are bright red, whilst green is used on tram stops and publicity, being the corporate colour of Croydon Borough Council, which was an enthusiastic partner in developing and funding the system for the Tramlink.

Croydon Tramlink system map
May 2000

Key

- **Tramlink Line 1:** Wimbledon – Elmers End, every 10 minutes
- **Tramlink Line 2:** Croydon – Beckenham Junction, every 10 minutes
- **Tramlink Line 3:** Croydon – New Addington, every 6-7 minutes
- **Connecting rail service**

Croydon tram

A two-section articulated tram unit during test running on one of the stretches of reserved tracks, on which speeds of up to 50 mph can be achieved.

Tram Number 2530

The first of the new trams, number 2530, runs through the Croydon town centre en-route to Beckenham Junction. CentreWest London Buses, as the operating member of the consortium, showed a sense of history by numbering the cars sequentially following on from the last of the first generation of Croydon trams withdrawn 50 years earlier.

link ⊖ Tramlink ⊖ Tram	
17APR00	11:09
From: East Croydon	TRM01
Child Single	40p
To: Beddington Lane	000003132
ble for inspection	Not transferable Retain ticket for inspection	Not transfer Retain ticke

Tramlink Travelcard

Redesigned bus services
2000

Considerable redesign of bus services was made possible by Tramlink, including a new interchange at Addington Village, where new feeder bus routes from various parts of the New Addington estate link with the trams, providing fast access to Croydon.

⌒ **Dial-A-Bus**
Photograph: Ian Bell

One of the experiments carried out in the 1970s with the financial support of the GLC was the operation of 16-seat Ford Transit minibuses on routes that served areas unsuitable for larger buses. The same vehicles were used for an experimental 'Dial-A-Bus' service around Hampstead Garden Suburb, based at Golders Green station. This was later converted to a normal minibus service.

⌒ **'The Londoner'**

Whilst functional and in keeping with its 1970s style, the DMS bus, known briefly as 'The Londoner', presented a very square box-like appearance. The now 20-year-old RT on its nearside has a much softer appearance, as the two types head down Whitehall away from Trafalgar Square.

⟳ **DMS bus at Bank**

The second phase of the Bus Reshaping Plan called for one-person operated double deckers, and, following trials in the mid-1960s, London Transport chose the Daimler Fleetline. The standard design incorporated the 'split-entrance' layout with self-service turnstiles on the nearside and payment to the driver on the offside. A total of 2646 were built between 1970 and 1978.

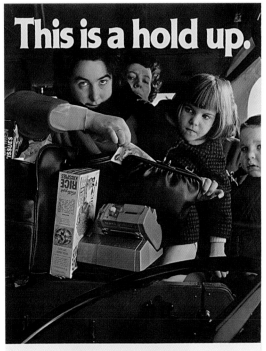

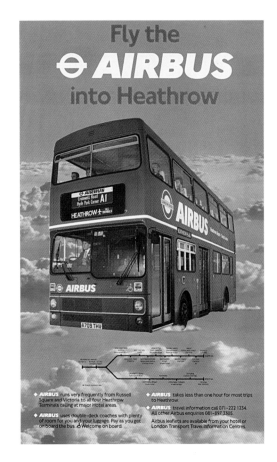

This is a Hold Up – Please Have your Exact Fare Ready
1971

The DMS bus was the first to be used for one-person operation on high capacity double-deck buses in London. The importance of limiting the time taken for loading passengers is demonstrated in this poster.

Leyland National at Chislehurst Common

The first Leyland Nationals were bought by London Transport in 1973 as part of an experiment to reduce noise emission from buses. The National became the standard single-decker from 1976 until 1981, by which time over 500 were in service.

Fly the Airbus into Heathrow
1991

Between 1979 and 1986 over 1400 metrobuses entered service. With their dropped windscreen, which improved the driver's vision, they became a familiar sight in north, west and south London. The metrobus also worked the Airbus service introduced in November 1980 to provide an express link between Heathrow and central London.

◑ **Streatham garage**

Streatham garage

London Transport embarked on a major programme of garage building and re-building in the 1980s. The rebuilt Streatham garage was constructed partly on stilts as the ground falls away sharply behind the frontage. Unfortunately, due to changing needs, it had a very short operational life, although part of the site is still used as a bus terminal.

◑ Leyland Titan

London Transport engineers co-operated with the British Leyland Motor Corporation to develop a new model of bus, the result being the Leyland Titan in 1978. In this respect it was the last new bus design to be influenced significantly by London Transport. This illustration shows a typical example at Piccadilly Circus.

◑ Ash Grove bus garage

Ash Grove garage, with its spacious interior, was opened in 1981. It has, however, had a chequered history, having been closed and re-opened twice. Used for a time to store the London Transport Museum's reserve collection, it has latterly been occupied by East Thames Buses, the trading name used by London Buses Ltd.

Leyland Olympian bus

An impressive line-up of new Olympians stands in Plumstead garage, which opened in 1981. When production of the Leyland Titan ceased, London Buses Ltd turned in 1986 to the Leyland Olympian, which, while similar to the Titan, had a separate chassis rather than being of integral construction. These buses incorporated the results of a study to develop the best design of entrance, exit and staircase layout.

Citypacer

Following the success of the early minibuses, more sophisticated vehicles were produced for this type of operation. One of these was the Optare Citypacer, seen here in simulated fog during the shooting of a promotional video for the new midibus range.

Bus route tendering

The introduction of bus route tendering under the 1985 Act was intended to introduce an element of competition into an otherwise regulated system. It allowed new operators to enter the London market, while ensuring that a properly co-ordinated network was maintained. The early success of the system in encouraging smaller operators to participate is demonstrated in this photograph showing buses of six companies, each in its own distinctive livery.

StarRider

The use of smaller buses to develop new routes in areas unsuitable for conventional vehicles spread rapidly from 1986 onwards. Purpose-designed 26-seaters were soon introduced. Typical of these is this Optare StarRider, seen at Downham on one of the local routes. The driver is wearing the new, less formal, but still smart, uniform that came into favour in the late 1980s.

Get on board ⊖ London's Buses.

⋂ Putney bus garage
1990s

An example of the architectural style of the 1990s can be seen in this photograph of Putney garage, in Chelverton Road, after it was rebuilt. The original garage had opened in 1912 but was extensively changed in the mid-1930s. It had the drawback of only one narrow entrance, a failing that has been rectified in the latest rebuilding.

⋒ *Shopping* by Alan Fletcher
1986

This poster is one of four produced at the time for London Buses. This one uses the novel theme of barcodes, a subject incomprehensible to the public only a few years before.

⋓ Dennis Dart bus

The early success of its small bus operations led London Buses Ltd to look for an improved design of purpose-built bus. Dennis Specialist Vehicles of Guildford had developed a new chassis, called the Dart, and this was ordered in considerable quantities. The bus illustrated here is one of the Wright-bodied versions, which replaced the smaller Mercedes Benz types that had launched the revolutionary Gold Arrow service on the busy high-frequency routes from Westbourne Park garage.

⤺ Refurbished Routemasters

When the Routemasters were refurbished in 1991, one of the most significant enhancements was the replacement of the original tungsten lighting with fluorescent. The considerable improvement achieved is shown in this night-time view of a standard Routemaster alongside one of the refurbished RMLs outside St Paul's Cathedral.

⌂⊃ Conductor training

Conductor training has changed little over the years, although the ticket machines, buses and conductors' uniforms have moved with the times, as can be seen in these two photographs of 1935 and 1997. More significantly, women are also part of the class of 1997.

⊃ New bus stop

A new design of bus stop was developed during the 1990s to replace old designs, some of which, although modified, dated back to the 1930s. The new modular design of post in metal

enables the timetables to be illuminated and has been praised by the Design Council. The bus stop flags give more information and also show the name of the stop and the direction of travel.

for new single deckers. This Dennis Dart demonstrates the high accessibility provided for both pushchairs and wheelchairs.

◊ Bus stop and shelter

London Transport has concentrated recently on improving its passenger infrastructure, and considerable investment has gone into new bus stops, shelters and bus stations. This shows a bus at one of the new stops beside a modern shelter at Wood Green station.

◊ Stratford bus station
1994

Stratford bus station opened in 1994, designed by LT architect Soji Abass. The inverted form of the tensile fabric roof canopy allows clearance for double decker buses and gives the structure a human scale. The supporting steel columns contain the roof drainage channels. Crystalline wall finishes and glass screens enhance the bright and welcoming appearance.

◊ Low-floor bus

By 1998 the low-floor accessible type of bus had become standard

⟳ Dennis Trident bus at Oxford Circus
Photograph: John G. S. Smith

Low-floor double-deckers began to appear in quantity during 1999, when specifications for all contracts for new double-deckers called for the low-floor type. The low-floor Dennis Trident shown here at Oxford Circus has been favoured by a number of companies.

Central London bus guide

Central London bus guide 2000

This map, published only a short time before London Transport became part of Transport *for* London in June 2000, shows the complex network of services available, and as the cover suggests, the numerous attractions served, including the London Eye.

Canning Town bus station

The new bus station at Canning Town was built as part of the Jubilee Line Extension project and shares the station's high standards of architectural design and finish. The bus station concourse is connected to three railways, the Jubilee line itself, the Docklands Light Railway and the Silverlink North London line, making it one of the most important interchanges in suburban London.

Gas bus

Three of the DAF SB220 buses bought to operate the special services to the Millennium Dome from Charlton station and Greenwich are powered by LPG, to test the practicability and cost of this low-emission system. This bus, with strikingly modern East Lancashire Myllennium [sic] bodywork in special Dome livery, is at North Greenwich station, with the Dome in the background.

Jubilee Line Extension route map and interchanges

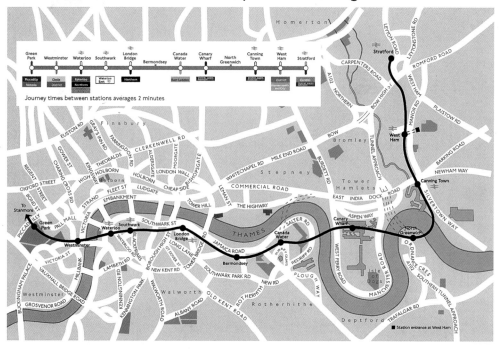

⊙ **Map of Jubilee line extension route**

🔄 **Illustration of Westminster Jubilee line station by Duncan Lamb**

Westminster was the biggest and most complex task of the Jubilee Line Extension project. The job involved the complete reconstruction of the existing District line station – without stopping the service – and the provision of a new building above. Proximity to the Big Ben clock tower required extreme care during construction, and the tight location required the Jubilee line platforms to be built one on top of the other. At 39m it is one of the deepest excavations in central London.

⮕ Emergency escape tunnel under construction
QA Photos
1998

This tunnel leads to the western emergency exit at Waterloo station. It is seen after completion of tunnelling but before installation of stairs, floors and finishes.

◑ *North Greenwich station under construction* by Richard Soden
1998

Richard Soden was commissioned to produce an artistic record of the construction of the Jubilee Line Extension. He chose to concentrate on the architectural features of the stations, rather than portraying the workforce or method of construction. There are 25 paintings in the series.

JLE STATIONS

The construction of the Jubilee Line Extension began in December 1993. The line was fully operating in time for the opening of the Millennium Dome on 31 December 1999 and is now referred to as the extended Jubilee line. As well as a magnificent feat of engineering, the extended Jubilee line is worthy of Charles Holden in its architectural vision, whilst the stations meet Frank Pick's aspiration of 'fitness-for-purpose'. The stations are characterised by high quality fixtures and fittings throughout the extension and actively exploit engineering aesthetics, such as the iron tunnel lining at Westminster station. Materials and style are extremely modern, co-ordinating well with the exciting new architecture of the Docklands area.

Canada Water station
Architects: Herron Associates (until 1993)
Photograph: Ian Bell

Canada Water station is graced by this glass rotunda, which admits daylight to the underground concourse.

North Greenwich station
Architects: Alsop & Lyall Architects
Photograph: Tim Soar

This is the station for the Millennium Dome, and is sited to encourage development throughout the Greenwich peninsula.

Underground roundel, Canary Wharf station
Photograph: Ian Bell

Westminster station platform
Architects: Michael Hopkins and Partners
Photograph: Dennis Gilbert

At around 95 feet below sea level, the westbound Jubilee line platform at Westminster is the deepest on the whole Underground.

Canary Wharf station escalators
Architects: Norman Foster and Partners
Photograph: Dennis Gilbert

Twenty escalators lead from semi-elliptical glazed canopies at street level to the spacious concourse.

Southwark station lower concourse
Architects: Richard MacCormac and Partners
Photograph: Ian Bell

Platform-level concourse clad in unpolished stainless steel

Canning Town station
Architects: Troughton McAslan
Photograph: Dennis Gilbert

Canning Town provides an interchange between the Jubilee line, Silverlink Metro suburban rail services and the Docklands Light Railway. Accommodating all three in a very narrow corridor, beneath high-voltage electricity lines, called for a radical design. The solution was to build partially underground, and to provide a cantilevered concrete deck supported on trusses to support the existing railway lines.

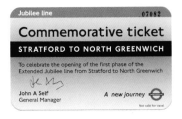

🎧 **Driver's cab**

Train design has for many years allowed passengers to be evacuated in an emergency using the cab doors. This view of a Jubilee line train cab clearly shows the steps and associated handrails that can be lowered by the driver should the need arise.

🎧 **Jubilee line 1996 Tube stock at Stratford station**

The first of a new fleet of 59 trains was delivered in 1996 for the Jubilee Line Extension, entering service in 1997. Through-running to Stratford finally started in 1999, in time for the Millennium celebrations.

🎧 **Jubilee line 1996 Tube stock seats**

The interiors of the new trains on the Jubilee line are finished to a high standard in bright, modern colours.

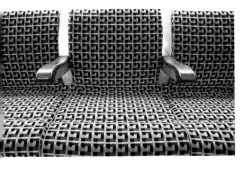

🎧 **Jubilee line platform-edge doors**

A major new feature of stations on the Jubilee line extension is the use of platform-edge doors. These provide additional safety and help prevent rubbish from falling on to the track, where it can interfere with equipment and cause delays. Train control is a critical issue, as trains have to 'dock' precisely at the platform, with train and platform doors perfectly aligned.

Jubilee line   07082

Commemorative ticket

STRATFORD TO NORTH GREENWICH

To celebrate the opening of the first phase of the
Extended Jubilee line from Stratford to North Greenwich

John A Self   *A new journey* 🚇
General Manager   Not valid for travel

🎧 **London Transport's newest Tube railway**

A commemorative ticket to celebrate the opening of the first phase of the Jubilee Line Extension from Stratford to North Greenwich on 14 May 1999.

Transport *for* London
2000

On 3 July 2000 control of London's public transport passed to a new organisation – Transport *for* London (T*f*L), part of the new Greater London Authority. T*f*L's responsibilities include London River Services, London's Transport Museum, buses and Victoria Coach Station, Docklands Light Railway, Croydon Tramlink, Street Management and the Public Carriage Office, which regulates London's black cabs. It will take over the management of London Underground early in 2001 when, for the first time, all of London's public transport is controlled by one strategic authority.

CrossRail map
1993

In 1989 the Central London Rail Study identified the extent of overcrowding on British Rail mainline services and the Underground. Among the recommended solutions was a radical project known as east–west CrossRail. This would enable mainline services to run right through the heart of London, linking the eastern and western regions without the need for passengers to change trains.

CROSSRAIL

The 21st Century connection

Linking major counties on the west and east sides of the Capital, CrossRail is set to change the face of rail travel in London and the South East.

A high-speed, high frequency service using a new generation of trains will deliver passengers from Reading and Aylesbury in the west and Shenfield in the east, into the heart of the City and West End without the need to change trains.

Designed to operate above and below ground, the rolling stock - built to comply with the latest standards of safety and quality - will speed under Central London through six mile twin underground tunnels giving passengers direct access to spacious new concourses at Paddington, Bond Street, Tottenham Court Road, Farringdon and Liverpool Street/Moorgate.

Once complete, CrossRail will reduce journey times, relieve congestion and satisfy the demand for a rail system that will carry the region's rail passengers swiftly and comfortably into the 21st Century.

For further information please contact:
CrossRail Project Office,
Telstar House, Eastbourne Terrace,
London W2 6LW Tel 071 918 0591

This information, correct at July 22nd 1993, may be affected by the continuing development of the Project.

ONLY CENTRAL AREA INTERCHANGES SHOWN

CrossRail, the 21st Century connection
1993

A considerable amount of design work for CrossRail has been completed, even though the project has yet to be given approval. An important difference between CrossRail and the existing Tube network is the use of large-diameter tunnels, sufficient to accommodate trains of mainline size. A new generation of dedicated rolling stock was envisaged. The tunnels themselves would start at Royal Oak in the west, running deep under the city to Bethnal Green in the east.

Possible routes and stations

CROSSRAIL

NOT TO SCALE

Model of proposed CrossRail station for Paddington
Photograph: Roderick Coyne
Architects: Alsop & Störmer

CrossRail station design presents many challenges: the size and length of the trains require very large stations, which would have to be threaded with great care through the dense maze of existing underground structures in central London, while maintaining connections to existing transport services. This proposal by Alsop & Störmer for Paddington Station includes an innovative 'light well' to bring daylight right into the deep station concourse.

Hungerford Bridge Millennium Project
Architects: Lifschutz Davidson
Engineers: WSP Group
Photograph: Hayes Davidson/Nick Wood

The Hungerford footbridge, which runs beside the railway line, spans the River Thames between Charing Cross and the South Bank. The architects plan to rework the bridge to create pedestrian walkways on either side of the existing railway line.

World Squares for All – Trafalgar Square
Architects: Foster and Partners

'World Squares for All' began as an international competition to improve access and enjoyment of central London whilst preserving the heritage setting. A team of consultants headed by Foster and Partners was commissioned to develop the proposals, beginning with phase one, the transformation of Trafalgar Square into a pedestrian space.

⊙ Hungerford Bridge Millennium Project
Architects: Lifschutz Davidson
Engineers: WSP Group

The inclined steel pylon and cables from which the new pedestrian bridge will be suspended pay homage to the architecture of the Festival of Britain, held on the South Bank in 1951.

⊙ Mile End Park Project
Architects: Park Building Architects Tibbalds TM2

Mile End Park in the East End of London, originally a residential area, was gradually transformed into a park as a result of extensive bomb damage in the Second World War. The mile-long park, however, was always under-used and neglected until recently, when the Mile End Park Masterplan was developed. The backbone of this plan is to link the disparate spaces through a serpentine pedestrian path/cycleway, opening up the Grand Union Canal and passing either under or over the major east–west transport routes that formerly divided the park.

⊃ Panorama of the Millennium Bridge
Architects: Foster and Partners
Engineers: Ove Arup & Partners

The Millennium Bridge is London's first new river crossing in more than a century. The 1140 feet-long pedestrian suspension bridge links St Paul's Cathedral on the north bank with Tate Modern, the art gallery housed in the former Bankside Power Station, on the south side. The Millennium Bridge, in conjunction with Tate Modern, is a key element in the regeneration of the London borough of Southwark.

⋂ Tottenham Court Road Underground station and Centre Point Plaza from the north
Architect: Hawkins-Brown

The plans to upgrade Tottenham Court Road station involve extensive changes and improvements to the existing site. Most significantly the ticket hall will be tripled in size by expanding under the forecourt of Centre Point tower.

⋂ Vauxhall Underground station
Architects: Rolfe Judd
Engineers: Ove Arup & Partners
Image: Melon Studios

The proposed design for Vauxhall station will connect the existing fragmented transport links by creating a new centrepiece to the station. This will be a high-tech oval interchange building, whilst the exterior traffic lanes will be landscaped with pedestrian crossings and a roundabout with integral bus and cycle lanes.

⌇ Brixton Underground station
Architect: Owen Cockle, Chetwood Associates
Image: Jonathon Hadcroft, Chetwood Associates

The design to upgrade Brixton station aims to relieve congestion and improve the surrounding environment for staff and passengers by replacing the box-like entrance with a high-tech steel and glass façade, allowing better access and more daylight into the station.

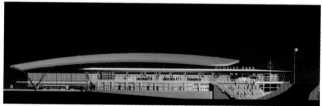

ⓘ **Vauxhall Underground station**
Architects: Rolfe Judd
Engineers: Ove Arup & Partners

Inside the pod: the envisioned interior of the interchange building from the entrance of the new bus terminus.

ⓘ **Wembley Park station**
Architects: Pascall and Watson Architects

A new Wembley Park station by London Underground Ltd is planned to provide better access, crowd control and a stunning 21st-century gateway to complement the spectacular new Wembley Stadium, which will dominate Olympic Way as spectators exit from the station.

Overleaf
The Thames
2000
Photographer: Hugh Robertson

This view shows Westminster Bridge, the Houses of Parliament and the new parliamentary building, Portcullis House, designed by Michael Hopkins and Partners.

Bibliography

LONDON

LYNDA NEAD, *Victorian Babylon. People, Streets and Images in Nineteenth-Century London*, Yale University Press, 2000

ROY PORTER, *London. A Social History*, Hamish Hamilton, 1994

GENERAL HISTORIES OF LONDON'S TRANSPORT

THEO BARKER, *Moving Millions, A Pictorial History of London Transport*, London Transport Museum and Book Production Consultants, 1990

T C BARKER and MICHAEL ROBBINS, *A History of London Transport*, George Allen & Unwin Ltd, Vol I, 1963, Vol II, 1974

ALAN A JACKSON, *Semi-Detached London*, second edition, Wild Swan Publications, 1991

CHARLES F KLAPPER, *Roads and Rails of London (1900-1933)*, Ian Allan, 1976

GAVIN WEIGHTMAN and STEVE HUMPHRIES, *The Making of Modern London 1815-1914*, Sidgwick & Jackson, 1983

LONDON TRANSPORT'S ARCHITECTURE

DAVID LAWRENCE, *Underground Architecture*, Capital Transport, 1994

DAVID LEBOFF, *London Underground Stations*, Ian Allan Publishing, 1994

KENNETH POWELL, *The Jubilee Line Extension*, with a foreword by Roland Paoletti, Laurence King, 2000

LONDON TRANSPORT'S DESIGN

KEN GARLAND, *Mr Beck's Underground Map*, Capital Transport, 1994

OLIVER GREEN, *Underground Art*, Laurence King, 1990

OLIVER GREEN and JEREMY REWSE-DAVIES, *Designed for London – 150 Years of Transport Design*, Laurence King, 1995

DAVID LAWRENCE, *A Logo for London*, Capital Transport, 2000

RAILWAY HISTORY

DESMOND F CROOME and ALAN A JACKSON, *Rails Through the Clay, A History of London's Tube Railways*, second edition, Capital Transport, 1993

ALAN A JACKSON, *London's Local Railways*, second edition, Capital Transport, 1999

ALAN A JACKSON, *London's Metropolitan Railway*, David and Charles, 1986

JACK SIMMONS, *The Victorian Railway*, Thames and Hudson, 1991

H P WHITE, *A Regional History of the Railways of Great Britain, Vol 3: Greater London*, David and Charles, 1987

BUSES

A L LATCHFORD and H POLLINS, *London General. The Story of the London Bus 1856-1956*, London Transport, 1956

JOHN REED, *London Buses Past and Present*, second edition, Capital Transport, 1994

VERNON SOMMERFIELD, *London's Buses: The Story of a Hundred Years*, St Catherine's Press, 1933

TAXIS

MALCOLM BOBBITT, *Taxi! The Story of the 'London' Taxicab*, Veloce Publishing, 1998

TREVOR MAY, *Gondolas and Growlers. The History of the London Horse Cab*, Alan Sutton Publishing Ltd, 1995

TRAMWAYS and TROLLEYBUSES

JOHN DAY, *London's Trams and Trolleybuses*, London Transport, 1977

JOHN REED, *London Tramways*, Capital Transport Publishing, 1997

RIVER THAMES

FRANK L DIX, *Royal River Highway. A History of the Passenger Boats and Services on the River Thames*, David & Charles, 1985

RIVER THAMES WORKING GROUP, *A Report into Transport on the River Thames*, River Thames Working Group, 1995

Index